A BEGINNER'S GUIDE TO
PARANORMAL
INVESTIGATION

A BEGINNER'S GUIDE TO
PARANORMAL
INVESTIGATION

MARK ROSNEY, ROB BETHELL & JEBBY ROBINSON

AMBERLEY

First published 2009

Amberley Publishing Plc
Cirencester Road, Chalford,
Stroud, Gloucestershire, GL6 8PE

www.amberley-books.com

Copyright © Mark Rosney, Rob Bethell and
Jebby Robinson, 2009

The right of Mark Rosney, Rob Bethell and Jebby Robinson
to be identified as the Authors of this work has been
asserted in accordance with the Copyrights, Designs and
Patents Act 1988.

ISBN 978 1 84868 234 4

British Library Cataloguing in Publication Data.

A catalogue record for this book is available from the
British Library.

Typeset in 11.5pt on 15pt Chaparral.

Typesetting and Origination by FONTHILLMEDIA.

Printed in the UK.

Contents

Acknowledgements and Dedications

There are a myriad of people to whom we owe a great deal of thanks both personally and collectively. Many of those people are listed here, but for those we have, for whatever reason, failed to mention, please accept our apologies and our gratitude in equal measure.

From the three of us, we would like to give our appreciation to Janette Fleming, Michael Hadfield, Sarah Flight, Roy Basnett and team at CityTalk FM, Tom O'Connell, Matt Chance, Carol Penney, Cheryl Marlowe, Iris Clayton, Julie Connolly, Carol Hughes, Ali McBride, Stephen Mercer and all at EPRI for your unending support, encouragement, enthusiasm and friendship – without which *Para-Projects*, *Spook School* and this book would never have seen the light of day.

In addition, we would like to thank the following people for permission to use their photographs or personal stories in this book: Niamh Rimmer and Jen Marks, Mike Jaega, Maureen Kidd, Clare Rooney, Tracy Brown, Dave Owen, Paul Howse, Roger Ellison, Julia and Paul Graham.

Mark's dedications: To the people who have shaped my life for the better and filled it with much love, friendship and laughter – my children Lee, Sarah and Tom; my granddaughter Ellie; my siblings Pat, Ged, Tony and Kathy; my friends Anita, Tracey, Jane, Dave, Shelly, Jenz, Nikki, Julia, Paul, Malcolm, Karena, John, Sharon, Carole, James and Neil; everyone who was ever in Ocadi Sunrise; everyone at Dandelion Radio and everyone involved with *Spook School* – much love to you all. Also, a special note to my ex-managers Steve McPoland, Elaine Jennings and Howard Rigby who helped me through some of the darkest hours I have known – mere words cannot express how grateful I am for your support and friendship. Finally, to Rob and Jebby, two of the greatest friends anyone could wish for, may our friendship and our adventures go on forever. Load up the Mystery Machine chaps . . .

Rob's dedications: I would like to dedicate this book to the following people: my parents Bob and Mary – you mean so much to me; all my love to my two brothers Peter and Alan; my partner for many years Teresa, you really are my soul mate; My son Daniel, a great mate as well; my beautiful granddaughter Maci, and last but not least, two of the best friends that anyone could hope for, Mark and Jebby – I owe you both so much, but you will just have to wait. Love to you all.

Jebby's dedications: There are many people that I have encountered in various parts of my life to whom I owe a plethora of thanks and never got around to doing it. Thank you all and may our worlds collide again in the not too distant future. To my children Rachael and Sean, being a dad to you isn't something that I've been particularly good at, but I want you to know that no matter what you may feel, I have always loved you and I always will, both of you have experienced a lot during your short lives and through all the good times and bad you have always made me feel nothing less than pride. To my family – Irene, Sheila, Billy and all the rest – I've not always been around but whenever I've shown my ugly face it has always been received with warmth and love, and it is greatly appreciated. One of the main people to whom I would like to express my thanks would probably wish to remain nameless, and for you, I'll always be there! Finally, Mark and Rob, the journey with you has been a blast, I feel honoured just to walk in your shadow; may there be many more miles in front of us!

Foreword

Upon hearing the word 'paranormal', what is it that springs to mind? Perhaps it's ghosts, flying saucers or poltergeists that you think of, or maybe Bigfoot, Lycanthropes or the Loch Ness Monster. Regardless of its associations, there are few topics that separate popular opinion quite like the paranormal. For many, talk of time-slips, extraterrestrials, witches and demons can lead to hours of passionate, excited discussion, while others dismiss the whole notion of such phenomena as nonsensical and a waste of time.

But what does the word 'paranormal' actually mean? Well, fundamentally, it is an adjective to describe something beyond the scope of contemporary scientific understanding. Scientists and mathematicians, although they may disagree, contend with the paranormal every day. It is only by expanding their understanding, by contending with that which seems 'unknowable' or 'unbelievable' that discoveries and, ultimately, progress are made. An excellent paranormal investigator called Mark Rosney, who happens to be one of the authors of this book, talked of his intentions in paranormal research as being to make the 'para' normal. I think this perfectly sums up what drives all serious research into the unknown.

I first came into contact with Mark Rosney, and the book's other authors Jebby Robinson and Rob Bethell, while filming a documentary series called *Spook School* for the Unexplained Channel. I observed them as they attempted to turn members of the public into competent investigators of the unknown at a community centre in Merseyside.

It was clear very early on that Mark, Rob and Jebby represent something quite unique amongst paranormal enthusiasts. Hard-working, level-headed, scientifically grounded, their fascination and passion for the unknown is matched only by their rigorous investigative practices. They're just as happy blowing a mystery apart as they are coming to the conclusion that it could be something genuinely anomalous. This can be infuriating for anyone desperate to pin their hopes on the existence of ghosts at all costs but is great news for anyone interested in getting to the truth and also means that if Mark, Rob and Jebby are stumped, chances are that it is a genuine anomaly!

They have over thirty years experience at the cutting edge of paranormal investigation between them, yet they are happy to pass on all their research and investigative techniques in order to help foster this passion for the subject in others. They're enthusiasm is contagious. Spending an evening on a hilltop in Cheshire in the dead of winter isn't most people's idea of a good night out, but when Mark, Rob and Jebby organise a skywatch, there is no shortage of volunteers eager to watch and learn alongside them.

They're also hugely inventive, having an almost A-Team-like ability to turn everyday objects into utensils for capturing the unknown. I've witnessed them using string and a protractor to monitor UFO activity and incorporate a duster in the exposing of 'fraudulent' photographed phenomena.

There are simply no better people to share information on investigation into the paranormal than Mark, Rob and Jebby. They've seen so much, experienced everything from big cats to poltergeists, photographic anomalies to time-slip phenomena, and they've done it all on a shoestring. Their greatest hope is that this book will encourage you to do likewise. I am under no doubt whatsoever that it will achieve this and much more.

Tom O'Connell
TV Producer, Antix

Introduction

In recent years, there has been an explosion of interest in the paranormal, thanks in part to the growing number of TV shows that grace our screens which follow 'fearless' investigators as they attempt to seek out 'strange' phenomena in the 'spookiest' locations on the planet. This has naturally led to many people wanting to know more about the paranormal and, more importantly, how to investigate it for themselves. If you are one of these people, this book is for you.

Written with complete beginners in mind, this book does not require any prior knowledge or experience. It contains useful and effective methods, techniques and handy tips that have been developed and refined from over thirty years of collective experience that the authors have gained from actively investigating the unknown.

The book is organised into handy topics that can be studied on their own, or in sequence, which cover five main paranormal areas ranging from Ghosts through to Unidentified Flying Objects (UFOs). Each topic outlines a basic history of the phenomenon, offers a range of alternative theories that researchers and enthusiasts are currently exploring and finally gives practical advice on how best to investigate that topic – from choosing the best methods and equipment your budget will allow, to using them effectively on your own investigations.

Considering the amazing amount of 'detection' equipment now available, paranormal investigation can be a very expensive activity, especially if you want to buy every gadget available. However, it is possible to do effective investigations on a shoestring budget, and we also show you how to do just that.

Before we embark on our voyage through the unknown, it is useful to define what is meant when we use the word paranormal. The *Oxford English Dictionary* defines the paranormal as anything that is beyond the scope of normal scientific understanding.

Since our understanding of the universe around us is still incomplete, it should be obvious to everyone that, by definition alone, there *must* be phenomena out there that currently defy rational explanation. Yet there are a large body of sceptical people who passionately deny that anything paranormal exists at all. Part of the problem lies in the fact that paranormal events are spontaneous – they come and go of their own accord. Because we cannot yet predict where or when things such as apparitions or UFOs will occur, they are difficult to study in any meaningful scientific way. This is one of the reasons why mainstream science remains largely disinterested and sceptical about the paranormal. The phenomena's unpredictability also brings along another problem: that of capturing good evidence. Not only do you have to be in the right place at the right time, but you also need to have something to hand in order to capture the event.

Recent advances in technology have now placed cheap and easy-to-use audio/video recording devices in most of our pockets in the shape of video-equipped phones and highly portable cameras. Thanks to their reduced size, it is easy to take them wherever we go, making them instantly available if any spontaneous phenomenon decides to pay us a visit. This has led to an amazing increase in the amount of footage and photographs purporting to show all manner of paranormal activity occurring around the globe. However, not all of this 'evidence' is reliable, or indeed useful, partly due to people not knowing how to use these devices effectively, especially when they are caught by surprise. In this book, we also show you how to be better prepared for the unexpected and how to get the best out of whatever equipment you have available. This, in a nutshell, is what this book is all about – open-minded, level-headed research and investigation techniques that will help you to determine if something *truly* paranormal has taken place, and how best to attempt to capture evidence to prove it.

How to use this book

Since this book has been written to convey the key skills required to investigate more than just one type of paranormal phenomenon, we have divided the book into five main subject areas: Ghosts and Hauntings, Photographic Anomalies, Electronic Voice Phenomena (EVP), Cryptozoology and Unidentified Flying Objects (UFOs). Each of these topics can be studied individually or, if you prefer, you can work through them sequentially. The choice is yours. However, before you get started, it is vital that you become acquainted with the information found in Section 1: Core Concepts and Skills, which is important for any type of paranormal investigation you choose to conduct. This includes elements such as developing the right attitude for paranormal investigation, putting together your basic investigation kit and learning a few basic rules to keep you safe.

Core Concepts and Skills

Key Attributes

When taking beginners out on investigations, we like to ask them what they consider to be the most important piece of equipment that an investigator needs. Many newcomers plump for answers such as EMF meters, infrared scanners or some other piece of sophisticated hardware, which, although extremely handy to have, are all a million miles away from the correct answer.

In our opinion the best piece of 'equipment' that an investigator will ever take to an investigation is an *open mind*!

The above answer illustrates beautifully that paranormal investigation is not solely about having the best gadgets, it is also about developing a healthy mindset. Once you possess that, you will be able to use whatever equipment you have at your disposal more effectively. The following is a list of key attributes that we feel you need to have, or to develop, in order to become a competent paranormal investigator.

Objectivity

There are a variety of reasons why people want to investigate the paranormal. Some want desperately to prove it exists; others want to debunk it completely. We feel that both of these approaches are wrong. What is needed is a neutral viewpoint somewhere between the two. This is known as objectivity. Being objective is not as easy as it seems, for everyone has their own ideas and theories about the paranormal, and these constitute what is known as a 'belief system'. If left unchecked, your personal beliefs will colour your perception of events. Metaphorically speaking, leaving your belief system at the doorstep of any investigation you undertake is *essential* if you want to remain objective. If you go into an investigation believing that you *will* encounter the unknown, then you are likely to misinterpret anything you see or hear as being a paranormal event. Conversely, if you go into an investigation thinking that the paranormal is complete rubbish, then you are likely to disregard evidence out of hand without taking a critical look. Developing an objective stance is vital if you want to do effective paranormal investigation.

A good example to illustrate the importance of having an objective mindset occurred on an investigation conducted a number of years ago by a team in Merseyside, England, where an elderly lady believed that her house was under psychic attack from a poltergeist. She reported that at roughly the same time each night, about an hour after she retired for bed, the 'poltergeist' would rap loudly on her walls, keeping her awake all night. After weeks of repeated activity she was on the verge of a nervous breakdown. In desperation, after calling out a medium and getting the house blessed by her local priest, she called out the investigation team. Sure enough, at the precise time she specified, the team could hear the strange raps coming from all the walls in her home. In no time at all, they got to the root of the problem. The sounds were not being made by a discarnate entity hell-bent on interrupting her sleep; they were being caused by air trapped in the central-heating pipes cooling down in the walls. By cranking her central heating timer back one hour, they were able to 'manifest' the 'phenomenon' an hour earlier, proving that the 'activity' had a more down-to-earth explanation – much to the lady's relief!

If the team had gone into the house expecting to find ghosts or poltergeists, then they would have almost certainly interpreted the raps as being paranormal in origin. Instead, they went in with open minds, which let the evidence lead them to the correct conclusion, not let them *lead the evidence* to what their belief systems wanted to find.

Problem Solving

The paranormal is like a huge jigsaw puzzle, and anomalous events are its pieces. Unfortunately, completing this puzzle is going to be very difficult because we have no idea what the finished picture looks like. To make matters worse, we don't even know if we have all the pieces – and some of the pieces we currently have might not even belong in the puzzle at all! Therefore, it is a paranormal investigators job to look critically at each piece to see if it really belongs.

We do this by looking carefully at alleged paranormal activity to see if rational explanations can be found before reaching for supernatural causes. For example, if on an investigation you hear the sounds of footsteps coming from a room that is supposed to be empty, try to think of all the possible causes. Is everyone in the building accounted for and away from the area? Could the sounds be coming from somewhere else, such as through the walls of an adjacent property? Could the sounds be caused by other living things, such as pets or rodents?

By asking questions like these, you are *testing* the event to see if a rational explanation can be found. By looking at all the alternatives, you are improving the quality of the investigation, and also the quality of any 'evidence' that you gather. You should be equally as happy finding rational explanations for alleged phenomena as you are in finding genuine anomalies. If you treat each alleged paranormal event as nothing more than a puzzle that needs to be solved, you are well on your way to becoming a competent investigator.

Expect the Unexpected

Because of the spontaneous nature of paranormal activity, it is very easy to get carried away with the moment and get excited or frightened, or both. We have lost count of the number of people we have seen running away in fear after being spooked by their own shadows; or others who have been so excited by the sudden appearance of a strange light in the sky that they forgot to use the camera they were holding! If you let your emotions run riot then you won't be capable of doing a proper job. That is why it is important to remain calm and focused at all times. Remember, your job is to observe alleged paranormal phenomena at work and to gather as much information about it as possible. Running away from the 'activity' or becoming hysterical does not achieve this!

Patience

Real-life paranormal investigations are often NOT as dramatic or action packed as they appear on TV or in movies. There will be long periods in every investigation when nothing out of the ordinary happens. In some investigations, you may find nothing unusual occurs at all! That is not to say that paranormal investigation is a boring activity – far from it! – but be prepared not to find anything anomalous straight away. In the world of the paranormal, patience is a virtue.

Develop a Good Working Philosophy

Don't believe everything you hear about the paranormal. It is sad to note that there are many myths, untruths and poorly tested ideas out there that have come to be largely accepted as fact. For instance, the popular notions that UFOs are spaceships from another world, or that apparitions are the spirits of the dead are taken as given by a majority of people without there being a shred of tangible evidence to support either notion with any certainty. As you will see in later sections, there are many different theories to consider carefully before anyone can say with assurance what the cause of each phenomenon really is. We believe that the best approach is to take one step backwards. Don't look for ghosts or alien spaceships – look for *phenomena* instead. That way, the evidence you gather will lead you, rather than you leading it.

As well as trying to capture evidence of phenomena, it is also essential to gather as much information about the conditions surrounding the events themselves. For instance, investigators have discovered that the spot where an apparition has been seen just instants before appears to be much colder than the surrounding area. We do not know why this is so, but in gaining valuable information like this, we are moving towards a better understanding of the mechanisms involved in causing the phenomena to occur where (and when) it does. In doing this, you will be helping to bring elements of the 'para' into the realm of the 'normal'.

To help illustrate the above point, consider rainbows. Ancient man may have regarded seeing a rainbow in the sky as a supernatural event, possibly as a sign from the gods. However, over time, and after observing many rainbows, someone, somewhere, started to see a pattern emerge – that a rainbow only occurs when sunlight shines through falling rain. Suddenly, the 'supernatural' rainbow becomes a perfectly natural phenomenon, and the new discovery pushes our understanding of the world around us out a little further.

A Sense of Humour

Is having a sense of humour essential in paranormal investigation? Yes, we think it is! There are two reasons for this. Firstly, the more you investigate, the more you will get to see that the paranormal appears to *play games* with people. Over 100 years ago, author and collector of strange phenomena reports, Charles Fort, posited the idea that maybe some form of higher intelligence was orchestrating highly strange and inexplicable events for people to experience purely for its own amusement. He called this intelligence 'the cosmic joker' because some paranormal reports are not only weird, they are comically bizarre. For instance, here is a UFO report from France compiled by legendary French UFOlogist Aimé Michel that many people would have discounted as nothing more than a bizarre hallucination had the incident not been observed by independent witnesses.

On 18 October 1954, Mr and Mrs Labassiere were driving home to Royan, in western France, along Route N150, when they spotted a pair of flying discs travelling overhead – one orange in colour, the other red. As soon as the discs overtook the car, they proceeded to land in a field close to the roadside. As the couple watched, dwarf-like creatures emerged from each craft, casually walked past one another and then boarded each other's saucer. Seconds later, both craft took off at incredible speed, leaving Mr and Mrs Labassiere feeling a little perplexed as to what they had just witnessed.

As a UFO incident, the creatures' actions seem bizarre and a little pointless, but as an elaborate practical joke, it is nothing short of comic genius. It is this element of highly strange absurdness that creeps into the paranormal again and again. The 'cosmic joker' factor has been subtly experienced by many investigators, ourselves included. Only too often do we get to hear stories from investigators of strange activity starting up 'just as the camcorder had run out of tape'; or worse still, 'just after the team had packed away all their gear and was ready to go home'. It is almost as if someone or something is saying 'Ha ha, you didn't catch me that time!' It is moments like these where a sense of humour helps to stop you from going gaga.

The second reason why we feel a sense of humour is important is that many investigators are in agreement that paranormal phenomena seem to occur more often when people are at ease, so creating a happy, relaxed atmosphere during investigations may be a key element in capturing phenomena. Yes, paranormal investigation is a serious business, but don't forget to have a little bit of fun along the way too.

Study All Phenomena

We recommend that you don't just confine your investigations to just ghosts or UFOs, but investigate the paranormal in its entirety. If you do, you will discover that there are amazing crossovers between the various phenomena that may provide vital clues to help get to the bottom of some of the mysteries.

Basic Safety/Common Sense Rules

The following are some very basic rules that cover all types of paranormal investigation. It is important that you observe them at all times.

Never, Ever Investigate on Your Own

This is essential for two reasons. Firstly, if you are the only one on an investigation and you have an accident, it may be a long time before you are missed! Secondly, if you are fortunate enough to experience something anomalous, the presence of another witness will add a bit more credibility to your report, and also make it harder for sceptics to discount your experiences as hallucinations or misperceptions. With these points in mind, it is a good idea to join a local investigation group, or to form your own!

Always Tell Someone Where You Are Going and When They Can Expect You to Return

The reasons for this are obvious. If you run into difficulties (say you and your team manage to lock yourselves in a cellar), having someone know where you are and what time you should have returned is very useful. Please remember to check in with them when you do return to avoid having an angry search-party battering down your door.

Always Have a Basic First-aid Kit

Even minor injuries like a cut finger can turn nasty if you do not tend to it as soon as possible. With this in mind, your basic first-aid kit should at least contain plasters and some form of antiseptic spray or cream.

Never Drink Alcohol Before or During a Paranormal Investigation

You need to be alert throughout your investigations and any amount of alcohol will dull your senses, make you feel tired and very possibly alter your perception of events. If you do encounter something anomalous while you are under the influence, you will be less credible as a witness and your experiences will be harder for others to believe.

Top Tip: Never investigate anything on 1 April. It will almost certainly turn out to be a hoax!

So, now that we have covered basic attitudes and safety, it is time to assemble your investigation kit!

Investigation Equipment

Paranormal investigation can be a very costly activity, especially if you want to use all the latest detection kit. However, it is possible to do a decent investigation using modestly priced equipment. If you are starting from scratch, we recommend that you start off small by assembling a basic investigation kit consisting of:

Camera	Camcorder	Tripod
Compass	Thermometer	A basic audio recorder
Watch	Torch	A pair of cheap motion sensors
A basic first-aid kit	A basic toolkit	Notepads and pens
A case or bag to carry it all		

The above kit will be enough to get you started in instrument-based paranormal investigation, as most of it is useful for investigating more than one aspect of the paranormal. For instance, the camcorder's zoom facility can double as a basic

magnifying scope on UFO skywatches or cryptozoological field investigations; your audio recorder can be used to pick up EVPs as well as to take field notes or to log temperature readings verbally; and your compass can double as a rudimentary gaussmeter when looking for anomalous magnetic activity.

Assembling Your Basic Kit

You may already have some of these essentials around the home, such as a camera and a camcorder. If these items belong to other family members, make sure you ask them for permission before you borrow them. Many years ago, a budding investigator we knew 'borrowed' his parent's camcorder for a skywatch without their permission and accidentally taped over footage of his sister's wedding. His family was not amused.

If you decide you want to buy your own equipment, but you don't have a big budget, don't fall into the trap of thinking you need to buy the latest makes and models. As technology improves, people tend to get rid of perfectly adequate devices in order to buy newer models with additional features. Many of the older models are still very good for paranormal investigation, and you may get lucky and spot a real bargain in your local second-hand/charity shops. You will be amazed at what you can pick up for a fraction of the cost of buying brand new.

Test and Familiarise Yourself with Your Equipment

When you do buy your own equipment, it is vital to test it out thoroughly as soon as possible after you have purchased it to make sure it is not faulty. Check out all the features and functions that the device has, even if you do not intend to use a particular function, as you may find you need to use it in the future. If you leave it too long and do find a fault, it will be more difficult to return it and get an exchange or a refund.

Top Tip: Never throw away till receipts!

Learn how to use your equipment. The best way to do this is to go through the instruction manual carefully and familiarise yourself with all the controls and functions. There is nothing worse than missing out on capturing evidence because you could not use your equipment properly. To that end, practise with your new device as much as possible before using it on an investigation. That way, you will learn its quirks and its strengths and weaknesses as a paranormal investigation tool. For instance, if you have a camera that can work in low light levels, test it to see how little light it can operate in effectively. For UFO investigations, if your camcorder has a manual focus facility, see how quickly you can set it up and focus on passing aircraft. Practice makes perfect, and knowing how to use your equipment properly will dramatically increase your chances of capturing evidence when the opportunity arrives.

Looking After Your Equipment

Follow the manufacturer's instructions for cleaning and maintenance, and set aside an evening a month to make sure your devices are still working 100 per cent. Make sure that all equipment is stored away from locations that get too cold, too damp, too hot or too humid. In addition, pay particular attention to storing devices with magnetic memory storage (hard drives, tapes, memory cards) away from strong magnetic fields such as hi-fi speakers, as these have been known to wipe memory and damage devices.

It is important not only to maintain your equipment regularly, but also to make sure that it doesn't get damaged in transit while going to/coming back from investigations. The best way to make sure your kit survives the journey is to buy hard cases to transport everything in. You can buy hard cases that come supplied with foam rubber inners that you can customise by cutting out gear shaped holes, so that all your equipment is stowed away securely. The holes also act as a sort of checklist when you

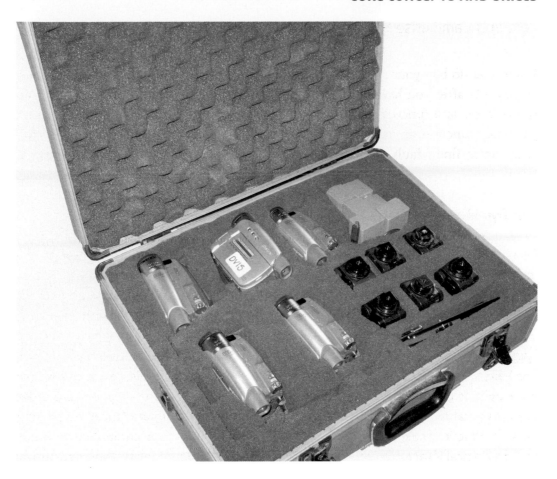

come to pack things away, as you will be able to tell at a glance if something is missing. Also remember to stow your case(s) securely in the vehicle you are travelling in. No matter how tough a case is, your equipment will not survive for long if the case is bouncing around the boot of a car.

Equipment Specifications

This section is all about the sort of equipment you can use to carry out effective paranormal investigations. Not all of it is essential, but you will find everything listed extremely useful to have. Every item listed also contains details about the minimum requirements and the features that each device needs to possess in order to be effective in a paranormal investigation.

Digital Cameras. Left to right: Compact with movable screen, mobile phone with 5 megapixel built in camera, Digital SLR.

Camera

Uses: Ghosts / UFOs / Cryptozoology

For almost as long as they have been around, cameras have been the central piece of kit that investigators have used on investigations to attempt to capture evidence of anomalous phenomena. Although investigators have far more equipment at their disposal nowadays, cameras are still an essential 'must have' in anyone's basic kit.

As well as capturing evidence of paranormal activity, cameras are useful for making visual records of your investigations, such as taking reference photos of equipment set-ups on ghost investigations.

Cameras come in two distinct types – traditional (film cameras) and digital. Although film cameras produce good results, they have large drawbacks compared to digital. For instance, you cannot see the pictures taken on a 35-mm camera straight away, as the film needs to be developed and then the shots printed; and both film and camera are more prone to catastrophic failures (mechanical seizures, light leakage, etc.), which could lead to you losing your photographs altogether. Because of these factors, we recommend that you choose to go digital. When choosing a digital camera, there are a number of factors you will need to consider:

Camera Type

Digital cameras currently come in two main types – digital compacts and digital single lens reflex (DSLR).

Digital compacts are cheaper, more portable and easier to use than their SLR counterparts, and they are good all-round cameras for most paranormal applications. If you are choosing one of these, try to pick one with a large, and preferably movable, view screen.

The next step up from a digital compact is a digital SLR or DSLR. These cameras are much more expensive, but they do have a few advantages over compacts. For one, they have interchangeable lenses, so it is possible to fit them with specialist lenses such as wide-angle, telephoto or macro tubes, which makes them very handy cameras to have in the field. Some of them also come with a removable flash that can be fired far away from the lens, which eliminates some of the problems that can be encountered by compacts (see section on photographic anomalies for more details). If you wish to go for one of these, see if you can try it out before buying it to get a feel for how comfortably it fits in your hand and also how much it weighs. Some digital SLRs weigh far more than others, and if you are on a lengthy investigation, the weight can really get annoying, especially if you have it hanging around your neck. No matter what you choose, compact or SLR, your camera needs to have the following minimum standards or features.

Camera Resolution

A digital image is made up of tiny dots called pixels. The more pixels that a camera can capture increase the sharpness and detail it can provide in its pictures. The level of sharpness and detail a camera can deliver is known as its resolution. Camera resolutions are measured in megapixels, where a megapixel equals 1 million pixels. For paranormal investigation, we recommend that you go for the highest resolution you can afford, but do not buy anything below 5 megapixels. A 5-megapixel camera can easily produce a decent A4-size print or on-screen equivalent.

Lenses and Manual Override

Any camera is only as good as its lens, so choose a camera that has good-quality glass lenses. Carl-Zeiss lenses are a very good choice. The camera you choose should also have some degree of manual override capability, where you can adjust the shutter speed, exposure settings and ISO setting (digital equivalent of 35-mm film speed).

Make sure that the camera has a minimum rating of 400 ISO so that you will be able to take photographs in fairly dark conditions.

Memory Storage and Latency

Choose a camera that stores its images on removable memory cards, such as compact flash or SD cards and make sure that the camera can handle some of the newer cards that can contain 4 gigabytes of information and beyond. Choose a camera that doesn't have too much latency between shots. Latency is the delay time the camera has between taking one picture and being able to take the next. The delay between shots is caused by the camera processing and writing (storing) the image data onto the memory card. This delay can sometimes be made worse by the brand of memory card you choose. Memory cards have different speeds for reading and writing data, referred to in megabytes per second (MB/s). If at all possible, go for cards with higher values, such as 10 or 12 MB/s. If the delay is too long between shots, i.e. 5 seconds or more, the camera or card may be unsuitable for some paranormal applications.

Rainproof Factors, Battery Consumption and Tripod Fittings

If you intend to use the camera out of doors then choose a camera that can survive in the wet. One of my first digital cameras stopped working after being left out in fine rain for a few minutes. If you need to use your digital out of doors and are unsure how robust it is, put your camera into a clear plastic bag, with just the lens sticking out, or carry an umbrella around with you just in case. Ideally, choose a camera that has fairly low power consumption so that it doesn't eat batteries too fast. Most Canon and Sony models are fairly economical to run. Make sure that the camera has a screw-thread hole on its underside so you can attach it onto a tripod if needed.

Check Reviews

The best way to find out about a camera's performance is to check out camera-user magazines, websites, online forums and user reviews for the makes and models that you are considering. All of the above info should be available, along with numerous other useful comments.

Basic: Digital Compact 5 megapixel
Better: Digital Compact 8-10 megapixel with movable screen
Best: Digital SLR 10+ megapixel

Useful Accessories

Lens cloth/camera cleaning kit – it is essential to have a lens cleaning cloth with you at all times, as there is nothing more annoying than finding that all your pictures contain unwanted specks because the lens has picked up some dirt. Always clean your lens before you start to take photos.

Spare memory cards
Protective case
Spare batteries

Shutter release cable (digital SLRs only) – this is a cable that attaches to your camera shutter button, so that you can take pictures without having to be near the camera. This allows you to keep your camera as still as possible, which is useful for taking longer exposures.

Camcorder

Uses: Ghosts / UFOs / Cryptozoology

A camcorder, or some sort of video capture device, is massively useful on any sort of investigation. Not only can you set them up to capture anomalous activity, but you

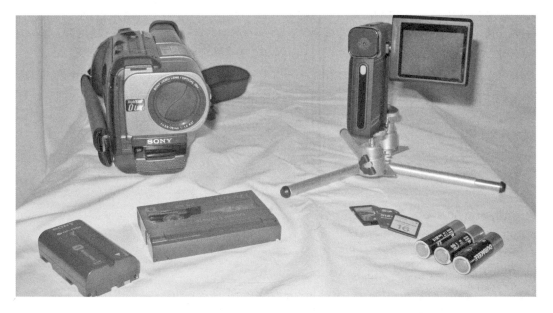

Camcorders. Left to right: Sony Nightshot 8mm analogue, Mini SD card Digital.

can also use them to record witness interviews (with permission, of course!), or to document details such as how/where you have set up equipment, or to record team activity/movements on investigations.

Technology is always on the move, and currently camcorders come in three main formats. The formats refer to which type of memory storage the camera uses. The most expensive are hard-disc (HD) camcorders; followed by removable storage devices such as DVD, SD and compact flash cards; followed by the tape formats: Mini DV, Digital 8, Hi8, and finally, 8 mm analogue.

HD recorders are convenient for depositing your footage onto a computer quickly, but if you fill up the memory halfway through the night, you will have to have a laptop with you to dump the footage onto in order to continue using it. For this reason, we recommend that you go for any device that records onto removable storage media, such as DVDs, memory cards or tapes, as it is much cheaper to buy spares than a laptop!

As previously mentioned, if you are looking for a decent camcorder but can't afford the price on the tag, don't be afraid to use older technology. As technology races ahead, people get rid of perfectly adequate equipment only because they want to own something with all the latest features. Older camcorders can, and do, provide more than acceptable results at a fraction of the cost. For instance, Sony NightShot Hi8 Camcorders can now be picked up for around £30-50 second hand. The very basic features that your camcorder will need are listed below.

Night Vision Capability

Sony NightShot camcorders are the preferred choice of most paranormal investigators due to their excellent night vision capabilities.

Optical Zoom

Camcorders are equipped with both optical and digital zoom capabilities. Choose the one with the highest optical zoom that you can afford. Using digital zoom reduces the picture quality.

Manual Focus

This is particularly useful for UFO investigation. When zooming in on objects in the sky, a camcorder's automatic focus facility can have difficulty in keeping the object you want to video in focus, especially in low light conditions. This is the main reason why most UFO footage is blurred. Having the ability to focus the camcorder manually will improve your footage, and it's usefulness as evidence, a thousand-fold.

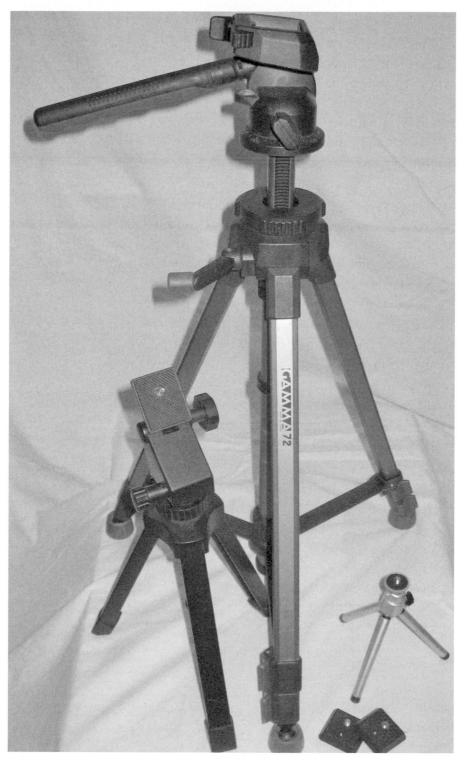

Various tripods you can use, ranging from large clip type leg locks with removable quick release plates to small tabletop varieties.

Basic: Analogue 8 mm/Hi8
Better: Digital 8 or Mini DV
Best: DVD camcorders / HD recorders (used in conjunction with laptop for storage)

Useful Accessories

Infrared light extender – this can extend the night vision capability of your camcorder from 3 metres (10 feet) to 100 metres (300 feet)

Spare high-capacity rechargeable camcorder batteries
Battery charger/mains transformer (and leads)
Lens cleaning kit
Tape Head / DVD Cleaner
Carry Case

Tripod

Uses: Ghosts /UFOs / Cryptozoology

Choose the sturdiest tripod you can afford, as cheaper models tend to be too flimsy and not as stable as more expensive models. The best tripods are fitted with clip-type leg locks that allow for speedy set-up and take-down. Choose a model that can accommodate quick-release plates, as this allows you to swap equipment on the tripod more quickly than using the older screw-thread models. It is a good idea to buy spare quick-release plates and to attach these in advance to each piece of equipment that you wish to use your tripod with. A good tripod can extend up to around 5-feet tall, which is ideal when using binoculars or spotting scopes in the field. Finally, if your tripod comes equipped with a built-in spirit level, please feel free to crack paranormal gags about it, even though we have heard them all before!

Top Tip: Don't forget to take the detachable plates along with you on your investigation, as failure to do so will render the tripod completely useless.

Compass

Uses: Ghosts / UFOs / Cryptozoology

Compasses are useful for all manner of investigations. They are useful in UFO investigations to find out the direction in which you are observing something

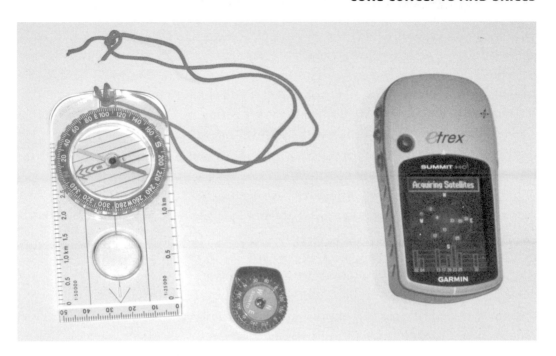

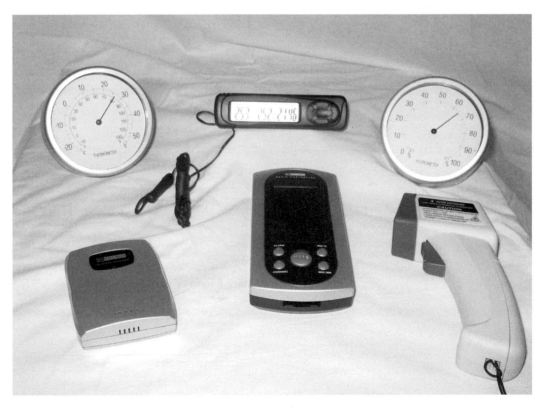

Top: various compasses, left to right: orienteering, button, GPS. Bottom: various types of thermometer ranging from analogue and digital to laser guided non-contact.

anomalous. In cryptozoology, they are used in conjunction with maps for finding your way around areas where big cats have been sighted, and in ghost investigations a compass can be used as a crude gaussmeter to detect magnetic 'hot spots' in allegedly haunted locations by looking out for unusual needle deflections.

The best compasses you can buy are the orienteering sort that are mounted onto a clear plastic base that is marked up with grid lines and rulers to help you calculate map distances. Good compasses have fast moving needles and good clear displays that are also luminous in the dark.

In recent years, traditional compasses have been joined by digital devices that boast more accuracy, and there are some that are now 'plugged' into the Global Positioning System (GPS) satellite network, which not only show you what direction you are pointed in but also plot your current position and give you global grid references, which you can later upload into software such as Google Earth. This is very handy for noting precise locations of suspect tracks or possible UFO ground traces, giving you the ability to find the locations more easily on return visits.

Basic: Magnetic needle orienteering compass
Better: Digital compass
Best: GPS position and direction finder

Thermometers

Uses: Ghosts

A thermometer is a very handy device to have on a ghost investigation, as you can use them to check out potential cold spots and help you to monitor the immediate environment for anomalous temperature drops. In paranormal investigation, a rapid temperature drop of 5 °C in a confined space is significant and worthy of further investigation.

Thermometers come in two types: traditional (mercury, alcohol and bimetal coil varieties) or digital. Both types have their merits and are relatively cheap to buy.

The bonus of traditional thermometers is that they do not need power to run. Therefore, they are not prone to malfunction caused by paranormal (or ordinary) power drains. They also react fairly quickly to changes in temperature.

Digital thermometers are small, lightweight and fairly accurate (as long as they have adequate power available (so change batteries regularly!). Because they are inexpensive, it is a good idea to buy a few, which you can either leave in each area under investigation or give one to each team member to carry around with them. That way, if somebody does encounter a cold spot, they can get readings immediately and also monitor what is happening from moment to moment. A good digital thermometer will respond quickly to temperature changes, will have a facility to log the minimum and maximum temperatures experienced during the investigation and also have a backlit display screen so that you can see the readout in the dark. The best digital thermometers have a data logging facility that automatically records the temperature at set intervals for a twenty-four-hour period.

Basic: Alcohol/mercury thermometer
Better: Digital, with backlit display
Best: Digital with twenty-four-hour data logger

Audio Recorders

Uses: Ghosts / UFOs / Cryptozoology

Audio recorders are primarily used on investigations to record anomalous sounds and voices (see section on Electronic Voice Phenomena (EVP)), but they are also useful for recording witness interviews, dictating notes, verbally recording instrument readings during baseline sweeps (see section on Ghosts), or describing your impressions and experiences while on investigations. There are two basic types of audio recorder: analogue tape recorders and digital devices. Both of these come in a variety of formats:

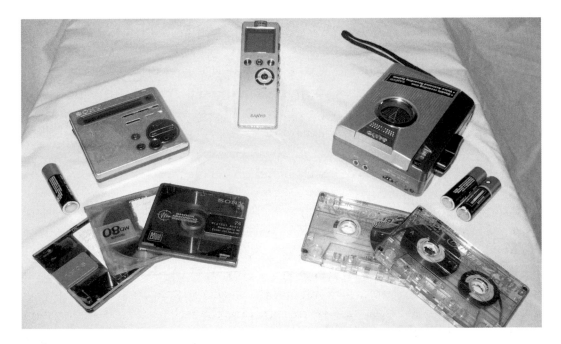

Audio Recorders. Left to right: Minidisc, Digital Memo, Analogue Compact Cassette.

Analogue: memo recorders, cassette recorders
Digital: minidisc recorders, MP3 recorders, digital memo recorders

Each has their advantages and disadvantages. But before we go into the nitty-gritty of choosing what format to use, here is something that applies to both types of device.

Recording levels

Whether you choose analogue or digital, try to pick a device that has the capability of recording using both manual and automatic recording levels. Automatic recording levels boost low sounds up and cut loud sounds down to the same pre-set volume, meaning that the sound of a pin dropping will be recorded at the same volume level as an explosion. Sometimes low-volume sounds can appear anomalous when boosted artificially, so it is important to have the ability of setting the recording levels manually, so that any sounds you capture are recorded at the volume level they occur at.

Analogue Tape Recorders

These can be picked up in most second-hand and charity shops incredibly cheaply nowadays, mainly because they are considered to be 'antiques' by many people. However, if used correctly, analogue tape recorders can provide very good results. Their main downside is that they contain many moving parts, so are prone to mechanical breakdowns such as motor burn-out or tape-head failure and have the annoying habit of chewing up tapes when you least want them to. Some recorders come with built-in microphones, which at first seem very handy, but because they are built into the body of the recorder, they are prone to picking up unwanted noise from the machines mechanism, which can completely ruin your recordings. To this end, buy a recorder that comes with an external microphone socket so that you can place the microphone as far away from the recorder as possible. If you choose a good microphone, even the cheapest of tape recorders can produce very good results.

Analogue Memo Recorders

These are handy for dictating memos and notes because they are small enough to slip into your pocket. Since many come with a built-in speaker, make sure to choose one that comes equipped with a headphone socket so that you can play back your recordings without disturbing other team members.

Analogue vs Digital

I'm sure some people are wondering why we have included such seemingly old-fashioned technology into a twenty-first-century manual when there are so many amazing digital devices out there that offer more reliable and higher-quality recordings. Have we gone mad? Not yet. The answer is that there is a difference of opinion between EVP researchers as to whether digital technology is capable of picking up anomalous voices. Champions of analogue recorders say that there is something about the way sound is recorded onto analogue tape that lends itself to be easily manipulated by the 'spirit world', which apparently is something that cannot be achieved as easily on digital formats. Our personal opinion on this, based on our own successes with digital methods, is that you can achieve good results using either types of device. However, there is one technical issue with some digital recorders that can be a bit of a problem.

All digital recorders use compression algorithms called audio codecs to reduce the amount of data they store into their memory. Compression works by cutting some of the higher and lower frequencies and any periods of silence from the recording. When compressing music, the loss of a few frequencies is hardly noticeable, but for EVP recording, the frequencies that have been removed can make natural sounds appear very different and lead some people to think that they have caught something anomalous.

Audio codecs use two distinctive types of compression: Lossy and Lossless. Lossy compression loses quite a bit of the original recording, which becomes noticeable if you want to do detailed investigation like frequency analysis. MP3s in particular are a lossy file format. Lossless compression is just that: lossless. No information is lost, although this makes the file size of the sound recording much larger. The best lossless file format is WAV, closely followed by ATRAC lossless, which is used by more modern minidisc recorders. Recording with devices that output lossless file formats is desirable if you wish to do more detailed study of your audio recordings. However, for beginners, digital recording using *either* type of compression will give you clearer recordings than most analogue devices, making it easier to pick out potential anomalies from the background hiss. For more about this, see the section on EVP.

Digital

In our opinion, this is by far the better medium to record in. Since most devices are solid state (no moving parts), they do not suffer from the problems that can plague tape recorders, such as mechanical failure and internal noise generated by the recorders moving parts. Here is a brief description of two useful devices.

Digital Memo Recorders

Most of these devices store their recordings on internal memory, meaning that once they are full you have to download their contents onto a computer. Usually they offer around 90-120 minutes of recording time in high-quality mode. There are different models available that record to memory cards which, although more expensive, have the advantage of allowing full cards to be swapped in seconds, making it less likely that you will miss something during an investigation.

Minidiscs

Although digital, minidiscs do have moving parts and some models can be a bit noisy when they operate. However, they can be picked up incredibly cheaply nowadays in second-hand shops (we have picked them up for as little as £10). They have an amazing recording quality, and unlike most digital memo recorders, can record in stereo. They are also cheap to run, as most of them are powered by a single AA battery, which can run for anything up to twelve hours continuously. This is still our budget portable device of choice for capturing anomalous sounds and EVP. If at all possible, see if you can pick up a more recent model that uses ATRAC lossless compression.

Basic: Analogue tape recorder
Better: Digital memo recorder
Best: Minidisc, ATRAC lossless format
Minidiscs don't come with their own microphones, so here is a brief rundown of what you will need to get to make it an effective EVP recording device.

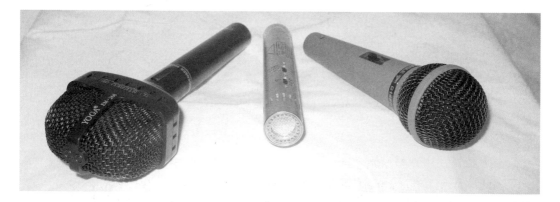

Microphones. Left to right: Stereo Condenser, Mono Condenser Omnidirectional, Mono Unidirectional (Cardioid).

Microphones

Do not be tempted to buy microphones that you find in pound shops. The recordings from these will sound as if you have done them through a thick, woolly sock! If you want to capture good results, you will have to buy a good microphone – there is no cheap alternative. There are three factors to consider when buying a microphone for paranormal investigations.

Frequency Response

The human ear is capable of hearing sounds with frequencies from as low as 20 cycles per second (also referred to as Hertz or Hz) right up to 20,000 Hz. When choosing microphones, go for the ones that can cover as much of this range as possible. The range between the lowest and highest frequency sound that a microphone can pick up is called its frequency response. Good microphones have a frequency response from around 40 Hz up to around 15,000 Hz.

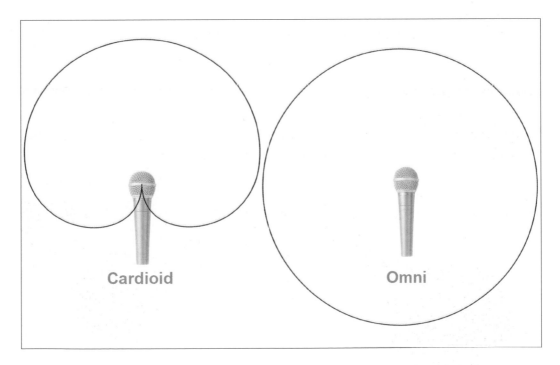

Cardioid microphones have a heart-shaped pick-up pattern, meaning that they are far less sensitive towards the rear of the body. Omnidirectional microphones are equally sensitive in all directions.

Sensitivity

As well as needing to have a wide frequency response, microphones used in paranormal investigation need to be sensitive. This is because a lot of the anomalous sounds that you will be interested in capturing may be very quiet. The most sensitive microphones are the type known as condensers. This type of microphone needs power to operate, and the portable ones that you will need usually operate off AA or AAA batteries.

Directionality

Another factor in choosing a suitable microphone for investigations is the microphone's directionality. This is the microphone's sensitivity to sound from various directions. The two types of microphone that are most useful in paranormal investigation are the following:

Omnidirectional – these microphones pick up sounds evenly from all directions, making them ideal for monitoring an entire room. (Omni means 'all' or 'every'.)

Unidirectional – these microphones pick up sound predominantly from one direction. They are also referred to as cardioids as their directional pick up pattern looks like a heart shape. These are less expensive than omnidirectionals, yet still give good results.

Connections

When buying microphones, make sure that the lead that comes with it has the correct connection for the device that you wish to connect it to. If it doesn't, don't panic, as you can buy adapters that will allow you to plug in almost any plug to any socket. You can pick them up from any specialist electronics or hi-fi shop. When it comes to choosing microphone leads, go for the longest you can buy. It is always a good idea to get the microphone as far away from the recorder as possible.

Useful Accessories

Microphone stand – these are useful for getting the microphone off the floor to reduce the possibility of picking up unwanted vibrations, such as team members walking around, and also to place it more centrally.

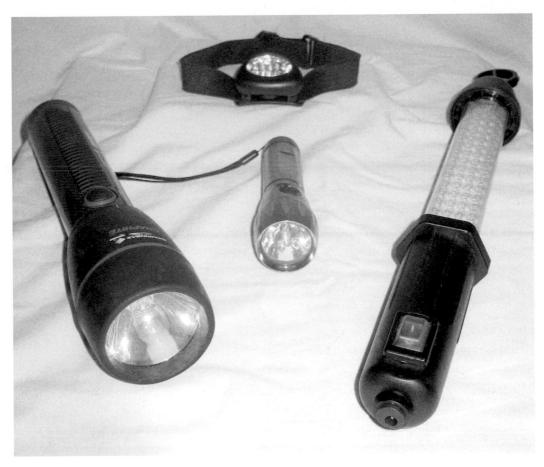

Various torches you can use, ranging from traditional bulb, head mounted LED to LED striplight varieties.

Gaffer tape (also known as duct tape) – this is useful for making sure cables are safely stuck down to the floor to avoid trip hazards, especially in access points where people have to walk through.

Basic: Condenser stereo microphone (around £20)
Better: Mid-range condenser microphone (around £50-60)
Best: Omnidirectional condenser microphone (£100+)

Torch

Torches are one of the most important things you will need on an investigation but are one of the most common things that people tend to forget to bring. Not all the places that you wish to investigate will have lighting, and in the ones that do, it is always possible for the lights to fail unexpectedly in traditional 'Scooby Doo' fashion. In these situations, having a torch handy will get you out of a lot of bother. Because paranormal power drains are one of the things you may experience, it is also a good idea to carry spare torches and batteries, or carry a wind up torch, which is powered by manually winding a handle.

If you feel that you will have your hands full with other equipment, buy a head-mounted torch that will keep your hands free and still provide light wherever you need it. If you go for one of these, please remember to take it off once the investigation is over as you can look very silly going home in the small hours with a lamp on your head!

Never ever use candles or any other naked flames for illumination on any investigation because of the potential to accidentally start fires. Burning down someone's home or inadvertently starting a forest fire will not endear you to many people.

Motion Sensors

Uses: Ghosts / Cryptozoology

Motion sensors are not used to detect anomalous phenomena. They are used to detect the presence of humans or animals that may stray into areas you are investigating and create noise or other effects that could easily be mistaken for paranormal activity.

Team members have been known to accidentally stray into rooms that are being monitored remotely by video or audio equipment, only to cast shadows on walls or make noises that are inexplicable to other team members who review the video and audio tapes a few days later! In addition, it is not unknown for unscrupulous people to hide in cupboards in order to hoax phenomena while teams' backs have been turned. Motion sensors will immediately alert you if either happens.

In some venues, small animals, such as rats, mice, squirrels, cats, bats and birds, may be the cause of alleged paranormal activity. Motion sensors will allow you to detect or eliminate these possibilities from your investigation.

There are two different types of motion sensor, passive and active. Both work on similar principles, i.e., they use an infrared beam to detect movement, but they differ in one important detail.

Passive sensors are single devices that use a wide beam, which can detect both the presence and movement of body heat over a wide area.

Active sensors are two-part devices that send out a narrow beam between the units, which activates an alarm when the beam is broken.

Passive type Motion Sensors.

In our opinion, the best motion sensors for paranormal investigation are the passive models, as their wide beams cover a larger area, meaning that they are especially useful for picking up the presence of small animals. For cryptozoology investigations, we recommend using trail monitors – although these can also be used in ghost investigations too. Trail monitors are infrared detectors that contain either digital still or video cameras which start recording as soon as anything passes them. The big drawback with these devices is that they can be expensive. Pick one with the best picture quality, currently around 6-8 megapixels, and one which can illuminate the furthest distance in infrared. Good models can send out a beam as far as 10.2 metres (around 35 feet). Depending on the specifications you want, a trail monitor will cost you anything between £150-700, so it is a good idea to shop around.

Basic: Any battery-powered unit available from places such as DIY superstores or hardware stores.
Better: N/A
Best: Trail monitor

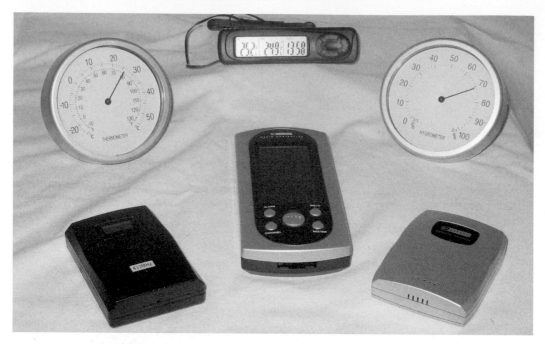

Various types of inexpensive weather stations you can buy.

A more sophisticated laptop-based weather station.

Popular EMF meters. Left to right: Trifield, K2, 2mG.

Weather Stations

Uses: Ghosts

As well as having thermometers, it is also useful to have some form of weather station, so that you can also keep an eye on the pressure and humidity of the areas under investigation. You can pick up very basic units for around £10 from bargain stores or electrical gadget sellers. These devices comprise of a base station and a remote sensor that transmits data back wirelessly, allowing you to keep a track of the conditions in two areas simultaneously. This is especially useful if you experience a cold spot or an anomalous drop in temperature in one area, as you can not only compare the difference in temperature, but also see if other factors such as pressure or humidity have also been affected. The main drawback of these devices is that sometimes it is difficult to get a connecting signal between the remote sensor and the weather station, often caused by the thickness of walls or the presence of a large amount of metalwork in the structure of the building you are investigating, which prevent signals from travelling very far. Another minor drawback is that someone has to manually log the readings from the base station every five minutes or so, but it is a worthwhile exercise, especially if you encounter something anomalous.

The next step up is to purchase a more professional system that uses a laptop to automatically acquire and log the data. These units often come with around four or five remote sensors, making it possible to keep track of weather data for whole sites. However, these can be quite expensive to purchase.

Basic: Weather station with backlit display and one remote sensor
Better: N/A
Best: Professional weather station with laptop data logger

EMF meters

Uses: Ghosts

We are constantly bathed in electromagnetic fields that are being generated by all the electrical devices and cables surrounding us that carry electric current. Electromagnetic field (EMF) meters are devices that allow us to measure the levels of electromagnetic radiation in our immediate environment. Electromagnetic fields, as their name implies, are a combination of electric fields and magnetic fields. Electric fields are always present wherever there is an electric charge, irrespective of whether that charge is static or flowing. A device can still have an electric field while it is plugged into the mains, even if it is switched off. Magnetic fields occur anywhere where there is flowing electricity. If you switch off the device, the magnetic component of the field should disappear.

EMF meters were originally designed for engineers and electrical hobbyists and only in recent years have EMF meters become synonymous with ghost hunting. Some investigators believe that ghosts either generate EM fields directly or can somehow affect EM fields already present in the environment. Hence, they believe that if you can detect changes in EM fields in locations during investigations, those changes *may* have been caused by something anomalous. The problem with this is that measuring EM fields is a difficult and time-consuming process, and consequently hard evidence in support of the 'Ghosts cause EMF activity' theory is currently lacking.

Magnetic fields run in three dimensions referred to as X, Y and Z. Single-axis meters, as their name implies, can only measure the field strength in one direction at a time, so to get a true reading of the field strength at a particular point with these, it is necessary to orient the meter in each of the directions, X, Y and Z, take a reading from each, square the readings (multiply each reading by itself), add the three results together and finally calculate the square root of the sum. This is a tricky and

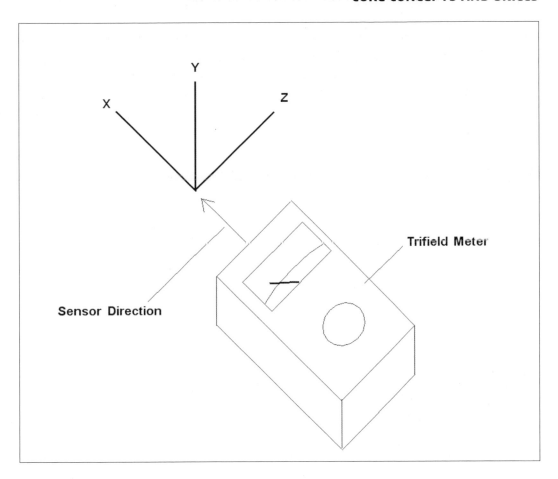

time-consuming business. EMF meters come in two main types: single-axis or tri-axis detectors.

Tri-axis Meters

These have three in-built sensors pointing in each direction, X, Y and Z, and so this meter is capable of giving an accurate field-strength reading without having to do all the measurements and maths. However, tri-axis meters are far more expensive than their single-axis counterparts.

Single-axis Meters

Most single-axis meters only measure magnetic fields. Magnetic fields occur wherever there is flowing electricity, e.g. along power lines and in switched on electrical devices. Magnetic field meters are also referred to as gaussmeters, which measure magnetic-

Binoculars.

field strengths in units known as milligauss (mG). This type of meter comes in a variety of makes and models. Some are analogue meters which have needle read outs and others have either digital read outs or progressive light-emitting-diode (LED) displays (a row of LEDs that light up in sequence to show field strength). Of these, our preferred choice is the needle variety, as these can show transient (fleeting) readings better, which some believe are indicative of paranormal activity.

The best-known single-axis meter is the Trifield Natural EM meter. This is often mistaken for a tri-axis meter because of the name, but it is called a Trifield because it is capable of measuring magnetic, electric and radio frequency fields either individually or collectively. Trifield meters are incredibly sensitive, especially when set to read everything (in the sum mode). In the sum and magnetic modes, the meter will give out a reading whenever it first detects an EM field, and then it will settle back down to zero until it detects a change in the field strength. This makes it handy for detecting even subtle changes in the EM fields in the immediate area. Since these meters are so sensitive (although you can adjust their sensitivity), it is not a good idea to walk around with them when taking readings. They are better left in a single position and read occasionally. For more information on how to use EMF meters in ghost investigations see Section 2: Ghosts

Basic: Progressive LED gaussmeter
Better: 2G gaussmeter
Best: Trifield Natural EMF

Binoculars

Uses: UFOs / Cryptozoology

Binoculars are as useful for sweeping across fields in search of big cats as they are for scanning the night sky for UFOs. The most useful binoculars for night-time skywatching are basic 7 x 50s, where the first number represents how much the binoculars magnify things by (in this case seven times), followed by the diameter of the lenses in millimetres (in this case 50 mm). It is the diameter that is the most important in night-sky viewing, as the bigger the lenses are, the more light will be able to enter them. Don't be fooled into getting the highest magnification possible, for as the magnification increases, the field of view decreases. Your binoculars should have coated optics to reduce reflections and to improve overall image quality.

However, we appreciate that the use of your binoculars will not be strictly limited to just paranormal investigations as they will possibly be used more in your other leisure activities, whether it be nature watching, walking, horse racing or such like. In activities such as these, the chances are that the binoculars will be hand-held rather than used on a tripod, and this puts certain limitations onto the specifications of the binoculars concerned. Zoom binoculars sound a wonderful idea but when held up to the eye you would need to be endowed with the arms of Arnold Schwarzenegger to keep them steady when used at maximum zoom. So, for the purposes of general all-round use, we recommend something of no more than ten times magnification, with the objective lens being no less than 32 mm to accommodate low-light viewing.

Useful Accessories

Lens cleaning kit
Tripod adapter mount
Tripod

Spotter Scope with angled eyepiece.

Spotter Scope

Uses: UFOs / Cryptozoology

Like binoculars, spotter scopes are ideal for all outdoor work. The spotter scope wins over binoculars in two important respects. They are quicker to set up and often have much larger-diameter lenses. In addition, you can buy special adapters that will allow you to attach digital SLR cameras to your scope, effectively making it a telephoto zoom lens.

There are two types of spotter scope that you can go for: angled eyepieces, where the eyepiece is at around 45 degrees to the body; and straight, where the eyepiece is in line with the body of the scope. The angled-eyepiece variety is good for skywatching, as it means that you can set your tripod lower, which will make it less prone to wobbling. Lens diameters typically come in sizes between 50-100 mm and magnifications of fourteen to sixty times. A typical set-up would consist of an 80-mm-diameter lens coupled with a twenty-five times zoom eyepiece. The more expensive scopes have a range of optional eyepieces that can be used along with it; however, the price of some of these eyepieces alone will cost more than a cheaper scope.

Useful Accessories

Lens cleaning kit
Tripod
SLR adapter mount

Surveillance CCTV Cameras

Uses: Ghosts

One of the methods we employ in our ghost investigations is to seal off an area and let the equipment do the investigation for us (see Section 2: Ghosts and Poltergeists). CCTV cameras are ideal for this purpose, as it is then possible to monitor the video output remotely from another location. CCTV cameras come in two varieties: wireless or hard-wired.

Wireless Cameras

This type provides the cheapest option, costing around £60 each for a camera and a radio receiver. This enables you to both see and listen into the room under surveillance. These cameras work well in most buildings, but because they are wireless, getting a

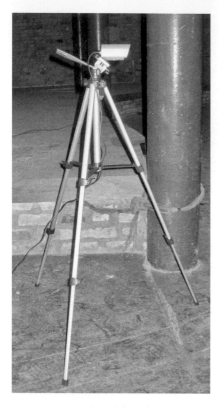

Hard wired CCTV camera strategically placed in an alleged haunted location.

On the left is a hard-wired CCTV camera complete with cable. On the right is a wireless camera and receiver.

good signal from the camera to the receiver can prove problematic on occasions. That aside, we have obtained some very good results in most of our investigations, including one where we successfully ran a camera from a room two floors below us, at a distance of over 100 metres (approximately 300 feet). To use a wireless camera like this, you will also have to have some sort of video recorder and a TV monitor, which does push up the expense a little. However, old video/TV combi units are ideal for use, and they can now be picked up very cheaply.

Hard-wired Cameras

The next stage up is to go for larger hard-wired cameras. They are a little more expensive, and their range is only limited to the length of cable you have. They are quick to set up and the results can be stunning. These units can be purchased from most gadget, electrical or DIY stores. Decent hard-wired cameras currently retail from around £80-100. Again, if you shop around you will find some incredible bargains.

If you have a bit more money to spend (£200-300), you can pick up a fully-fledged, semi-professional close-circuit television (CCTV) set-up, including four cameras and a dedicated hard-disc recorder with the ability to show all four camera outputs on screen at the same time. For a little more, you can buy extension cables for the cameras and run them further away with no appreciable loss of signal in runs over 100 metres.

Basic: Wireless spy cam
Better: Hard-wired home CCTV
Best: Semi-pro CCTV

Video Recorders

As stated above, in order to run any CCTV camera you will need to be able to record the camera's output. Using an old VHS video recorder is cheap, and will provide you with good results.

The next step up is to consider getting a hard-disc (HD) video recorder. A HD recorder has the ability to burn the camera footage to disc, meaning that you could burn a copy for every team member to take away and scrutinise at home. If you do decide to obtain a HD video recorder, make sure that you get one that is able to 'split titles'. This will allow you to break up longer pieces of footage into DVD-sized chunks in order to burn it successfully to disc. Not all HD recorders have this facility, so check carefully when you buy.

If you want to run more than one CCTV camera at a time, you will either have to buy each camera a video recorder, or purchase a dedicated CCTV hard-disc recorder,

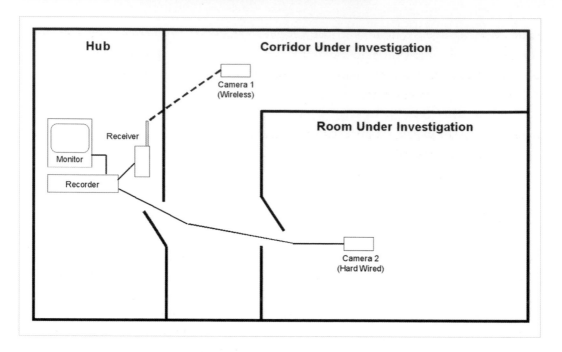

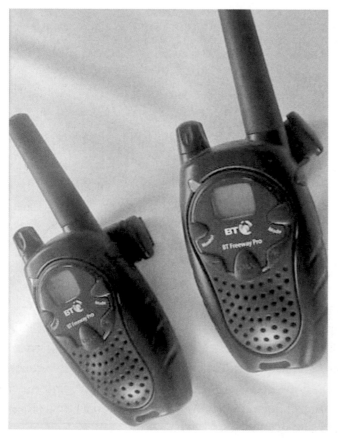

Above: In order to set up a remote video feed you will need a camera, a recorder and some form of monitor. This set-up shows both a hard-wired and a wireless camera linked to the hub (the centre of operations in an investigation). *Left:* Walkie Talkies.

which will allow you to run and record up to four cameras at a time. However, these can prove to be a little bit expensive. If you do choose to get one of these, make sure that it records each camera channel at full size, even if you are viewing the camera outputs in split screen mode.

Basic: VHS video recorder or TV/video combi
Better: HD video recorder
Best: CCTV hard-disc recorder

Monitors

As well as needing to record the output of your cameras, you will also want to be able to see the output live. This means that you will have to have a monitor screen of some sort.

Again, a video/TV combi unit is a cheap way of achieving this, but these can be a little bulky to take along to an investigation. A lighter and less bulky alternative is to obtain a flat-screen monitor. A 15-inch monitor will currently set you back something in the region of £40-50.

Another alternative (although more costly) is to obtain a digital projector to project the camera outputs onto a wall or screen. The advantage of this is that the whole team will be able to watch the video feeds without having to huddle over a small monitor screen. If you do decide to purchase a projector, make sure that the cost of a replacement lamp for it doesn't exceed the original cost of the projector.

Basic: TV/video combi
Better: 15-inch flat-screen monitor
Best: Digital projector

Walkie-talkies

Uses: Ghosts / UFOs / Cryptozoology

Walkie-talkies are one of the most useful things to have with you on an investigation with you. If your team splits up into smaller groups during the investigation, it is handy to know where they are in relation to you if you hear any noises, so that you can eliminate any natural causes. They are also useful if you need to set up remote cameras, where one person can check on the video picture at the hub (see Section 2: Ghosts and Poltergeists) while instructing someone in the investigation area where to position the remote camera in order to get the best coverage.

A basic pair of walkie-talkies is ideal for small teams. These will set you back no more that £20, and for that you will get two units which have around eight channels for you to communicate on, with an effective range of around 3 km.

For larger teams, you will possibly have to go for a set of four handsets which will cost something in the region of £70. These will offer more channels and quite possibly have longer ranges. Once you have purchased them, you will find a million and one uses for them.

Top Tip: Attempt to find walkie-talkies that have backlit screens so that you can easily see what channel you are on in the dark, and ideally the set you choose should have a headphone socket so that their noise output can be reduced if necessary.

Investigation Skills

One of the most common mistakes made by newcomers to paranormal investigation is that they tend to go off and investigate sites (buildings, hills, fields, etc.) just because they look *spooky* or feel *creepy*. Before you even set foot in an allegedly haunted property, run a UFO skywatch or start scouring the countryside for big cats, it is vital to establish beforehand that there is a reasonable chance of you actually finding something to investigate. If you don't, you will almost certainly be wasting your time. Experienced paranormal investigators follow a tried-and-tested process that allows them to carefully determine if a site investigation is worth mounting. We call this the 'Investigation Life Cycle'.

The Investigation Life Cycle

To investigate any alleged paranormal activity properly, you will need to go through a set of clearly defined stages. These stages are called the Investigation Life Cycle. Not all reports of activity are worth pursuing through to the final stages, and at each point in the life cycle you can decide, based on what you have learned, if you wish to proceed onto the next stage. Going through each stage in sequence will ultimately save you from wasting valuable time on things that don't deserve it. Depending on what you are investigating, you will be doing slightly different tasks during each stage, but overall, every investigation should go through the following stages in order. Here is a brief overview of each stage:

Initial contact – Most investigations will start with you being approached by someone who has experienced something they consider to be paranormal, e.g. they claim to have seen an apparition, UFO or big cat and they want you to investigate it for them. If you are initially satisfied that they may have experienced something unusual, the next step is to arrange to conduct an interview with them.

Witness interview – This is where you will be able to gather important information regarding the incident, and will be your chance to assess the witness's credibility in person. If everything seems OK at this stage (i.e. no obvious hoax or misperception), carry on to the next stage.

Background research – No matter what you are investigating, you will have to conduct some background research. For ghost reports, this could mean checking out the location's history. For UFO sightings, you will need to find out about weather conditions, positions of stars/planets, etc. For crypto investigations, you will have to study area maps. This is where you can gather important information to help you get the most out of the next stage, which is visiting the location for an initial reconnaissance.

Initial location reconnaissance – This is where you see the incident location for yourself first hand. Based on information gained from the witness and from the research, you will be in a better position to look around and see if you can find rational explanations for what has been reported and also to assess the location to see if conducting a site investigation is going to be worthwhile. If it is promising, the next stage is to plan the site investigation.

Planning the site investigation – You will need to plan when you intend to conduct the site investigation, who is going to attend, how to get there, what equipment you will need, who is taking what, how many consumables do you need, i.e. tapes, batteries, discs, food, etc.

Pre-brief – This is where you assemble your team, agree what roles everyone will be playing and the responsibilities they will have during and after the investigation.

Running the investigation – Here is where you set up your equipment and conduct the site investigation. Hopefully all the preparatory work you will have done in the previous steps will make your investigation run smoothly and provide you with some interesting results.

Analysis – Although the team will have been monitoring some of the equipment live during the site investigation, it is necessary to carefully review all recordings, both audio and video, to see if anything anomalous has been caught.

Report – Once all the recordings have been analysed, it is then a good idea to put together an account or a report on what you found, and your conclusions.

Publishing your report – Once you have written up your account/report, it is important to get the information out into the paranormal community so that others can benefit from your findings. Remember that the paranormal is like a big jigsaw puzzle. You may be holding onto a vital piece that someone else is looking for.

If you stick to doing things in this order, your investigations will be much more professional and rewarding.

Initial contact

Irrespective of whether someone is contacting you to discuss their paranormal experiences or you are contacting them to enquire if a location has been experiencing activity, it is very important to make a good first impression. Here are some handy pointers.

Remember that the other person is the VIP and you are merely an investigator. It is vital to listen to them very carefully and give them time to tell you their story. Try not to interrupt too much.

If the other person is contacting you by telephone, be mindful of how much the call is costing them and don't try to keep them on the line any longer than they want to be.

If you think it is worthwhile taking the investigation further, don't be pushy. Explain to them that the next step would be to set up an interview with them, and that the purpose of this interview would be to gather more in-depth information about their experiences. Never ask for their contact details. If they want you to have them, they will offer them to you. Instead, give them your contact details and ask them to consider if they would like you to investigate further and let them get back to you in their own time. Putting the ball in their court will act as a natural filter. Chances are that if the people weren't entirely honest or sure about what they claimed to experience, you probably won't hear from them again.

If you haven't had a chance to make notes during the conversation, jot down brief notes as soon as you can. The longer you leave it, the more you will forget. These notes will come in handy should you wish to set up an interview with them later. To this end, always carry a small notepad and pen with you at all times and also leave one by your phone.

Witness Interview

One of the most important of all these stages is learning how to conduct effective witness interviews. Whether you are interviewing someone who has seen a UFO or ghost or big cat, it is important to conduct the interview in a professional manner in order to get all the information you need to be able to assess the incident thoroughly. The information you gain here is essential in helping you to decide if it is worth taking the investigation forward to the next stage.

Things to take along with you:

Fully charged mobile phone
Witness address and contact phone number
Maps or directions (even if you have a Sat Nav)
Notes you made during the Initial Contact
Watch
Notepad and pens
Audio recorder (tape or digital)
Sufficient batteries, tapes, discs or memory cards
Microphone (if necessary)
An open mind!

If the person agrees to an interview, arrange to meet them somewhere where they feel comfortable and at ease. With this thought in mind, offer them the chance to have one of their friends attend too. The more at ease the witness is, the more useful the interview will be. For your own safety, never, ever go to an interview on your own.

There is always a slim possibility that the witness may turn out to be emotionally off-balance. The chances of this happening are low, but please be aware that the possibility exists. In our thirty years of investigation experience, we have only had one interview situation where we were fearful for our own safety, when the female witness we were interviewing became excitable and attempted to use a team member to physically illustrate how she had wrestled a 'ghost' to the ground. Luckily we managed to escape unharmed. It sounds funny now, but at the time it was an alarming experience. With this possibility always in mind, **never go to a witness interview alone**. If you can't take a fellow investigator, find a willing friend.

If you are male and wish to interview a female witness, try to take along another female to make the witness feel more at ease. If you are female and are interviewing a male, try to take along a male companion. As another precaution, always tell somebody where you are going, and roughly how long you will be away. Get them to call you at a prearranged time (say, one hour into the interview) to make sure that you are OK. This phone call also serves another purpose, as it will give you an excuse to leave without appearing too rude should you wish to terminate the interview for any reason.

Let the witness know who you are bringing along. Never take more than three people with you to an interview, as taking a crowd will only intimidate the witness. Make sure you have the correct address of the arranged meeting point and also the witness's telephone number, and work out in advance how you are going to get there and how long it will take you. Set out a little early to give yourself plenty of time and, if travelling by car, factor in extra time to find a parking space. If, despite your best efforts, you find you are running late, call the witness to let them know.

Never arrive too early. This can sometimes be more irritating to people than arriving late. No one likes to hide the vacuum cleaner behind the sofa in a blind panic. When you do arrive, greet the witness by name and introduce your companions. If you are visiting the witness's own home, don't announce on the doorstep that you are paranormal investigators. The witness may not want their neighbours knowing their business, and in some people's eyes, there is still a small amount of stigma surrounding people who claim to have witnessed paranormal events. Once inside, take a few minutes to allow the witness to relax before plunging headlong into the interview. Exchange a few pleasantries about the weather or how difficult/easy your journey was to break the ice. Once everyone is relaxed, let the witness know that you don't want to overstay your welcome, and inform them that they can ask you to leave at any time. The witness will have as busy a life as you have, and you should not encroach on too much of their time or their hospitality.

A witness interview in progress. Note that the investigator is both recording the interview and taking notes, just in case the recording does not turn out.

Interview Goals

There are three main reasons why it is important to interview witnesses before attempting to conduct a full-blown site investigation (known in ghost investigations as a vigil, UFO investigations as a skywatch, etc.).

Interview Goal 1: Assessing Witness Credibility

In most investigations, witness testimony is the only 'evidence' that an investigator will walk away with; therefore, it is vital to determine beyond reasonable doubt that what the witness is telling you is credible.

Assessing the witness's credibility is not just about working out if the witness is lying or not. It also encompasses factors such as: is the witness prone to exaggerating? Is the witness's recall of events accurate? Does the witness have a belief system that could colour their perception of events? Does the witness have mental-health issues that could cause them to be delusional? (e.g. hearing voices, hallucinating, etc.)

Was the witness under the influence of alcohol or taking perception-altering drugs (prescription or otherwise) at the time of their experience?

Let's look at each of these in turn.

A – Lying

In our own experience of conducting interviews, the majority of the people we have interviewed have been honest and sincere individuals. However, there are a minority of people out there who are not. People lie about having paranormal experiences for a variety of reasons, such as they may want attention or they may be seeking publicity. In some cases, people have been known to fabricate paranormal encounters in order to get their local council to re-house them in better accommodation.

Sadly, there are no foolproof techniques available to determine 100 per cent if someone is trying to deceive you, but as you conduct more and more interviews you will start to see a pattern of behaviour that 'genuine' people exhibit when they have encountered something that they cannot explain.

Testimony feel – People who experience the paranormal at first hand tend to be stunned and/or confused by what they have experienced, and in dramatic encounters with the unknown some people even start to doubt their own sanity, which is a perfectly natural reaction for someone who has encountered something that is far removed from the safe and familiar world that they are used to living in.

They will tend to ask you if you can explain what they have encountered, or if you (or anyone you know) have experienced anything similar yourselves. They will have a thirst for knowledge to fill the recently opened gap in their understanding. They may have also undergone a significant shift in their attitudes, where the attention they now give to the everyday world and its day-to-day matters, pale into insignificance against their attempts to rationalise what they have encountered. Some people become more creative, some people more spiritual, and people around them tend to notice and comment on it. This is another good reason to persuade the witness to have a friend with them, so that you can gather their opinion on the impact the event has made on the witness.

Witnesses who try to deceive you will tend to come at things from a more clinical angle, where they will emphasise the details of the 'encounter' more than its effect on them. Usually, they won't ask you to explain what they encountered, since they know full well what they encountered – absolutely nothing! This is only a rule of thumb, and it does take time – and lots of interviews – before you get a feel for the characteristics exhibited by genuine and false witnesses.

Body language – Another useful (but again NOT 100 per cent reliable) way of determining if the witness is lying is by looking at their body language. As a general rule, people who lie (unless they are pathological liars) don't like to make eye contact with the person to whom they are lying. Their physical movements will be more limited and appear stiff, for when we are under stress our muscles tighten up. Watch out for people who try to excessively touch or cover their mouth when speaking, as it is common for liars to want to put up 'barriers' between you and them. Other 'barrier' traits employed by people not telling the truth are when they have a tendency to turn their body away from yours slightly, and/or deliberately move physical objects, e.g. coffee cups, books, etc. between you and them.

Visual accessing cues – Another useful body language 'tool' to indicate if someone is lying is a technique called visual accessing cues. Discovered by Dr Richard Bandler and Dr John Grindler, this technique uses the witness's eye movements to determine if someone is recalling events (using their memory) or if they are using other parts of their brain to 'create' something new, such as a lie.

When we are recalling information, our eyes tend to look left as we gather the information from our memory. If we are being 'creative', our eyes will tend to look right. If the witness is left-handed, then the directions are reversed. Again, like all of the techniques we have mentioned, this method is not 100 per cent reliable, but in tests we conducted with colleagues, we found this method to be around 90 per cent effective!

Verbal clues – Sometimes people give out unconscious verbal clues when they are not telling the truth. People who have made up a story tend to include a lot of unnecessary

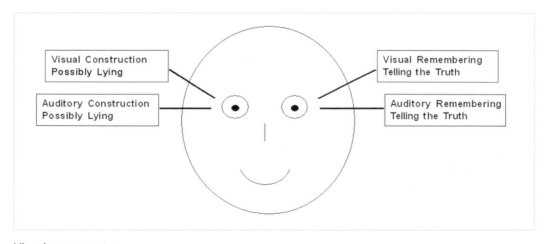

Visual access cues.

detail in their accounts, such as: 'It happened just after 9 p.m., and I know that because my friend had just called me and she had to be in bed by nine because she had an early start the next day'. Truthful people will tend to just tell you the important bits, such as what they experienced, with you having to ask further questions to elicit the extra details. People who are not telling the truth often trip themselves up by contradicting themselves. To that end, when interviewing, a good trick is to subtly cross-examine what the witness is telling you by asking the same questions a number of times in subtly different ways throughout the interview, and then compare the answers you get. For instance: How did you first become aware of the event? What caught your attention first?

You can also compare the information you gathered at the initial contact with that which you gain at the interview. Another verbal lying trait is that, if challenged, liars tend to become incredibly defensive, whereas people who are telling the truth (or what they believe to be the truth) tend not to be. The reasoning behind this is that people who are lying are over-worried that they will be caught out and, if they think that you do not believe them, will be likely to overreact and become overly defensive. People on the defensive tend to use phrases such as, 'you don't believe me, do you?' or 'but it's true, I tell you', emphasising words that counter your suspicions such as 'believe', 'true', etc. A person telling the truth will more likely go on the offensive, saying things like 'I know what I saw' or 'that's exactly how it happened'. However, it is not good practice to challenge the witness, and this should only be resorted to if you pick up a lot of inconsistencies in the witnesses statements.

B – Exaggeration

People tend to exaggerate if they really want people to listen to what they say, or if they have strong feelings about something. Both of these behaviours drive people to over-emphasise and to make accounts of paranormal activity appear more dramatic than they really were. This can lead you into thinking that the location you are considering to investigate is more active than it really is, and that the effects or evidence you are 'likely' to pick up will be outstanding. Exaggerated claims caused us (the authors), against our better judgement, to spend several fruitless nights investigating a pub in Cheshire, England, where the only 'spirits' we came across were in the bottles behind the bar! It was only on the third investigation that we got talking to some of the pub regulars, only to discover that the last sighting of the apparition that we were told was 'very regular' occurred over eight years previously.

The only way to assess possible exaggerated claims is to cross-examine the witness's statements and ask for more specific details. For instance, if you ask someone how often they have experienced something at the location, and their answer is 'lots', try to get them to qualify exactly what 'lots' means by asking them to break it down into how many occasions they have experienced something in a month, followed by a week. By drawing out more specific detail, you will get a much clearer picture of the potential the location has for further investigation.

C – Recall/Perception Assessment

The best way to assess someone's recall or perception abilities is to get them to describe something that you have also experienced to see how they fare with detail and accuracy. One subtle way to do this is, if possible, to switch the topic of conversation at some point to TV shows that you watch, e.g. a soap opera, and pretend that you missed a recent episode. By asking the witness to describe what happened on the show, you will be able to get a rough idea of how well they perceive and recall events. This isn't a very scientific test, but it will give you a rough idea of the witness's abilities. Poor perception on behalf of the witness may, in their mind, make more mundane events appear to be supernatural ones. Poor recall ability means that you will not be able to rely on the details being told to you. Both will require a lot of cross-examination to get a better idea of what actually occurred.

D – Belief Systems

If someone has a strong belief system, it will naturally colour their interpretation of the events they experienced. Try to find out as early as you can what the witnesses take is on all things paranormal. Here are some useful questions to use: Is this your first experience? Before your experience, did you believe in the paranormal? What do YOU think you experienced?

Each of these questions should allow you to gauge what the witness thinks about the paranormal and therefore what sort of slant/bias they are likely to put on their testimony.

E – Mental State/Mind-altering Drug Use

One of the most important things to do when gauging a witness's credibility is to determine if the witness:

Has a mental health condition
Is taking any perception impairing prescription medication
Was under the influence of any mind altering drugs that could be responsible for them having their 'paranormal' experience

Mental-health conditions – People who have bi-polar and schizophrenic conditions are capable of experiencing delusions/hallucinations from time to time, both visual and auditory, which will appear very real to them. Being able to tell with certainty that someone has a mental-health condition is a highly specialised business which is best left to the professionals. However, there are signs that sufferers sometimes exhibit that are useful to look out for:

A sudden behavioural change during the course of the interview, e.g. the witness suddenly becomes excitable, withdrawn or distracted/disinterested without real reason.

Expressions of strange or extravagant ideas, such as claiming with the utmost sincerity that they had been to the outer planets (yes, this did happen to us during one interview).

Displays of sudden anger or emotional outbursts.

Conversations change rapidly from topic to topic, sometimes with no logical connecting thread.

Thoughts and sentences become disorganised and incoherent.

The above are not sure-fire ways to tell that someone has a mental-health condition with any certainty, but they may be sufficient enough to indicate that there **may** be a problem with the witness's credibility from a mental-health angle. If you feel that someone is suffering from a mental health condition, it is wise to make polite excuses and leave as soon as possible, as you won't be helping the witness at all by exploring their experiences.

Mind-altering substances – People who were under the influence of either perception-impairing medication or mind-altering drugs such as LSD, cannabis, magic mushrooms, alcohol, etc. at the time of their experience are also highly likely to have had their perceptions impaired to the point of rendering their paranormal experience claims useless. We have found that the best way to determine if the witness has taken something that may be responsible for what they experienced is simply to ask them. This can be a cringingly embarrassing thing to have to do, but you can soften the blow by saying something along the lines of: 'I'm sorry, but we have a few questions that we have to ask everyone, and you don't have to answer if you don't want to, but are you currently on any medication, or were you drinking or taking any recreational drugs at the time?'

More often than not, witnesses will be open and honest with you. We have never found anyone who has taken offence to the question . . . yet. If they give you the name of a medication that you are not familiar with, take a note of it and check out the medication's side-effects (listed under contra-indications) in a copy of the *British National Formulary*, the medical professions 'Bible' of medicinal knowledge. You can find copies of this at your local library. It is important to note that people with mental health conditions, people who are on some forms of prescription medications or mind-altering drugs may have had a genuine experience, but unfortunately, unless they have good physical evidence to back up their claims, their testimony will always be in question.

Interview Goal 2: To Determine if Conducting a Location Investigation Is Going to Be Worthwhile

Sometimes it is not worth conducting an investigation at a location for a number of reasons, such as:

The witness's credibility may be in question, meaning that you are unsure if there really is anything anomalous taking place, or the reported activity may have occurred a long time ago with nothing else having been reported since.

The location of the activity is at the witness's home and not all the family members agree to an investigation taking place there (which could lead to attempted hoaxing or equipment sabotage), and/or the family home is too busy with the comings and goings of people to allow you to conduct a satisfactory investigation.

It is very important to assess witness testimony carefully if you wish to avoid wasting time running potentially fruitless site investigations.

Interview Goal 3: To Gather as Much Useful Information as Possible about the Incident

The following guidelines will help you to develop a good interview technique that should allow you to get the best out of any interview you conduct.

The interview is not just for your benefit alone. As an investigator, you have a responsibility to take care of the witness's needs as well as your own. If they have genuinely experienced something anomalous, they will have issues that they may want you to help them with. Make sure that you also make time for the witness to ask questions too! Try to answer these as plainly as possible without using too much technical jargon. However, if the witness asks for your opinion about what they have experienced, politely decline, telling them that 'at this stage, you wouldn't like to commit yourself, but it sounds intriguing' or words to that effect. This is done so as not to colour the witness's perception of events with your own personal interpretations while the interview is in progress.

Before you start the interview it is important to let the witness know the following:

The interview is going to be more like an informal chat, and that its purpose is to dig a bit deeper into the events to hopefully gain an insight into what they have/are experiencing.

The information the witness gives you will remain confidential and will only be passed to other team members for investigation purposes. The investigator will ask for the witness's permission if they wish to relay details of the testimony/incident to anyone else. This is helpful in gaining the witness's trust and also in providing a more relaxed atmosphere where they know that they can speak openly and confidentially.

The witness doesn't have to answer a question if they don't want to.

As an investigator, you are unable to 'get rid' of any phenomena, and if that is what they ultimately want then you are the wrong person to ask. Tell them that you are here to study the phenomena in order to attempt to understand what causes it and why. You could add the fact that sometimes a rational explanation can be found, which more or less does the same thing.

Ask the witness if they mind the interview being recorded. If you are allowed to record the interview, take notes as well, just in case the recording doesn't turn out.

Interview Recording Tips

Put fresh batteries in your recorder and take spares. Make sure you have enough tapes/memory cards or sufficient internal memory to record the whole interview.

Listen to the background sound in the room for a few seconds. Is there anything in the room that is creating noise that might drown out the recording of the interview, i.e. a TV or radio blaring away in the background? If so, ask if the witness doesn't mind switching them off during the interview.

When starting the recording, make sure you announce the date, time, location and all present at the start of the recording. This is useful when you start cataloguing recordings.

Make a mental note of what time you will have to change the tape/memory card and keep your eye on the time.

Questioning

When interviewing the witness it is very important not to use *leading questions*. Leading questions are those that suggest an answer to the witness, which may also bias the witness towards giving an answer that the interviewer wants to hear. Instead, use *open questions*. Open questions are ones that allow the witness to answer in their own words, without having their responses channelled towards certain answers. Here are some examples of leading questions and their open equivalents:

Leading: Was the ghost translucent or did it appear solid?
Open: What did you see?

Leading: Was the sound like footsteps on the stairs?
Open: What did you hear?

Leading: Were you afraid?
Open: How did you feel?

Starting the Interview

The first question you must start with is this: 'Tell us in your own words what you experienced.'

Listen carefully to what the witness has to say. Let them tell the whole story. Do not interrupt them and do not attempt to put words into their mouths if they are struggling to explain anything. Take note of any pertinent points as they talk, and jot down questions you would like to ask.

It is always a good idea to bring along a basic checklist of core questions. Core questions are questions that ideally you need answers for. Having a list of core questions at hand is useful, for if the witness doesn't provide the answer for one or more of them while they recount their story, you won't forget to ask those questions at some point. Remember that you are trying to gain information about the witness themselves (character, beliefs, and attitude), their experiences and also the location where they had their experiences.

Here is a basic core question checklist:

Location information:

Where did they experience the phenomena? (Address or location and specific room/area within the location.)

When did they experience it? (Date and time.) If time is approximate, how did they gauge this?

Were there any other witnesses? If so, who were they and are their contact details available?

Does the witness know of anyone else who has experienced anything anomalous at the location prior to their experience?

If yes, what did they experience?

Does the witness know if the location has a paranormal history?

The witness's experience:

What happened?

How did they first become aware of the event?

What did they See, Hear, Smell, Feel, Taste?

How did the event cease/stop?

How long did they experience it for?

What were they doing just prior to the experience? For instance, if the witness was asleep and suddenly awoke to find an 'apparition' in the room, it is entirely possible that they could have been in a hypnopompic state (a state somewhere between being unconscious and being awake) and were experiencing a hallucination. When in hypnopompic states, people can have both visual and auditory hallucinations.

Were they in good health at the time of the experience? Viruses and flu conditions can sometimes make body temperature extremely high, leading to people having hallucinations.

What characteristic(s) of the event made the witness come to the conclusion that it was paranormal in origin?

Did the event affect anything in the surrounding area? e.g. did objects move of their own accord? Were there any electrical equipment failures, e.g. lights, computers, radios, TVs? Were there any animals present, and if so, how did they react?

Did the witness manage to gather any physical evidence, i.e. photo/video/audio?

The witness's character:

What does the witness think that they have experienced?

Does the witness believe in the paranormal? If yes, what aspects?

Did the witness believe in the paranormal prior to this event?

Has the witness had any other paranormal experiences prior to this one? If so, what? And when?

Concluding the Interview

Once you feel that the interview has run its course, give a visual clue to the witness that you have concluded your business by closing your notepad and switching off your recorder. Tell the witness that you think you have got everything you need for now, but ask them if it is OK for you to contact them again if any further questions come up.

Unless you are 100 per cent certain about the witness and what they have had to say, do not commit yourself to taking the investigation a stage further. Let the witness know that you will be in touch soon to see where things will go next.

Ask the witness if they have anything they would like to ask you, and let them know that they are free to contact you should they need to over the next few days.

On the way out, thank the witness for their time, patience and hospitality.

After the Interview

As soon as you can, write up your thoughts, feelings and observations from the meeting and cross-examine the answers given to assess if it is worthwhile taking the investigation to the next stage. Arrange a meeting with your team to discuss the interview as soon as possible afterwards.

Don't leave the witness in limbo for too long. As soon as you have made a decision about whether or not the investigation should proceed to the next stage, let the witness know.

The next few stages in the Investigation Life Cycle are a little different depending upon what you are investigating, so these will be covered individually within each topic.

Ghosts

I would like, if I may,
to take you on a strange journey!

The Narrator
The Rocky Horror Picture Show

A Brief History

Ever since mankind has been pottering about on the planet the human race has been fascinated with the concept of life after death and what form it could possibly take. What happens to the soul when the physical body ceases to function anymore? Does it simply die along with the body, or is it that the soul, life-force, spirit, call it what you will, is somehow transferred or imprints itself onto another life or even onto an inanimate object?

Could it be that a ghost, as is popularly believed, is the soul of someone that has died? This belief in the soul is the foundation of animism, which is to say that every natural thing has a soul whether it is a human being, an animal, every living thing from the smallest plant to the largest mountain, from wind to wave and everything in-between. This belief system is present in one form or another in the majority of the world's religions, and if you find it hard to believe that a religion would entertain the notion of ghosts, etc., there are a few mentions of them in the Bible; Jesus had to persuade his followers that he had indeed risen from the dead and what they were seeing was, in fact, not a ghost. Many people believed that to witness a ghost was some sort of evil omen or a premonition of death to occur in the not too distant future, and to see a ghost that actually resembled themselves was a sure sign that their own death was imminent.

In a way, the most public incarnation of animism in recent years has been the 'Force' that was an integral part of the *Star Wars* series of movies, where the Jedi could sense any alterations or disturbances in this life energy, such as the destruction of the planet Alderaan by the Death Star in the original *Star Wars* movie. But this belief, of a ghost being the soul of some person that is now dead is not solely linked to modern times and cultures, far from it; it is a notion that has been around for centuries. Various ancient cultures depict the soul to be an exact replica of the dead body from where the soul originated, even down to the clothing that the person wore.

But this poses a further and a fundamentally far more serious question: if the soul does indeed manifest itself in the clothes that were worn at the time of death; do we have to look forward to wandering around the hereafter exposing our buttocks just because some of us happened to have died in a hospital somewhere wearing one of those not-very-flattering gowns that tie at the side or back. Let's face the truth here, this look may very well work for some Hollywood starlet or the likes of Kylie Minogue, but the majority of us don't expect the concept of exposed ghostly bum cheeks or bum cleavage to win us many, if any, friends in the afterlife. How would that look on *Most Haunted*? It would certainly make interesting viewing though!

Another popular belief about ghostly apparitions that has been almost constant throughout recorded history is that the soul of the departed is somehow trapped on Earth looking to avenge some wrong-doing that was either done to them whilst they was alive, or alternately, some misdeed that they themselves were guilty of. Quite often it seems that it is the spirit of someone that had their life taken due to murder or some other such act of violence. In Scandinavian mythology, this belief that the murdered soul of a person could not rest in peace until retribution had been achieved is given the name of *Gjenganger*, which appears to be a curious mix of ghost and poltergeist. But the violent death aspect is borne out with the sheer quantity of spectral sightings and reports from around the areas where battles have been fought, and from every continent all around the globe. The loss of life doesn't have to be on a horrendous scale for these reports to occur, it ranges from major battles during the World Wars, such as the Battle of the Somme where the death toll of British, French and German servicemen was something astronomical and the likes of which will hopefully never be seen again, to the smallest skirmishes that occurred during the likes of the English and American Civil Wars, such as at Newton-le-Willows in Merseyside, where, on the anniversary of the Battle of Winwick Pass, 19 August 1648, it is said that the sound of drums and marching feet can still be heard in the area around where the fighting and dying took place.

Again, another popular theory is that, rather than a violent or murderous end, it could be that the death happens so unexpectedly, so completely out of the blue, that the person in question fails to realise that they are actually dead and continues to carry on their everyday life, completely unaware that it is doing so as a ghostly manifestation.

A popular misconception is that ghosts and poltergeists are one and the same thing, but there are differences between these two paranormal phenomena. Whereas a ghost is said to be seen but rarely heard, and ghost-like activity is said to 'haunt', a poltergeist phenomena is said to 'disturb' because it is heard rather than seen; in fact, the literal translation of the word poltergeist is 'noisy spirit'. But in fairness to all concerned, it is quite difficult to differentiate between these two because some of the activities associated with both of these phenomena can be very similar.

This bridge commemorates the Battle of Winwick Pass. Even to this day, on the anniversary of the battle, the sounds of marching troops and music are said to echo around Newton-le-Willows.

As with ghosts, poltergeist activities have been mentioned and recorded throughout the annals of worldwide history and again are not necessarily linked to one particular culture or religious belief system. One of the earliest reports of a poltergeist comes from Germany in the ninth century and the activities recorded are typical of those associated with this kind of case. The family in question were subjected to banging noises, objects being moved and thrown around, and as you can imagine in this environment, a fun time was not to be had by all the family. Poltergeists, due to their activity traits, can be one of the most terrifying and nerve-wracking aspects to encounter in the world of the paranormal.

One of the most famous cases of poltergeist activity happened only thirty years ago, during the 1970s in the north part of London. The incident happened over the course of a gruelling thirteen months for the family concerned. The 'Enfield Poltergeist' was a landmark case as it was widely publicised at the time of its occurrence through the various media of the day. The events in question even spawned a mock documentary by the BBC called *Ghostwatch*. Broadcast at Hallowe'en in 1992, it in turn caused something of a stir among the viewing public as it had an alarming effect on many of those who watched it, much as the Orson Welles radio broadcast of *War of the Worlds* had had on the American public many years before. One of the advisors for the show was Guy Lyon Playfair, who was the lead investigator, along with Maurice Grosse, on the Enfield Poltergeist case. Though the programme has never been broadcast again by the BBC since its initial airing, with a bit of digging, it can be found on the internet and still makes very interesting viewing!

But the fascination and investigation into the world of the paranormal really took off during the Victorian era. It was an age of fantastic development scientifically, but if you take a look at some of the great works of literature from around that period – Mary Shelley's *Frankenstein*, Bram Stoker's *Dracula* – you'll see that the world of the supernatural was never very far from the forefront of the Victorian mentality. It was not uncommon for accusations of witchcraft still to be heard; in fact, it was not until as late as 1944 that the last person was jailed in England for offences under the Witchcraft Act. For the Victorians, it wasn't simply a case of believing in a spirit world, they also wanted physical proof too! In 1848, three sisters from New York State came under the spotlight of the public's attention. The Fox sisters, Leah, Margaretta and Catherine, became famous for their ability to communicate with the world of the dead, their method of table rapping enabled the sisters to ask questions of the spirits, who duly replied with a series of knocks, each sequence of knocks, taps and raps represented the ghostly equivalent or yes or no, and so on and so forth. In fact, their skills came to the fore as a result of a poltergeist infestation in their childhood home in Hydesville. Supposedly, they were in contact with a spirit that had been murdered and later buried under their house that went by the name of 'Mr Splitfoot'. As their reputation grew so did their clientele, with many eminent dignitaries of the day taking part in séances with the sisters, all of whom were convinced that what they had experienced was totally authentic and beyond question. Both Cate and Margaretta became mediums and all three siblings were influential in the creation of Spiritualism, the religious movement, and this, along with the fame and notoriety of the Fox sisters, led to an influx of mediums popping up all over the United States of America. The phenomenon eventually crossed the Atlantic and landed up on the shores of the British Isles in the early 1850s. Despite the fact that many of the mediums, including the Fox sisters, were eventually proven to be fakes (in 1888 two of the sisters, Cate and Margaretta, admitted that they had fraudulently caused the communications with the world of the spirits, though they came to retract this statement a year later), the Spiritualist movement continues to this day.

One of the side effects of mediumship was the creation of ectoplasm, which is noted to have been excreted by the medium during a trance-like state, and is said to aid in the formation of a ghost. There are many accounts of people who witnessed the phenomenon and there are many photographs supposedly showing the manifestation of ectoplasm; in fact, many of the people attending mediums and séances felt as though they had been cheated if no ectoplasm was evident during the event, such had its popularity become. Reports of ectoplasm in recent years seem to have died a death, though it did have a resurgence in the 1980s due to the *Ghostbusters* movies, and it still pops up from time to time in one guise or another in things like the *Hellboy* comics.

A great debunker of mediums and spiritualists was the legendary escapologist Harry Houdini. He uncovered various scams run by mediums, and the way that some of them made ectoplasm seem to appear from out of the ether. Various tricks were used to perform this feat, from a hidden bladder that was squeezed to make it appear that the ectoplasm was being projected from the mouth, to strips of cloth covered in some form of grease that could be hastily applied to the body of the medium, which in the dim light in which séances were normally held, would appear slimy, gooey or otherworldly. Houdini, along with other investigators of the period, deduced that the greatest feat performed by the mediums in relation to ectoplasm was the power of suggestion. It was during this period that Houdini met and befriended Arthur Conan Doyle, the creator of the great detective Sherlock Holmes. In contrast to Houdini, Arthur Conan Doyle was a great believer in the skills of the mediums to such an extent that Houdini thought him 'hopelessly gullible'. Doyle became a member of the Society for Psychical Research and investigated the case of the Cottingley Fairies and was convinced that the fairy photographs were completely genuine.

Ironically, Houdini's wife, Beth, held yearly séances at Hallowe'en for ten years following Harry's death in 1926. But, alas, Harry Houdini never appeared.

In the last twenty years, we have seen interest in the paranormal and its investigation again hit an all-time high. Ghosts have become, and in a way always have been, the pin-up girl for the supernatural. Almost everyone can tell some sort of ghost or spooky story, whether they believe in the phenomenon or not. Just like the Victorians, the paranormal has pervaded into our consciousness like never before, and all things spooky have now become big business. How many ancestral homes, country pubs and hotels now advertise the fact that they have a haunted room, gallery or such like? With television shows like *The X-Files*, *Supernatural* and *Medium*, along with the reality paranormal investigation shows like *Most Haunted*, *Ghost Hunters International*, *Spook School* and many others, the pursuit of ghosts and paranormal investigation has been brought right into our living rooms; it has awakened a dormant interest in many of us and has entertained us at the same time. But what if you want to take it further, what if you want to investigate it yourself?

Unless you live in a haunted house, sitting in front of your television set is not the place to be. But just how do you go about it . . .

Alternative Theories

What is a ghost? What is an apparition? The simple answer is that no one knows for sure. Some ghosts appear to interact with the living, responding to our presence directly, whereas some don't and seem to be nothing more than 'recordings' of past events. There have also been reports of people seeing ghosts of the living, where individuals have allegedly been sighted simultaneously in two places at once. Since ghosts seem to exhibit different characteristics, most researchers have come to the conclusion that the experiences collectively described as 'ghosts' represent not just one, but a whole range of phenomena. In this section, we take a critical look at some of the theories about ghosts and their various categories, and weigh them up against the reported evidence.

Life After Death – Survival of the Spirit or Soul

The most common belief, held by a majority of people around the world, is that a ghost or apparition is the soul or spirit of someone who has died. The soul or spirit is believed to be the part of us that contains our consciousness, memory and personality; it somehow is able to survive the death of the physical body and continue to exist in its own right, where it then has the ability to interact with the living. However, in absence of hard, scientific evidence to support the reality of life after death, where did this idea originate? The belief in life after death is as old as recorded history, and there is good evidence to suggest that the notion goes back even further, possibly to the dawn of mankind. So what gave ancient man such a strong conviction that part of us lives on once the body has expired?

Some researchers say that ancient man knew a lot more about death and the processes that followed afterwards because they were closer to it than we are today. In our modern, technological world, we tend to shy away from death, and the recently departed are covered up and whisked away to be buried or cremated as soon as possible. However, for reasons now lost in the sands of time, the dead of some ancient cultures were kept for a long time amongst the living.

From archaeological studies of Neanderthal burial sites, approximately 60,000 years old, evidence has been found to show that Neanderthal tribe members made frequent visits to their deceased's graves to leave regular offerings of food, clothing, weapons, totems, jewellery and flowers. It appears that there was a need in their culture to continue to provide for their dead long after their physical deaths, even though tribes were undoubtedly hard pushed for food and other resources. In particular, there is a very interesting burial site that was discovered deep in a cave in France, where the pollen of no less than twenty different types of flowers and plants was discovered in the soil. Some of the pollen belonged to plants that were not native to the area, which is testament to the extraordinary effort the tribespeople went to in order to provide for their dead. To ancient man, the dead, and the tending of them, was of the utmost importance – in some cases appearing to be more important than the need to tend for the living. Why was this so? Luckily, contemporary clues still exist today.

Anthropological studies of tribes who reside in remote parts of the world, where twenty-first-century civilisation hasn't wiped out ancient traditions and beliefs, show similar practices to those of the Neanderthals. In particular, while conducting studies of the Makabeng tribe in South Africa, anthropologists discovered that there were very close ties between the living tribe members and their departed relatives. The living claimed that they were constantly pestered with demands from the dead for food and trinkets, so much so, that if they didn't comply they were, essentially, *haunted* by them. However, in return, the tribe were also able to ask their departed for advice or help whenever the need arose. Just as important as the dead themselves were their final resting places, for it was believed that the location where the deceased were laid to rest was the place where the spirit or soul would most readily commune with the living.

It is interesting to note that the Makabeng's ability to communicate with the dead was not confined to select individuals in the tribe, but was an ability that all claimed to possess. Could it be that our move away from nature to our technologically dependent society has caused most of us to lose our ability to feel and communicate with the spirits around us, and that when we see apparitions we are experiencing rare instances when our deeply buried abilities surface for an instant? If this is so, does the best proof for the existence of ghosts come from mediums? Mediums are people who claim that they are able to communicate with, and in some instances actually see, spirits of the dead. They claim that their abilities allow then to act as a conduit between the world of the living and the afterlife, which allows spirits to 'come through' to our plane of existence and make their presence known. But is this really the case?

One of the biggest problems faced by paranormal investigators is proving that anomalous phenomena really do exist. Far too much of what is presented as 'proof' is anecdotal, being formed mostly from personal accounts with no supporting physical evidence. Unfortunately, evidence from mediums falls squarely into the anecdotal category because not everyone can experience what a medium claims to be experiencing. Non-mediums literally have to take the medium's word for it that there is a 'presence in the room'. On occasions, mediums do provide impressive results, for instance, names of former deceased occupants of a building, the manner of their deaths, etc., which can often be backed up by historical research. However, sceptics are keen to point out that there are many conventional sources that a medium's 'information' could have been gleaned from rather than the 'spirit world'. Techniques such as cold reading (a method of using subtle trial-and-error questioning to gather information from a person that, unless you know the trick, appears to have been gained from supernatural sources), inspired guesswork, and conducting private research have all been cited as more realistic sources of a medium's information than communication with the spirits of the departed. Another alternative explanation offered by some is the possibility that mediums aren't actually contacting the dead, but using extra-sensory perception (ESP) to subconsciously read the minds of the living!

Our personal take is that we do feel that there is something to a medium's abilities that is worthy of further study, but until more is understood about the mechanisms and workings of mediumistic processes, the evidence gained from mediums alone will always be anecdotal, and as such is not appropriate to use as conclusive evidence of the existence of life after death. Are ghosts really the spirits of the dead? The debate continues.

Imprinting/Residual Haunting (aka The Stone Tape Theory)

When independent witnesses report seeing the same 'ghost' perform the same activity at the same location time and again, some researchers believe that what is actually being seen is not a ghost, but a 'recording' of a person or an event that has somehow become imprinted into the fabric of a building or a location. This imprint is said to be able to 'replay' itself when the conditions are right. This type of ghost sighting differs from other kinds in one important respect: the apparition does not appear to be aware of the presence of the witnesses or of its immediate surroundings. It has often been reported that apparitions have been seen to walk through walls as though they were not there, and in some rare reports it has been claimed that they have actually walked right through the witnesses themselves. When an apparition is found to have walked through a wall where a door or corridor used to exist, this seems to add weight to the notion that what is being observed is some form of 'recording' of a past event.

It is interesting to note that most of these recurring apparitions appear to be of people who, when alive, went through the same routine on a regular basis. Could repeating the same actions, over and over, eventually lead to the activity imprinting itself into the surroundings? After all, reports of phantom police officers walking the beat and long-deceased night watchmen patrolling factories are fairly common, and they appear to support the 'repetition imprint' idea. If this is the case, will some of us one day appear as 'ghosts' ourselves, simply by going about our daily routines?

However, the imprinting theory has its critics. Some researchers say that, although regular sightings of ghosts do seem occur at specific locations, there is no reliable evidence to show that what is being witnessed is exactly the same event time after time. Another problem with the imprinting theory is that no one has come up with a satisfactory explanation of how it is possible for a person to actually 'record' themselves into a wall, or explain how that 'recording' can subsequently be played back.

Over the years, researchers have suggested many possibilities, such as that microscopic quartz crystals found in bricks may be capable of absorbing and storing electrical energy given off by people, or iron particles in walls may have the ability to record sounds and moving images in much the same way as they can on magnetic tape. Another intriguing idea is that water may play a role in the imprinting process, as recent scientific research suggests that water may have some form of rudimentary 'memory'. It has been found that if you place anything in water, e.g. a chemical compound, and then dilute the mixture to an extent that not even a single molecule of the chemical remains, the water continues to behave as though the chemical is still present. Some paranormal researchers have speculated that the water in our bodies may be capable of storing our 'essence', which then imprints itself into the fabric of our surroundings as we exhale or perspire.

Maybe one of the above ideas may eventually be proved to be correct, but there is a long way to go before all of this becomes a satisfactory explanation for what is going on.

Bilocation or Multilocation

Over the past few hundred years, there have been reliable reports of people seeing 'ghosts' of the living, where individuals, and in some cases, inanimate objects, have been seen to inhabit two separate locations at precisely the same time. In some instances, the 'double' has looked partially translucent, but in others has seemed as solid and as real as the actual person and, more importantly, some doubles have even interacted with people and objects around them. The people to whom bilocation occurs are usually not aware that the event is taking place, but they report that they feel increasingly tired as the incident progresses.

The following is a typical example of a bilocation incident that was told to us by the witnesses themselves. Interestingly, this bilocation did not occur to a human, but to a dog. Paul Graham was sitting in the downstairs lounge of his home in Wales ,where he was relaxing reading the newspaper. The family dog, an eleven-year-old Collie-cross called Boots, was lying curled up by his feet. His (now ex) wife, Sue, who was upstairs having a lie down, suddenly shouted at Boots for jumping up onto the bed and waking her up. As she continued to scold the dog, Paul looked down at his feet, and sure enough, Boots was still lying there, but this time the dog was awake and alert because he had heard his name being called. Paul gave Boots a reassuring pat on the head, and then shouted upstairs, 'What are you going on about? Boots is down here with me.'

His wife shouted down angrily, 'No he's not, he's up here pestering me!' To prove that the dog was with him, Paul got Boots to bark. Perplexed, Sue did the same with the dog in the bedroom.

Thinking that possibly a stray dog had wandered upstairs, Paul asked Sue to bring the dog she had with her downstairs, which she agreed to do. Seconds later, the dog emerged at the foot of the stairwell and padded towards Paul with its tail wagging furiously. There was no mistaking the fact that the dog that had been in the bedroom with Sue was indeed Boots. But when Paul looked down, the dog that had been at his feet, whose head he had patted only minutes earlier, had now mysteriously vanished, despite Paul only taking his eyes off him for a second. Paul and Sue were completely stunned. Each of them is still convinced that, for a period of around five minutes, their dog had inexplicably existed simultaneously in two places at once.

There are a whole host of other phenomena that may be linked to bilocation, such as out of body experiences (OoBEs), where people report that they have floated around outside their body for a short while and existed independently of it, or near death experience (NDE), where some people that are very close to death report that they leave their bodies and eventually fly down a dark tunnel towards a bright light. However, unlike bilocation, both OoBEs and NDEs are not witnessed by others.

Critics say that the reported instances of bilocations are either hoaxes or misidentifications, where the individuals concerned look identical to each other and their simultaneous appearances get mistaken for a bilocation. This may happen some of the time, but in our humble opinion, under the right conditions, part of us may very well be able to exist independently of the body, for a short time at least.

Crisis Apparitions

Another puzzling class of apparition, and one that appears to be a commonly reported experience, is when people see an apparition of a friend or relative who, at that precise moment, is in a crisis situation and almost at the point of death. Often, the witness reports suddenly waking up from a deep sleep to find their friend or relative standing at the foot of the bed. Critics are quick to point out these apparitions could merely be 'waking dreams' caused by individuals worrying in their sleep about their sick and dying friends or relatives. However, in some cases, witnesses have not been aware that the person who 'paid them a visit' was in a life-threatening situation, and have only found out when calling them the next day. Once again, it appears that under certain conditions, our consciousness is capable of projecting itself outside of the body, but it still does not confirm that our consciousness can survive the body's physical death.

Time Anomalies

One of the ideas put forward to explain the presence of ghosts is that we are not actually seeing spirits of the dead, but are in fact witnessing time anomalies, where, under the right conditions, different periods in time can somehow 'overlap' for short intervals. These overlaps open up 'windows' that allow us in the present to experience events in the past, giving rise to appearances of monks, Roman soldiers, cavaliers and other spooky effects such as anomalous sounds or smells.

From recent discoveries made in quantum mechanics, it has been postulated that the flow of time as we understand it, i.e. past to present to future, may be a construct made by our minds, and that time may operate very differently to how we perceive it. If that is the case, are paranormal occurrences showing us aspects of its true nature? As counterintuitive as this idea may at first seem, it does appear to offer a good explanation for some of the activity experienced by ourselves and others whist investigating what has been called the most haunted house in England, Chingle Hall.

Chingle Hall is an eleventh-century farmhouse that has survived the ravages of almost 1,000 years of local unrest, ranging from plague and civil war to the infamous Reformation, where priests secretly performed outlawed Catholic masses, an act that carried the death penalty. With so much dark history, most people are not too surprised to discover that the hall is reputed to be the home of over twenty different apparitions and ghostly effects that have been experienced on a fairly regular basis.

The original hall was constructed with a moat running all around it, complete with a rising drawbridge whose winding mechanism was housed in an upstairs room at the front of the property. The drawbridge and mechanism have long since been removed and the room now serves as a bedroom. Despite this, on occasions, the sounds of a chain running through a winding mechanism can still be heard in this room, and these sounds have been successfully captured on audio on more than one occasion. Downstairs in the Great Hall, the smell of burning candles has suddenly filled the room, only to vanish as quickly as it has appeared. Could both these occurrences be effects of different times overlapping? As well as phantom winding mechanisms and candles, one visitor to the hall experienced something that only makes sense if you accept a time anomaly as being the cause.

On the stairs leading up to the second floor, there is a handrail mounted on the right-hand side as you look up the stairs. On one investigation, conducted in the hall in the mid-1990s, investigator Mike Jaega began descending the stairs in the dark so as not to disturb the night vision of colleagues who were on the landing. In the gloom at the top of the stairs he spied the handrail and placed his right hand on it and used it to guide him down to the bottom. It was only when he reached the last step and had let go of the rail that he realised it should have been on the other wall! Fumbling in the dark, Mike tried to touch the rail he had just let go of, but couldn't find it. Reaching out with his left hand he soon located it on the other wall. The handrail was now back on the side it was supposed to be on. When he told the owners about this they stated that the handrail used to be on the other side, but was moved over to the other wall in the early 1970s. Did Mike start off in the '90s, descend the stairs in the '70s and re-emerge back into the '90s at the bottom? Could these events be indicators that time anomalies are indeed the cause of some of the occurrences at Chingle Hall?

More recently, Mark Rosney had another experience where, once again, different times appear to have overlapped for a short while. Whilst working as a civil servant in Runcorn, Mark's daily bus journey took him along the same route for over four years. During that time, he became very familiar with all the buildings and scenery along the way. On a bright January morning in 2008, Mark suddenly spotted an old, dilapidated building that he was sure he hadn't seen before, standing on its own at the edge of an industrial estate. He remembered noticing that most of the tiles were off the roof, and that the windows were all smashed in, allowing the net curtains to flap around helplessly in the breeze. The building looked very old and he was puzzled why he hadn't seen it before. Mark got the distinct impression that there was something very odd about the house, for it looked very out of place where it stood. He made a mental note to look out for it again when he next passed by.

On the journey home, Mark failed to see the house. Thinking that it must have slipped by unnoticed because it was growing dark, he decided to try again the following morning. When he failed to see it the next morning, he talked to work colleagues about it. One of them suggested that maybe the house had been pulled down during the day. This prompted Mark to check out the location using Google Earth, as the images used to construct the maps for the immediate area were around two years old. If the house had been knocked down on the same day he first spotted it, surely it would show up on these? But at the location where Mark had spotted the house, there was nothing at all, except for a strip of grassland. Could this have been another occasion when something from the past momentarily popped into the present before returning to its own time? More importantly, if there had been occupants in the house, would they have seen a vision of a ghostly express bus hurtling past their windows?

Low Frequency Sound (Infrasound)

Sound is generated whenever anything vibrates. This vibration causes the air molecules around us to firstly bunch tighter together (compression), and then to spring apart (rarefaction), pushing the energy of the vibrations outwards from the source in much the same way as ripples move across the surface of a pond when you toss a pebble into the water. These 'ripples in the air' are called sound waves. The distance between the peaks (compressions) of the ripples is called the sound's wavelength. The longer the wavelength, the lower in pitch the sound is. For example, the lowest frequency sound that the human ear can hear has a wavelength of 16.6 metres or 54 feet, whereas the highest frequency we can hear has a wavelength of just 1.7 centimetres or 0.67 inches.

Imagine that we were able to see sound waves pass by us. Counting how many complete waves go past us each second gives us the frequency or pitch of the sound we are hearing. Because low-pitched sounds have much longer waves, far fewer of them will be able to go past in a single second than higher-pitched sounds. We measure the frequency of sounds in cycles per second (referred to as Hertz or Hz for short).

We are capable of hearing sounds as high as 20,000 cycles per second right down to a mere 20 cycles per second. Anything below 20 cycles per second is referred to as infrasound. Infrasound waves are very large. Blue whales are capable of generating sounds as low as 5 Hz, where the sound waves have a length of 67 metres or 220 feet. Although we cannot hear infrasound, we are capable of feeling it, usually through picking up vibrations or feeling pressure in the chest. But we can also experience infrasound in other ways.

In 2003, experiments conducted at the Southbank Centre in London showed that adding infrasound at frequencies of 17 Hz into classical music performances made people feel uneasy, anxious, sad or even experience feelings of irrational nervousness or fear, which are not the normal things you would expect people to feel at a music concert. Researchers are not that surprised by this, as infrasound is generated in nature by things such as impending earthquakes, tsunamis and large herds of stampeding animals, which may be the reason why we instinctively link infrasound to feelings of unease and fear.

As well as creating feelings of unease, infrasound can also cause people to have visual hallucinations. Vic Tandy, a lecturer at Coventry University discovered that a faulty extraction fan in his lab caused him to experience effects that would have normally been classed as being paranormal in origin had he not investigated the incidents very thoroughly. As Vic was working alone late one night in his lab, out of the corner of his eye he became aware of a strange grey, floating shape hovering in the distance. However, as soon as he turned to look at it directly, the mysterious shape disappeared completely. The next night, Vic was in the same lab, this time doing some DIY on his fencing foil, which he had placed into a vice. Inexplicably, the sword started to vibrate and then swing wildly. Vic was perplexed.

After a few days of detective work, Vic discovered that the extractor fan in his lab was generating infrasound at a frequency of 18 Hz, which explained not only the fencing foil's weird vibration, but also why he saw the grey apparition out of the corner of his eye. 18 Hz just happens to be the resonating frequency of the human eye! Eye vibrations can, and do, cause visual hallucinations, especially around the edges of our field of vision. Parapsychologists and other researchers have successfully detected infrasound at some of the well-know, reputedly haunted venues around the UK, and they are now convinced that some of what we perceive as 'ghostly' activity can be explained by the presence of low frequency sound.

As well as being created by natural events, infrasound can also be generated by man-made activity such as distant traffic, heavy machinery or wind turbines.

Poltergeists

Poltergeist activity usually starts off small but, over the course of a few weeks, becomes more dramatic and sustained, before tailing off slowly back to normality. On average, the activity tends to last around four to six weeks. During the peak, people experience frequent large-scale activity, usually in the form of furniture and other household items moving around of their own accord. Often objects will hurtle around rooms violently, as though being thrown by invisible hands. Personal possessions can disappear and reappear of their own accord, usually in the unlikeliest of places and sometimes foreign objects such as stones or old coins can inexplicably fall from above, seemingly coming through the ceiling. Sometimes these foreign objects (known as apports) can feel very hot to the touch if picked up soon after they appear.

Unlike ghosts and hauntings, which are primarily location focused, Poltergeist activity seems to be person focused, usually occurring around children who are going through puberty. Many psychologists believe that the activity is created by the human mind, which, under conditions of stress, is capable of invoking psychokinetic effects on the immediate environment.

However, there is an opposing viewpoint to this from other researchers. They believe that what is actually taking place is that the person who is the focus for the activity has become susceptible to being possessed by a spirit or other entity, which uses them as a channel with which to unleash their torments on the living world.

Of these two viewpoints, we tend to stray towards the 'created by the mind' school of thought, as this appears to be the most straightforward. It is a rule of nature that the simplest solution is usually the correct solution! As we shall see next, there is some compelling evidence to support the living angle.

Created by the Mind?

There are some researchers who are coming to the conclusion that the living may have the ability to create physical ghost or poltergeist-like effects and activity with mind power alone. In an interesting experiment conducted in Canada in the 1970s, a team of researchers from the Toronto Society for Psychical research decided to see if it were possible for them to make their very own ghost. They attempted this by creating a totally fictitious person whom they christened 'Philip', and then created an equally fictitious life story for him, making him an aristocratic Englishman living in the sixeenth-century.

The team met weekly and spent long periods discussing Philip's character and personality. At these meetings, they would concentrate on aspects of his fictional life, developing his character and life history more and more, in the hope of producing ghost-like activity. After a few weeks, the team bonded and began to regard Philip as a real-life character that they felt they knew very well. The experiment continued for a few months without any results until one fateful session when Philip made his 'presence' known by knocking on a table. At first the knocks were very faint but over the next few weeks the knocks became stronger and more audible. The team then devised a method of communicating with Philip – one rap for yes, two for no, and in no time at all they began to have amazing conversations with their 'made-up' ghost. Philip soon expanded his 'ghostly' repertoire by moving the table all around the room, and making lights turn on and off by themselves.

The success of the Toronto team has spurred on other teams across the globe to try the experiment for themselves, and most have been successful in creating an impressive array of phenomena, seemingly to order. However, like poltergeists, some people ask the question, was the activity created by the minds of the living or by a 'genuine' spirit mimicking the fictitious one? Again, we favour the 'living' over the 'spirits' as the source of the activity. This leads us to wonder, if our minds can create ghost-like effects around us, what else might they be capable of?

How to Conduct a Ghost Investigation

Ghosts and hauntings have become a boom industry of late, with many organisations offering 'ghost hunting' nights at allegedly haunted locations. Here, you are often charged a small fortune to wander around in large groups looking for paranormal activity. You are often led around by guides who usually claim to be psychic, who build up the atmosphere by telling everyone about the location's spooky past or how they are 'feeling presences' in the room. Eventually, the attendees are let loose on their own to 'investigate' the venue. Although these events can be a lot of fun, they are a million miles away from how a ghost investigation should be conducted.

As stated earlier in this topic, one of the biggest problems faced by paranormal investigators is proving that anomalous phenomena really do exist. On a typical ghost hunt, even if you are lucky enough to 'catch' something eerie on audio or video, there

Investigation Life Cycle

Initial Contact
Witness Interview
Background Research
Initial Location Reconnaissance
Planning the Site Investigation
Pre Brief
Running the Investigation
Analysis
Writing Up Your Findings
Making Your Findings Public

are so many people wandering around the venue making noise and generally spooking each other that it becomes impossible to eliminate the people present as being the cause for a majority of activity you have 'caught'. Is that EVP or just someone in the background whispering to a friend? Is that an apparition in the distance, or just another investigator who has wandered into shot?

After a while, people who want to investigate more seriously begin to get frustrated with the lack of control in these situations. The methods we recommend will help you organise your investigations better with a view to raising your chances of capturing good evidence. As introduced in the core concepts and skills section of the book, the best method to use in any paranormal investigation is to follow the stages in the Investigation Life Cycle.

So far we have shown you how to conduct yourself at the initial contact stage and also how to get the most out of a witness interview. After conducting the interview, if you decide that you wish to proceed with running a site investigation at the location where the activity was reported, it is important to do some background research before you attempt to set foot in the location.

Background Research

Equipment:

Pens
Notepad
A4 wallet
Highlighter pens
Library card
Patience!

Whether the location you wish to investigate is the witness's house, a pub, a derelict building or an old castle, it is important to do thorough research. This is a painstaking job but can be very rewarding and enlightening. If you are intending to investigate the witness's own home, you already have a good source of information at hand: the witness. They will be able to tell you how long they have lived there, the names of the residents and also tell you about all the significant events that have occurred there during their stay. They may even know something about the previous occupants (if any), such as names, occupations and also a bit about what happened to them.

It is a good idea to have only one person from the team look into the historical information, as this will act as a control element in the subsequent site investigation. The reason behind this is simple. If the whole team knows the history, it is likely to influence their perception of events – i.e., if they know that an elderly lady died there in a specific room many years ago, they may interpret what they experience as the spirit of the old lady. If some of the team are not aware of the history, then it allows for them to perceive without bias, and their accounts can be scrutinised for comparisons/differences.

Firstly, look carefully at the information you have gathered from the witness interview to see if there are any obvious leads that will help you to dig into the location's historical background. The sort of information you need to find is:

When was the location (house, hall, castle, etc.) built/established?

What was the location used for before? (Church, graveyard, cottage, hill fort, shop, farmland, battleground, site of antiquity, etc.)

Have any significant events occurred there? (Deaths, murders, fires, other tragedies, battles, plague, etc.)

Any structural changes/renovations (adding/removing rooms/wings, demolition of building, rebuilding, etc.)
Structural change details are very useful; for instance, if there are reports of an apparition walking through a wall, was there a door in situ in the past?

Former occupants' names/details.

As well as trying to find the names of the occupants, and what happened to them, try to find pictures or portraits of them as well. These are useful for comparison purposes if apparitions are seen and/or captured on video/film.

Is there any history of paranormal activity at the location?

Sources of Historical Information

Libraries – These are wonderful sources of local historical information. You will find local history books, maps (both current and historic), some census information, and contact numbers for local history societies and possibly even the staff will have personal local knowledge! First of all, take stock of the resource material you have available. It is always a good idea to start with the most recent information and work backwards.

When researching, keep meticulous records of your sources of information (book title, author, page number, ISBN number), as others may wish to cross-check your information in the future.

Maps – Start with the newest maps and then chart how the location has changed throughout the years. Ordnance Survey maps are ideal for this, and they go back as far as the early nineteenth century. Your local library may have older local maps that may help you too.

Historical references – Check out local history books for any mentions of the location. Wherever possible, try to check out the primary sources of the information you gather. Primary sources are documents or other sources of information (including portraits and photos) that were created at the time under study, which are more reliable than historical accounts written many years/decades/centuries after the event. A good historian will always include their primary source references in the text of their books.

Census information – If you come across any names, census information (the first census was in 1801, and has been repeated every ten years to the present day) may help you to establish if they actually lived at the location. In addition, census information will give you the names, relationships, ages and occupations of everyone who lived at the location.

Civil records – Once you have some names, checking civil records (marriages, births and deaths) will give you additional information. In particular, death certificates will give you the person's age and the cause and location of death, from which you may find some correlation with what people have experienced at the location, e.g., the apparition of an old woman appearing in a particular bedroom, etc.

Newspaper archives – If you get any interesting leads on dramatic events occurring in the past at the location, check out the library's local newspaper archives for any news reports that may have been written at the time.

Local history societies – Other useful information can be gained from speaking to the local history societies in the area. The library should have their contact details at hand.

Internet – Also, check out the internet for both historical and paranormal websites that may hold information on the location. In particular, see if any other paranormal groups have investigated the location before you and see what they came up with. However, treat everything you read on the internet with caution, as the information may not be accurate or true! Always check the facts, and if possible, check out their primary sources of information.

Write-up

Once you have completed your historical research, write it up and cross-examine it against the witness testimony. Make a note of any possible correlations.

Initial Reconnaissance Visit

Equipment to take:

Notepad and pen
Tape measure
Plug in night-light
Torch
Camera/Camcorder
Thermometer (digital or analogue)
EMF meter, if possible (alternative: compass)

Before taking the whole team and all your equipment to the location for a full investigation, it is vital to visit the place beforehand in order to plan out your site investigation more effectively; however, make sure that you get permission to go there if needed. Never, ever turn up unannounced, even if the location is a derelict house in the middle of nowhere. The authors know of one instance of a paranormal group who turned up completely unannounced in a convoy of cars and coaches late one night to investigate a supposedly derelict house on Pendle Hill, Lancashire. Within seconds of arriving they were chased off the land by an irate land-owner wielding a shotgun. The moral of this story is: always get permission before you attempt to set foot anywhere. Always respect people, their privacy and their property.

If done effectively, a reconnaissance (or recce for short) can save you a lot of time and hassle when you eventually get to do your site investigation. The following is a checklist to help you get the best out of the recce.

Check out the best route to the location – Valuable investigation time can be lost if you are not entirely sure how to get to the location, so making a dry run is always a good idea. In addition, you will be able to check out where best to park in relation to the location's access points to help you get your investigation kit inside with the minimum amount of effort/hassle. Walking a quarter of a mile or more from a car park to the location with a lot of equipment is no laughing matter.

Get a feel for the place first hand – If possible get the witness to accompany you to the location so that they can show you exactly where they had their experience(s). Look around carefully and also listen to the background sounds. See if you can come up with any rational explanations for what the witness has reported. In the case of reports of apparitions that walk through walls, are there any indications of structural changes to the building (i.e., a bricked up doorway or corridor)?

Have a walk through as much of the location as you have permission to access, taking notes, sketching room/area floor plans, taking photographs for later reference, etc. Also, make note of how you are feeling as you do your walk through. Are there specific areas at the location that feel eerie or odd? This may indicate that there are psychological factors at play that might account for some of the reported activity.

Select the areas/rooms where you feel you have the best chance of capturing activity – Based on what the witness has told you, look at the area(s)/room(s) where activity has been reported and look for things such as: entrances and exits, windows, ambient background noise, lighting and plug sockets. Let's look at these in turn.

Entrances/exits – Ideally, the area(s) under investigation should be located where human activity can be kept to an absolute minimum. Ask yourself the following: will setting up in a particular room or area block access to toilets, kitchens or fire exits? Will there be others (non-team members) present during the investigation? If so, will they need access to the areas you intend to set up in?

Windows – If necessary, can the windows be blacked out to prevent stray light/ reflections from producing false effects? In one investigation we conducted, stray light from car headlights coming in through a far window was found to be the cause of 'light anomalies' witnessed and captured on video by a previous investigation team. If blackouts are needed, measure up the windows with a tape measure and make a note to bring along something suitable to do the job. Also think about how you are going to attach the blackout to the window without causing physical damage or leaving marks on walls or window frames.

Ambient background noise – Listen carefully to the background noise. Is there anything that may cause problems when trying to record anomalous sounds, i.e., noisy air conditioning, machinery, traffic, or other external noise? If the area is heavily contaminated with background noise, can you live with it, or should you find another place to set up your equipment?

Lighting – Does the area have working lighting? If not, will that hamper setting up or taking down the equipment? Will it hamper the investigation itself, i.e., can your video equipment work well in low light conditions? If public access is required, will the equipment produce potential trip hazards or be safe from damage by people passing through?

Plug sockets – Does the area have plug sockets? If so, make a note of how many there are and where they are located. Also check to make sure that they work! Bring along a plug-in night-light to test them. There is nothing more annoying than finding out that one or more of the sockets you had spotted in the recce doesn't work during the investigation. Trust us, we've been there! Think about how much of your equipment needs to be plugged in. Will you need extension cables and/or multiple adapters to run the power to where you wish to place your equipment? Use a tape measure to gauge how long your cables will need to be.

Select an area where you want to set up the investigation base – We call this the 'hub'. This will be your base of operations for parts of the site investigation, where your team can stay and remotely monitor the areas under investigation (more about this in 'Planning the Investigation'). Ideally, you need to set up your hub as far away as possible from the areas you are investigating to reduce the possibility of stray noise from the team being picked up by your audio recorders. If you intend to run cables from the hub to other areas, use a tape measure to work out how long your cables need to be. Also, check to see if there are enough tables on which to set up your monitoring equipment, enough chairs for the team to sit on and adequate space for the team and the equipment to fit in the area comfortably. Remember, you and your team will be spending quite a bit of time located in the hub!

Planning the Investigation

With the information you have gathered from the witness interview, historical research and recce, you should have all you need to plan your investigation. The first consideration is what sort of investigation you intend to run. There are four main methods of ghost investigation that can be carried out. Each has advantages and disadvantages.

Types of Investigation

Method 1: Instrument-based passive investigation (Lockdown)

The principle of this method is simple. Investigation equipment is placed in the most promising area(s) within the location, and the video and sound outputs of the equipment are remotely monitored by the whole team from another area, known as the hub, which ideally should be located as far away as possible from the room(s)/area(s) under investigation.

Unlike anecdotal evidence, everyone present gets to 'experience' the evidence for themselves, from seeing the movements of a needle on an EMF meter, through to

Members of a paranormal group conducting an instrument-based passive investigation. Here they are gathered in their hub, remotely monitoring rooms in another part of the venue using CCTV.

watching the temperature suddenly drop on a thermometer. What's more, video and audio evidence can be played back, scrutinised and independently analysed in great detail. This sort of evidence is known as physical evidence.

The main advantage of this method is that if anything unusual is captured on video or audio – for instance, a shadow on a wall or the sound of footsteps in a room – and you know for certain that everyone present at the location were located far away in the hub, you have immediately eliminated the possibility that those particular 'anomalies' have been created by the movements of team members. The disadvantage of this method is that, by staying put in the hub, you are unlikely to detect cold spots, apports, dematerialisations, anomalous object movement/rearrangement, out-of-place smells, anomalous battery drains, or pick up EVP in other parts of the venue.

Method 2: Passive remote

This method is almost like the instrument-based passive method but with one difference. The equipment is set up as before, but once everything is recording, the

A spare camcorder is used solely to monitor temperature sensors and EMF meters during a passive remote investigation.

team vacate the location, usually overnight, and return the following day to pick up the equipment and take away the recordings for review and analysis. This method can be used in residential properties where having a team in place is impractical, i.e., due to space constraints. Temperature gauges and EMF meters can be placed in view of a dedicated camcorder, so that their readings can be retrospectively monitored alongside other video footage and audio from the area under investigation.

However, there are big disadvantages of leaving equipment to do its job unaided. If you do pick up anomalies, hoaxing will be more difficult to rule out as the team are not there to keep their eye on the overall investigation, and you must also consider how safe the equipment will be from damage or theft. That said, we have found this method useful and it has provided interesting results.

Method 3: Active investigation (Walkabout)

Active investigation is the exact opposite to passive investigation: a team gets to walk around the areas under investigation to see what they can find. Although this leads to 'human contamination' of the areas under scrutiny, there is no other way to do detailed EMF or temperature sweeps. When undertaking this sort of investigation it allows you to use all your senses: sight, hearing, touch, taste and smell. All are capable of picking up anomalies. Your skin can detect temperature fluctuations and static fields, your sense of taste can detect ionised air (metallic tangs) and your sense of smell can detect out-of-place smells such as burning candles, perfumes, cigarette smoke and other anomalous smells that have no rational source. Of course, all of this is subjective, but some of these events can be backed up by instrument readings, e.g., thermometers, EMF meters and, if you are lucky enough, ion counters. In addition, our own senses can help us to determine the explanation for that 'odd sound picked up on the recorder' or the source of that 'weird patch of illumination spotted earlier on the camera feed' far better than the most sophisticated piece of investigation kit. We have, in the past, put people in rooms so that they can use their ears to work out the source of weird sounds picked up earlier in an investigation. In one instance, we were able to quickly determine that the cause of an occasional metallic 'chirping' sound heard faintly on a microphone feed was being caused by faulty starter circuits in overhead strip lights. If we hadn't sent a couple of team members into the area then we would never have got to the bottom of that particular mystery.

The disadvantages of this method are obvious. Human presence will produce unwanted noise (footsteps, chatter), unwanted light sources (torch beams, camera flashes) and the possibility of the team unconsciously moving objects (opening doors, moving chairs or tables) which may be construed later on as paranormal events. What is more annoying is that the 'human contamination' may also mask genuine anomalous activity. There is nothing more frustrating than knowing with 90 per cent certainty that a closed door you passed earlier has now opened on its own, but not being able to rule out totally other team members' movements. However, there are ways of making a walkabout more 'controlled', which we will cover later.

Method 4: Passive and active

This is a combination of methods 1 and 3, where the investigation is divided up into sessions. One session is run as a 'lockdown', with all team members present in the hub, and the next session run as a 'walkabout', where the team is split into smaller groups and assigned to separate areas to actively investigate. These sessions can then be alternated for the duration of the investigation. This is our preferred method, and the one that we will cover in more detail in this book.

Team Size

The second consideration is your team. How many people do you take along? That will depend on where you are investigating. If the venue you are going to is large, say an old manor house or castle, then you can afford to take a larger team along with you, especially if you have a lot of areas to investigate. However, the adage 'too many cooks spoil the broth' is very apt, as it is much harder to maintain good discipline with a large group, and with the best will in the world, large teams create a lot of noise whilst going about their tasks.

Our rule of thumb is to have as many people as there are 'jobs' to do. (See 'Team Roles'). The key to a successful investigation is keeping the whole team busy as much as possible. Bored team members can, and do, cause problems. We heard of one investigation Stateside where a bored team member innocently wandered off to another part of the location that was not under investigation (and was supposedly off limits), where he managed to lock himself in a strong room, which led to the team having to call out the building's key holder to release him. This not only put an end to the investigation but was also very embarrassing for the group, as they ultimately lost the trust of the location's owner. Idle hands really do make mischief. We suggest that the maximum team size you should take anywhere is ten people.

If the location is a domestic house, then you really need to keep the team size to an absolute minimum for reasons of space constraint and out of consideration for the home-owner. Our rule of thumb for a typical house investigation is to have no more than four team members. As an alternative, it is also possible to do a 'passive remote' session, which we will cover in more detail later.

What Equipment Do You Need to Take?

This depends on factors such as the size of the location, what sort of activity has been reported and how many team members you wish to take. Ideally each room/area under investigation should have in place: video camera or device for capturing moving images; an audio device for capturing sounds and EVP; environmental sensors, such as temperature gauges, pressure or humidity sensors; movement sensors; trigger objects (these need not be set up in all areas).

As well as making sure each room has as much of the above equipment in it as possible, you will also need to draw up a list of everything else you will need to take, such as:

Equipment accessories: power leads, remote controls, instruction manuals, chargers, adapter plugs, extension leads.

Consumables: recording media, batteries (take lots!), gaffer tape, Blu-tack, Post-it notes, tape measure, food and drink, rubbish bags.

Personal kit: torches (as many as possible), watch, first-aid kit, basic toolkit, EMF meter or compass, pens, notepads.

When to Investigate

Have you ever wondered why ghost investigations are conducted at night? Although there are a small minority of investigators who believe that ghost activity only occurs after dark, most agree that ghost activity can occur at any time. One of the main reasons why investigations are conducted at night is that most people have commitments during the day, such as jobs or domestic responsibilities that prevent them from being able to do daytime investigations. Also, at night-time, buildings you wish to investigate will be less occupied and more suitable for running the kind of investigations we recommend. There is also a third reason why you should investigate at night. One of the effects that have occasionally been reported is something known as spooklights – small balls of light that are visible to the naked eye that have been seen to float around buildings for short durations. These would not be easily visible in full light. The next step is to arrange a suitable date with the location's owner to run the investigation. Give yourself at least two weeks' notice to plan the investigation, assemble your equipment/consumables and brief your team.

Pre-brief

Once you have decided which parts of the site you wish to investigate, have worked out how much equipment you need and how many team members you require, it is important to get your team together to discuss the logistics of the investigation. This includes choosing team roles, discussing how to get there (How many cars do you need for the equipment and people) and working out what to do when you get there.

Team Roles

It is important to assign roles to all team members. Giving everyone an area of personal responsibility will make the investigation run more smoothly and will help to maintain team discipline. If you have more team members than roles, you can always double up the people responsible for each role. Your team should consist of the following:

Team leader – The team leader should ideally be the person who conducted the recce. It is the team leader's job to make sure that the investigation runs smoothly and that team members stay focused on the tasks they have been assigned.

Timeline logger – In order to keep track of who goes where during an investigation, someone needs to take on the role of timeline logger. This person records the movements of the team at all times. This is a vitally important task, as you will be able to compare the team's whereabouts against where alleged anomalous activity occurs to see if team members could have inadvertently caused it.

Sound monitor – If you have the capability of remotely monitoring sound from the rooms/areas under investigation, one person should be assigned to listen in and keep a record of everything they hear in the room/area. If you haven't got the capability to monitor live, this person should be responsible for maintaining the audio recorders during the investigation – changing tapes, cards, batteries when needed.

Video monitor – If you have the capability of remotely monitoring video from the rooms/areas under investigation, one person should be assigned to look and keep a record of everything they see in the room/area. If you haven't got the capability to monitor live, this person should be responsible for maintaining the camcorders during the investigation – changing tapes, cards, batteries when needed.

Environmental monitor – If you have set up a weather station, you will need someone to keep a record of the temperature, humidity, etc., at both the hub and the area/room(s) under investigation. This person should take a note of readings at the start of the investigation, and then at regular 5-minute intervals throughout. In addition, this team member should also make a note of any sudden temperature changes or take additional spot readings if another team member thinks that something anomalous is occurring. The readings you take in the hub act as a 'control' compared to what is happening in the rest of the location. If you get a sudden temperature drop in just one area, it may be an early indication that you are about to experience some paranormal activity.

On one of our investigations, we used temperature data to assess what could possibly be causing batteries to drain completely in one particular room at the site we were investigating. One of the main causes of battery malfunction is extreme cold, where batteries drain much quicker than normal. By checking our weather data, we quickly realised that the temperature all over the building was 11 °C, which is not cold enough to cause battery drainage. Since the drainage was only occurring in one particular room, we concluded that something anomalous was taking place. Hopefully from this example alone you can appreciate how essential it is to log temperature data throughout your investigations.

Antix crew member capturing evidence of possible paranormal activity at work, as a mysterious power fluctuation affects one of their hi-tech cameras during the filming of *Spook School.*

Photographer – It is important to assign someone the task of keeping a photographic record of the vigil, such as taking pictures of how/where you have set up the equipment, general shots of rooms, etc. These act as reference photos, should you notice that anything has moved of its own accord. Reference photos helped us in one investigation where a remote camera perched on top of a TV monitor moved by itself. By checking the reference picture we were able to show that the camera was fastened down securely with Blu-tack, making the movement anomalous. Also, it is good to have someone document the activities of the team members throughout the course of the investigation.

All the roles apart from the team leader can be interchanged throughout the night to make sure that no one gets bored with their jobs. You will notice that we haven't included the role of medium in the team. This is not an oversight. As we have already discussed, evidence from mediums, although intriguing, is not considered as hard evidence because not everyone can experience what a medium is experiencing. However, this doesn't mean that there is no place for a medium in an instrument-based paranormal investigation. Some investigation teams employ mediums or sensitives to tell them which areas/rooms seem to be the most promising, and then set up investigation equipment at these points. Some teams claim that they have achieved interesting results using this method. Although the medium's claims cannot be used as hard evidence on their own, if what they 'experience' can be backed up by capturing something interesting on video or audio or if there is a corresponding temperature drop or EM field anomaly, this is something that can be considered to be stronger evidence, and may go some way to supporting what the medium experiences. Backing up a medium's claims with instruments is both good for the investigation and the medium. It may also lead, one day, to a better understanding of the mediumistic process.

Getting to the Location

When it is time to travel to the location, make sure that each team member knows how to get to the location. Even if you have a Sat Nav, make sure that you also take along a map, as Sat Navs have been known to send people in completely the wrong direction sometimes. Make sure that everyone knows who they are travelling with and that there is sufficient space in the vehicles for both equipment and team members.

Running the Investigation

Once you arrive, don't waste any time; get started as soon as you can. It is always a good idea to take all your equipment and supplies to the place where you intend to set up your hub. Before you begin to unpack and deploy your gear, it is important for the team leader to walk the team around the location to get them familiar with its layout, identify the areas/rooms which are to be investigated and the areas that are off limits (if any). As soon as everyone is familiar with the location, it is time to return to the hub and start unpacking.

Setting Up

Setting up can take up a lot of time unless you tackle it in an orderly fashion. Remember: paranormal activity is spontaneous and can occur at any time, even when setting up. With this in mind, try to work in pairs when deploying equipment. If you are alone, you will not have a second witness to any event.

We find it is best to set up your equipment in the following order:

Synchronise equipment – The first task is to synchronise all the internal clocks on every device the team has brought along, including any watches worn by team members. This is done so that it is possible to construct an accurate timeline of events during the site investigation. This will be covered in more detail later.

The hub: nerve-centre of any instrument-based paranormal investigation.

Set up the hub – Set up any monitoring equipment you have: video recorders, TV monitors, listening devices, etc. Make sure that they are placed sufficiently near plug sockets or that your extension leads can reach. If you do not have any means of remotely monitoring sound and video from the hub, don't worry, as there is still a lot you can do in the 'passive' parts of the investigation.

Set up video cameras

CCTV – Connect up any remote CCTV cameras you have. Once plugged in, check to see that you are getting a picture. Once you know that they are working, start walking them out to the rooms/areas you wish to investigate. If you have done your homework properly during the reconnaissance, your cables should reach. If not, you may have to rethink where to position your hub.

In the room/area you wish to place them in, set up your tripod and mount the camera onto it, making sure it is secure and that the tripod is stable. Using walkie-talkies or mobile phones (or shouting), get someone at the hub to help you position the camera so that you get the best overall view of the room/area. The view should take in the floor as well as the walls so that if you pick up anomalous sounds you can check for small animals.

Wireless – Connect up any wireless cameras you have and tune in the receiver at the hub so that you get the sharpest picture possible. Once tuned in, start walking them to the room/area you wish to place them in. Using walkie-talkies or mobiles, someone at the hub can monitor the picture quality as you progress, and let you know if the picture starts to break up. Wireless cameras can be problematic, as some buildings stop the signal from reaching the receiver. If the picture breaks up, you know you have reached the limit of the camera's transmitting range in that particular building.

Camcorders – If you don't have any video devices that you can monitor remotely, set up a camcorder in the room. Make sure that the battery is fully charged, or where possible, plugged into the mains. Insert a new tape/disc/memory card, make sure that the time/date display is visible in the picture, and then set to standby.

Set up Audio – If you have a microphone cable long enough to stretch from the hub to the investigation area, plug your microphone into the recorder and test that it is working. Next, walk the microphone out to the room/area you wish to investigate.

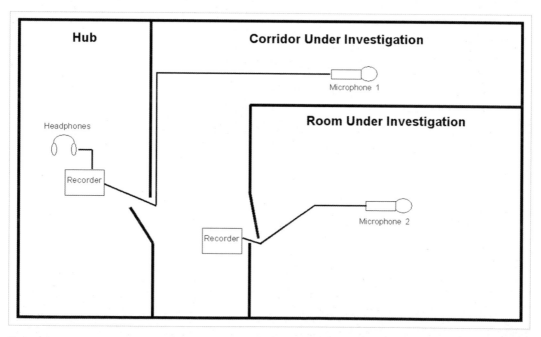

Two different microphone set-ups. Microphone 1 can be monitored live. Microphone 2's recording can be reviewed later.

Place the microphone as close to the physical centre of the room as possible. If the microphone has a cardioid pick-up pattern, point the head away from the entrance/exit you will be using to access the room.

If you do not have long enough cables to run all the way back to the hub, set up your recorder in the room and set up the microphone as far away from the recorder as possible. If the room you are investigating has a door, try to place the recorder outside and the microphone inside. Insert a new tape, disc or a blank memory card in the recorder and place on standby.

Set up weather station – If you have a weather station, set up the base station at the hub and check that it is picking up the remote sensor. Take the sensor to the room/area under investigation. If you have walkie-talkies, get someone to check that you are still receiving data at the base station. Set up the remote sensor in the room away from radiators, air conditioning outlets, or anything else that will give you false readings. If you don't have a weather station, you can always set up a data-logging thermometer in the room or set up a thermometer in front of a camcorder (if you have one spare). The readings from the thermometer can be viewed and logged later on playback.

Paranormal investigator setting up a dedicated camcorder to film a trigger object experiment.

Set up movement sensors – Set up movement sensors in all the rooms and areas under investigation. Set them up so that they cover all obvious entrances or exits, such as doors, windows, ceiling, wall vents, etc. Test them to see how effective they are around the room, in particular, at ground level, in order to detect rodents or other small animals. Once you are happy with their positions, disarm them for the time being.

Trigger objects – Set up some trigger objects in one of the rooms/areas you are investigating. Trigger objects are any small inanimate objects that are placed in a room in the hope that they will be moved by supernatural means. Traditionally, it was believed that if you place an object that has some significance to the spirit thought to occupy the location, it would encourage the spirit to interact with the object.

When choosing trigger objects, select flat, substantial things such as coins, large buttons or small picture frames that don't move easily on their own. Pick a flat, stable spot, such as a handy table or shelf, where the objects won't be disturbed by draughts or breezes, vibration or other objects in the room that have the potential to fall onto them (loose plaster included). Ensure that your trigger-object experiment is in full view of the camera that you have set up to monitor the room as a whole, so that you can check for accidental movement or hoaxing. To date, we have not had much success with trigger objects, but other investigators tell us that they have had very interesting results, so we persevere.

How to Set Up Trigger Objects

Place a piece of paper or card onto the table or shelf and attach it securely with tape or Blu-tack. Arrange the trigger objects onto it in a well-spaced regular pattern. Carefully draw around the outline of each object with a pen. Make sure that you do not disturb any of the objects while you do this.

Next, take a picture looking vertically down at the objects using a digital camera. Make sure you also get all the edges of the card into the picture as well. This is your reference picture. You will use this later to compare what you find at the end of the investigation.

If you have a spare video camera, mount it onto a tripod and point it vertically down at the objects, making sure that all objects and the edges of the card are in view. This is to eliminate the possibility of someone attempting to hoax activity by pushing or pulling the edge of the card and giving your objects a shove. If the entire card is in view, then it rules out this possibility. If practical, you can extend this measure by including the entire table or surface that your trigger objects are sat on in the shot to eliminate the possibility of anyone having nudged the table/surface as well.

Baseline sweep – Baseline sweeps are a way of providing a bit of control to your investigations. They record the conditions present in the room or area prior to the start of the investigation. These measurements can be used to compare against any other measurements you take throughout the evening. If anything anomalous does occur, any changes you detect may be directly linked to the activity. The two main types of readings that are commonly taken on site investigations are EM field values and atmospheric data, such as temperature, pressure and humidity. Because you have placed equipment in the rooms that is capable of generating EM fields, it is important to do your sweep after everything has been set up.

How to Make a Baseline Sweep

A: EMF readings

If you possess an EMF meter, take readings in all the rooms/areas you are investigating. Since taking accurate readings is a complex and time-consuming business (unless you possess a tri-axis meter), beginners can use the following method. This won't give accurate readings of the full field strength but will determine if any change has occurred.

Method – Once all the equipment has been set up in each room, take a pack of Post-it notes and a tape measure and lay out the Post-it notes in a grid pattern in the room or area, about three feet apart from each other.

Switch on all equipment in the room that will be operating during the investigation. Magnetic fields are only present while devices are switched on.

Point your meter in one direction and keep it oriented in this direction for the whole room sweep. As you walk over a Post-it, write the meter reading (even if it is zero) on it and repeat until you have taken readings at all Post-it-marked points in the room.

If you are using a Trifield meter, set it to either sum or magnetic. Place it on the ground and step away before taking a reading, as this sort of meter is incredibly sensitive and will react to even the slightest movement. Note: In sum and magnetic modes, the meter only detects changes in the field strength, not the field strength itself. Once it gets used to the levels of an EM field in a particular location, the needle will drop down to zero. If the EM field changes, the needle will react to it.

If you don't have an EMF meter, use a compass instead. Write down the compass readings on the Post-its.

B: Temperature

In the same room, also make a sweep with a thermometer. Take your time, as some digital thermometers take a few seconds to provide an accurate measurement. Again, take readings at the Post-it points and write them down beside the EMF values.

As a precaution, also mark up the Post-it locations on your room plans along with the EMF and temperature readings, just in case any Post-its are accidentally moved in the course of the investigation.

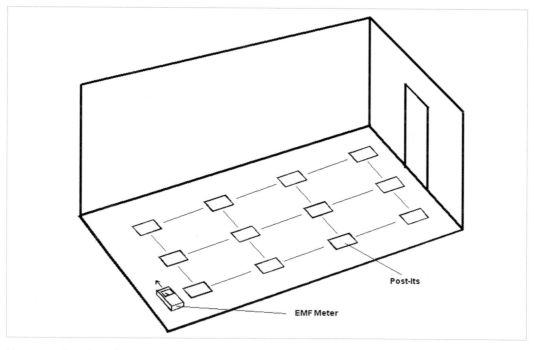

How to make a baseline sweep with an EMF meter: keep it pointed in the same direction for the entire sweep. When you come to investigate the room later, make sure you take measurements with the meter pointed in the same direction.

Reference pictures/equipment log – Once all the equipment has been set up and the baseline sweeps have been completed, go round all rooms/areas to take reference pictures. A reference picture is a photograph of each piece of equipment in situ and also general shots of room layouts. These are useful for comparison purposes if you think that something may have moved on its own. On your site floor plan, make a note of what equipment you have set up in each area/room. Once everything is in place and all notes have been taken, assemble the whole team in the hub.

Beginning the Investigation

Start equipment recording – At the hub, select two team members to go to each room to start all equipment recording. As they leave each room, they need to stand in front of the video/audio devices and state the current time and announce that the team is now leaving the room. This is done so that when the tape is being analysed later, any off-camera sounds made shortly after the team leave the room can be discounted. On their way out of the room they need to arm the movement sensors. From this point on, anything that occurs in the room/area cannot be attributed to team members. Once they have switched everything on and returned to the hub, the team leader can hand out investigation log sheets to all team members.

Investigation log sheet

Location	Heritage Market			Date	16/04/08	
Name	Mark rosney			Sheet	1	of 5

Time	Location	Event	Notes
19:30	Hub	Changed Batteries in Mini Disk	
19:40	Hub	Vigil Start – Session 1 – Lockdown	
20:02	Hub	Camera Failure	Picture feed from CCTV Camera in upper room stopped.
20:07	Hub	Voice heard on Audio feed	Voice heard on Cellar 1 audio feed. Possible Intruder?
20:09	Hub	Breaking Lockdown	Breaking lockdown conditions to check site for intruders.
20:10	Cellar 1	Checking for people	Rob and me in Cellar 1 – no sign of people, no way for anyone to break into area without passing us first!
20:45	Hub	End of Session 1	

Investigation log sheet.

Log sheets – Log sheets are for marking down anything of note during the investigation, which includes any sounds or visual observations you make, where you saw/heard them and also what you think may have caused them. You can also make note of other things such as sounds that you hear that are explainable, for instance, if you drop something on the floor in one room, the sound might have carried to other rooms and been picked up by the recording devices located in them. By noting the time you made the sound, it will be possible to eliminate it from the investigation when reviewing the recordings.

It is also vitally important to log your movements from room to room throughout the investigation. These can also be written down on your log sheets. The person who is assigned the job of timeline logger needs to record everyone's movements as a backup in case team members forget to log their own movements. It is *essential* to know exactly where people were in relation to any alleged activity picked up during the whole investigation. Once the investigation is over, the log sheets are used to construct an overall timeline of what went on during the investigation.

Switch off Mobile Phones – Just before the site investigation gets underway, the team should switch off all mobile phones they have brought with them. This is done because mobile-phone signals can bleed into any recordings you make, even if they are set to silent. There is also another reason for switching them off. On recent investigations we have found that sometimes team mobiles mysteriously turn themselves on all by themselves. On one occasion both Mark's and Rob's phones switched themselves on halfway through a walkabout session. One of the phones was a 'lobster' variety that could only be switched on by flipping it open first. Because we experienced this at exactly the same time that other equipment failed on us, we believe the event to be anomalous. We now use switched off mobile phones as another means of testing for paranormal activity.

First Session (Lockdown)

The first session needs to be run as a lockdown with all team members located in the hub for the duration. Lockdowns are especially good for capturing evidence of imprinting-type ghost phenomena, where the lack of noise and movement gives you a better chance of catching something should it occur.

Once everyone is ready, the team leader announces the time, and declares the first session to be running. The start time is then noted down on everyone's log sheets. The session should only run for as long as the shortest tape/disc that you have placed in any of your equipment. We recommend that sessions should run for no more that 45 minutes at a time unless you start to see/hear suspect activity, in which case, you should continue for as long as you can.

During the first session, keep the team as quiet as possible. If you do not have any way of remotely monitoring equipment, you can still listen carefully to see if you can hear anything anomalous, and also take local temperature readings at the hub. If anything is picked up by any team member, make sure they write down the time it occurred and all the details on their log sheet. Once they have done this, they can inform the rest of the team that something has happened by clearly saying 'event' without elaborating on what they have picked up. This then allows other team members to check their equipment feeds (if any) for any possible activity, without biasing their perceptions.

At the end of the first session, the team leader announces the time and draws a close to the first session. The timeline logger notes the end time down on their log sheet.

Changing Tapes

The team is then free to go and change tapes and batteries. Make sure that team member's work in pairs at all times, and that their movements around the site are recorded on their log sheets. As the team members enter rooms or areas, they should first disarm the movement sensors. Next, they should announce into the equipment the current time and the names of all present and then set to work checking the equipment. As tapes/discs are changed, make sure that all items are marked up with the date, the time of removal, the location (e.g., room 1, etc.), and stow them away in a separate bag or case. Insert new discs, tapes, etc., check battery levels and change as appropriate, and put equipment on standby. Once all the equipment has been checked, the team should reconvene at the hub for a quick break.

Preparing for the Second Session (Walkabout)

The second session is everyone's chance to walk around the areas under investigation. As this is going to invalidate a lot of what may be picked up, it is doubly vital to keep an accurate record of who is where at all times. The best solution we have found is to allocate someone the task of following the team around with a spare camcorder or audio recorder to record the team's movements and activities around the site. The walkabout will give you the opportunity to look for effects that you won't be able to look for under lockdown conditions.

As well as seeing apparitions, there are a number of other effects that are considered by many people to be other facets of ghost (and poltergeist) phenomena. Although not as earth shattering as seeing full-blown apparitions or heavy furniture being flung across a room by unseen forces, these effects can be deeply puzzling. The following is a list of the main effects that people have experienced in allegedly haunted locations.

Smells – Anomalous smells differ from real ones in two important respects. Firstly, they appear in an instant; and the smell fills the room completely and is often incredibly strong and overpowering. Moments later, the smell disappears as quickly as it came, leaving no hint of a trace. Secondly, the smell you are experiencing is *out of place* in the room or building you are experiencing it in.

It is not uncommon to experience scents or smells associated with a location's past – for instance, at Chingle Hall, many people have experienced the smells of lavender, incense and burning candles, which have no source in the present but which used to be part of the daily life of the hall. Other out-of-place smells that have frequently been reported on investigations are roses, perfumes, cigarette, cigar or pipe smoke, decaying flesh, and smoke from fires.

You must be careful to eliminate down-to-earth sources for any smells you feel are anomalous before coming to the conclusion that you are experiencing anything paranormal. For instance, if you are picking up the smell of flowers, check for open windows or vents that could be carrying the smell in from the outside, or for plug-in air-fresheners in the room or adjacent rooms or corridors. Also, check to see if any of the team is wearing strong perfumes or aftershaves or deodorants/body sprays that could be the source of the mystery smell.

In fact, it is a good idea for all team members to refrain from wearing strong scents, as not only could they be misconstrued as anomalous, but could also mask truly anomalous smells that may be present. If you want to go the whole hog, ban team members from eating strong-flavoured aromatic food before an investigation as well, not only for the above reason but also out of common decency for your fellow team members. Here is another important tip: if any team member does smell anything that appears out of place, they must eliminate the possibility of auto-suggestion taking place in others by announcing that an 'event' has occurred, but not what they think it could be. That way, team members can make up their own minds about what they think is happening, if anything. If the people present are in agreement, and no rational source can be found, then you have almost certainly experienced something anomalous.

Touch – Sometimes, when on investigations, people report that they feel as though something invisible has touched, poked or prodded them. Some people have even reported that they have had their hair or clothing tugged by invisible hands. The first thing to do is to check the environment immediately around you. One individual we know felt that something was preventing him from lifting his foot, only to discover that he was standing on his own shoelace that had come undone. It is important to check that you haven't backed into other team members elbows or managed to hook your clothes onto any snagging hazards such as belt clips, equipment carrying straps, or nails/screws in walls, etc.

Static fields and static discharges can also produce odd feelings in people and clothing. For instance, a statically charged jumper can also make arm hairs suddenly stand on end, creating weird feelings of being brushed against. On the whole, feeling as though you have been touched by things unseen is highly subjective, unless everyone present experiences the same thing at the same location.

Object movement – Sometimes in allegedly haunted locations, it is reported that objects can move by themselves, independent of any living activity. In several of our investigations, we have come across chairs and tables that have mysteriously rearranged themselves in rooms that were completely void of human occupation between visits; and on one occasion, in a theatre auditorium in Blackpool, a sprung seat in the stalls that was checked to be in an upright position before the start of a session was later found to be down when the team re-entered the room. In that instance, we had cameras covering the whole auditorium for the duration of the investigation which proved, to our satisfaction, that no one had been anywhere near the seat in question.

If you feel that objects have moved, take pictures with a camera before you touch anything and then check temperature and EMF readings (if possible). The pictures you take can be compared against the reference photos taken earlier to see if anything has changed. Also, if the suspect movement occurred in front of a video camera, you will be able to check to see if hoaxing or accidental movement by team members could be the cause.

Anomalous equipment malfunctions and battery drainage – It is not uncommon for paranormal investigators to experience seemingly inexplicable equipment failures while conducting investigations. Any serious investigator will tell you that devices, which they know to be in 100 per cent working order prior to an investigation, can cease to function when at an allegedly haunted site, only for them to start working again when they get them back home. The question is, are these failures actually paranormal events?

Equipment can fail for a variety of reasons. Sometimes devices can fail to work if they get too cold or if the humidity (dampness in the air) is high. Some devices fail if they get overly contaminated with dust or if placed near anything that outputs a strong electromagnetic field, such as high-voltage power cables or mobile-phone masts. Since ghost investigations often occur in the most inhospitable of places, such as derelict buildings with no heating, or old ruins partially exposed to the elements, all of these conditions are likely and can impair your devices' performance if you are not careful.

The most frequent devices that fail on investigations are things such as digital cameras, camcorders, walkie-talkies and audio recorders. All these devices have one thing in common: they are all battery powered. Rapid battery drainage is the biggest cause of equipment failure at allegedly haunted locations. Is battery drainage a sign of paranormal activity at work? No, not always. Batteries come in two distinct types, rechargeable and disposables. Rechargeables can be more problematic than their throwaway counterparts, especially if you do not allow them to drain fully before recharging, as this will result in the battery not receiving a full charge, despite reading full on a battery tester or volt meter. This problem is made worse if you then stick the batteries into high-energy-consumption devices like digital cameras.

As a rule of thumb, most paranormal investigators tend not to use rechargeables, but instead go for heavy-duty alkaline disposables. Although more expensive than using rechargeable batteries, the results are much more consistent, and the drainage problem is smaller. Nevertheless, all batteries can fall foul of extreme cold. When a battery is cold it tends to drain more quickly.

However, not all equipment failures are caused by the environmental factors listed above. Some equipment only fails when placed in a specific location, and starts working perfectly again once removed, even though temperature, humidity and EMF readings remain consistent throughout the site. It is these intermittent device failures that are of most interest to investigators.

If a piece of equipment fails at an investigation, remove it from the immediate area to see if that cures the problem. If it does, compare the temperature, humidity and (if possible) the EMF readings you get in both the problem area and your current location. If there is no significant difference in the temperature readings then you may be experiencing something anomalous.

Cold spots – One of the most reported features of allegedly haunted sites is the occurrence of cold spots. A cold spot is an area within a room where people feel a sudden and large drop in temperature the minute they walk into it. The best way to describe walking into one is to imagine that you are walking into a cold meat locker. Immediately outside you are warm, the next step you feel instantly cold! Some people believe that cold spots are where ghosts have removed energy from the surroundings in order to help them manifest themselves. But are cold spots really indications of ghostly activity or are they something more mundane?

We feel cold for a variety of reasons. Some of those reasons are physiological (i.e., we get physically colder) and some of them are psychological (i.e., we only feel colder). Physical reasons why a spot in a room could be colder than the surroundings could be attributable to things like breezes and draughts coming from openings in walls, ceilings, under doors, etc. In particular, cold air flowing in under a door can cool your ankles, making the rest of you feel much colder. It is important to check for breezes even at floor level. Remember, feeling cold is a relative thing. Some people feel cold in rooms that others find warm, so it wouldn't take much change in air temperature to make some people feel colder.

Psychology can also affect how cold or hot we perceive things to be without there being any physical difference in temperature. For instance, some people can be made to feel colder simply because of visual cues, such as being in a room where the walls are all painted blue can make some people feel that the room is colder than the rest of the house, despite it having the same ambient temperature throughout. Also, the power of suggestion can play a very big part in how we feel too. When on investigations, it is easy to allow others to influence our perception. If someone declares that they have found a cold spot, it is easy to allow that suggestion to make us perceive something that isn't really there. So how do we know when a cold spot is anomalous?

The cold spots that we have encountered have two important hallmarks: the cut-off point between feeling warm and cold can be very sharp. On occasions, we have encountered cold spots that are so sharply defined you can feel the difference in a single footstep. We have been able to go from feeling warm to intense cold and back again instantly by stepping in and out of the spot repeatedly. We are not just talking about feeling a bit cooler either. Anomalous cold spots feel intensely cold compared to their surroundings.

There are a number of things that we can do when we come across cold spots. Firstly, we can measure the air temperature in the spot and compare it with the surrounding area. Secondly, we can measure a person's skin temperature both inside and outside the spot to see if there is a physical difference. You can use either a cheap strip thermometer (for less than £2) or a laser-guided thermometer to do the job. If you possess an EMF meter, try that inside and outside the spot to see if there is an electromagnetic field directly associated with it. Keep monitoring the spot to see if it diminishes over time. If there is a distinct temperature difference, see if it is possible to map the extent of the cold spot to get an idea of shape and size.

Light anomalies – On some investigations, people have reported seeing tiny balls of light, no bigger than around 10-15 mm, moving around rooms. They tend to be short-lived, lasting a few seconds at a time. These are visible to the naked eye, and are therefore not the same as the orbs you can pick up on a digital camera. Because they are not usually very bright, they are best detected in low light conditions. (See 'Photographic Anomalies' section for an example caught on camera in an investigation in Liverpool, England).

Other light anomalies that are often seen are blue flashes of light that can illuminate a whole room for a fraction of a second in much the same way as sheet lightning. Both the above effects tend to occur in connection with other anomalous events such as cold spots, battery drainage and equipment failure.

Walkabout groups

If you wish to split your team into smaller groups, make sure that all groups have some way of recording their movements. In addition, if you have walkie-talkies, make sure that each team has one, so that teams can keep in touch throughout the walkabout session.

Designate each group a separate room or area to investigate, and make sure that they stick to it for the duration of the session. Also make sure that everyone knows what time they have to be back at the hub.

When you do set your teams loose in the investigation areas, make sure that they remember to announce their presence and the current time as they wander past any equipment, so that any off-camera sounds can be easily identified as team members passing through.

Each team member should take a torch, log sheets and pen with them when they set off. In addition, each team should have a thermometer, EMF meter or compass, camera or camcorder and an audio recorder.

Before sending the teams off to investigate, get two team members to start all the equipment recording again. If possible, two team members should stay at the hub to monitor the progress of the teams whilst they are on walkabout. They should also continue making a note of the hub temperature readings.

The Second Session (Walkabout)

To make sure that the walkabout is as controlled as possible the groups will have to be disciplined at all times. This means:

All team members need to be as quiet as possible whilst walking around the site.

They will have to keep an accurate log of their movements.

If a team member comes across anything they consider to be anomalous, they should say 'event' and not elaborate on what they have experienced. This allows other team members to make up their own minds without subjectivity creeping in to colour their perception.

If anything anomalous is detected, stay calm and focused and try to get as much information as possible using all equipment you have with you. For instance, temperature readings, EM field readings, etc. Be sure to note down the time and as much detail as possible on your log sheet or make voice recordings of the readings.

When in rooms under investigation, make sweeps with your EMF meter in exactly the same way as you did on the baseline sweep. Make sure that you have the meter aligned in the same direction as you used to take the baseline readings. If you do pick up odd readings, check them against the nearest Post-it. Make a note of any changes you come across. Do the same for temperature readings.

If you have a portable audio recorder, try some EVP experiments (see Section 3: EVP for more details). Whilst recording, ask questions and leave gaps for responses.

If you hear or see anything unusual, try to find out where everyone else is in relation to you. Could they be the cause of the noises you hear? Do other team members hear them as well?

On an investigation in Old Hall in Sandbach, Cheshire, our team was split into two groups who were located in adjacent bedrooms. We kept in touch via walkie-talkies as we heard the sound of footsteps come down the corridor. One team member looked out through a crack in the door and noticed a dark shape pass by. Next, the latch on the other bedroom door moved slightly. Since everyone in the investigation team were located in one of the rooms, team members could not have been responsible for what we saw and heard. We did not attempt to open the doors and look out as we had a video camera covering the landing where the activity was happening, which we were convinced would have captured the whole event. However, on playback, nothing was seen or heard. Although frustrating, we were convinced that the activity actually occurred due to the number of witnesses, and because we could instantly check that all present could not have caused the noises, we have no choice but to declare it as a paranormal event.

If you notice that something appears to have moved, take a photograph first before going nearer to investigate. The main rule in paranormal investigation is: collect evidence first; try to explain things later. You will be able to compare the photo with the ones you took before the start of the investigation to determine if anything has changed.

At the end of the session, make your way back to the hub as quickly as you can.

The Rest of the Investigation

By running alternate lockdown and walkabout sessions you will hopefully gather useful and reliable evidence. As long as you log observations, instrument readings and your movements accurately, you will be in a position to construct an accurate timeline of events, which will be useful when you come to analyse your sound and video recordings.

Ending the Investigation

Some investigators run their site investigations all night. Others only run them for a few hours. Our rule of thumb is that we usually only run an investigation for a maximum of four hours unless it is an active night, when we then continue for as long as possible. However, be aware that the longer you run your investigation, the more video and audio you will have to review when it comes to analyse everything. If you do decide to call it a night, take time to pack everything away neatly. To that end, make sure you allot enough time to do a leisurely 'get-out'. Pack away gear carefully making sure that everything goes into its specific case or bag. Wind up and tie off all cables properly so that they don't end up as a tangled mess the next time you come to use them.

Once you have cleared every room, do a sweep of the entire site to make sure that you have collected everything. Put all rubbish in a bin bag and take it home with you. Put back any furniture that you have moved, remove all traces of gaffer tape or Blu-tack. Ensure that you leave the location in the same way that you found it.

The team leader should collect all log sheets from team members and arrange a time to meet up with the timeline logger as soon after the investigation as possible to construct a master timeline.

Team members should agree as to what tapes/discs they are going to review, and make sure they are all labelled and packed away carefully.

Once everything is packed up, make one last sweep of the location to make sure that nothing has been left behind. You will be amazed at what some people can forget

Heritage Vigil: 18/06/2008

Timeline

Time	Event	Location	Noted by	Notes
21:23	Team go to Cellar via Night Club to show Roy around tobacco 1 (Rob, Sarah, Mark)	Night Club to Cellar	Mark	
21:29	Weather station sensor placed in Night Club			By Rob ?
21:30	Baseline temp at Hub 24.3 c (???)			No signal from Night Club Sensor
21:35	Temp not registering on hub station			Humidity 70%
22:12	Official Vigil Start – Video started			
22:18:30	Activity in front of camera	Night Club	Clare	Probably insects
22:20	Percussion sound	Night Club	Ben	
22:21:45	Car Headlights in Window?	Night Club	Clare	Possible anomaly, as window is at least 60 ft up!
22:22	Percussive sound picked up on microphone	Night Club	Eileen	
22:23	Minidisc stops!	Hub	Eileen/Ben	The new battery placed in the device just before the start of the vigil is drained! After only 11 mins of operation.
22:24:45	Flash in Bottom Left Hand Corner	Night Club	Clare	Torch from Team?
22:25	Battery replaced in Minidisc and device restarted	Hub	Eileen/Ben	
22:27	Mark and Sarah go to the Night Club to set up motion sensors	Night Club	Sarah	
22:30	Mark and Sarah back in Hub	Hub	Sarah	
22:·		Night Clu·		

Investigation timeline .

if they are not careful. On one of our investigations, a team we were working with left a case of investigation kit worth a few thousand pounds. If we had not conducted that last sweep, there is no telling where the case would have ended up.

Finally, especially if you are departing in the wee small hours, leave as quietly as possible so as not to disrupt other people living in close proximity to the location.

Analysis

Constructing the Timeline

Once you have caught up on lost sleep, it is a good idea to go through all the log sheets completed during the investigation as soon as possible while the investigation is still fresh in your mind. By systematically going through each log sheet and compiling everything in time order, you will be able to build up a picture of the sequence of events that occurred during the night. Once it has all been typed up, you will then need to send copies to all team members for them to use when they start to analyse the recordings.

Recording Review

Although some of the footage and audio may have been monitored live throughout the site investigation, it is still important to review all recordings made on the night. There is no alternative but to sit patiently and watch or listen carefully to see if anything odd has been captured. You will be able to use the investigation timeline to help determine if any of the activity captured was caused by the presence of team members. Here are some top tips:

Checking recordings properly takes a lot of concentration and a bit of patience. Before you embark on reviewing anything, make sure that you are not likely to be disturbed. Only review for stretches of thirty minutes at a time, then take a short break before resuming. This will help keep you more alert.

Note down the time and a brief description of anything you find interesting. If you have synchronised the internal clocks (if any) on your devices, the time displayed should be correct. If you didn't, then you will have to manually time the event from a point in the recording where a team member announced the correct time.

Once you have reviewed all tapes, type up the list of events that you have found and put away the tapes in a safe place for the time being.

Send your lists to the team leader or timeline logger for them to incorporate into the investigation's timeline.

The whole team should arrange to meet up as soon as possible to review the investigation and any evidence that may have been captured. If at all possible, try to make copies of the interesting segments from the original recordings, but do not get rid of the originals. If you have managed to capture anything interesting, then you will need to retain the originals for others to review. Similarly, if you have any interesting photographs, do not remove them from the camera's memory card or internal memory, as doing so may destroy vital file information (See Section 4: Photographic Anomalies).

Since the final stages in the Investigation Life Cycle: 'Writing up your findings' and 'Making your findings public' are identical for all types of paranormal investigation, we will cover them in more detail at the end of the book.

By sticking to some very basic rules, your chances of capturing something significant will be dramatically increased. We hope that your next Ghost Investigation is an outstanding success. Good hunting.

Electronic Voice Phenomena (EVP)

The truth is incontrovertible,
malice may attack it,
ignorance may deride it, but in the end;
there it is!

Winston Churchill

A Brief History

The jargonistic terms Electronic Voice Phenomena and Instrumental Trans-Communication basically refer to methods of alleged communication with the dead via an electrical device, usually some sort of audio recorder along with other such similar devices. The anomalous sounds recorded on these machines are believed by some people to be the voices and snippets of language from 'the other side' by the spirits of people that have died, sometimes quite recently, and in a lot of instances, these voices are of people that the listener is in some way related to. The actual recordings are typically fairly brief in length, consisting of only one or two words, and at the very most, a short phrase of some description or other, and are not heard at the time when the recording is made but become audibly apparent once the recording is reviewed. The quality of the recordings is also liable to vary in the extreme. On most occasions the recordings are inclined to be exceedingly faint and sometimes distorted too, but on the odd instance, one comes along where the speech is easily heard and it is easy to make out what is being said and quite often the speech is delivered in a curious cadence and usually faster than in normal conversation.

Electronic Voice Phenomena and Instrumental Trans-Communication are collectively one of the most discussed and completely fascinating aspects of research of all paranormal phenomena. On the internet alone, in excess of 50,000 sites are devoted to the subject, many of which will attempt to entice you into buying some sort of EVP recording gadget or gizmo, but buyer beware! The practice of attempting to record EVP has become, on the whole, a mainstay technique for many of those individuals and groups wishing to attempt to make contact with the spirits of those people close to them who have unfortunately passed away, whether it is good friends or dearly departed loved ones, and also as a general ghost hunting *modus operandi.*

As with various facets of the paranormal, EVP and ITC have, in recent years, attained a lot of airtime on both the big and small screens, the Michael Keaton movie *White Noise* being a particular case in point, where the central theme running through the movie is Keaton's character trying to make contact with his recently deceased and much-loved spouse; another example is the hugely popular film by director M. Night Shyamalan, *The Sixth Sense*, where the psychologist played by Bruce Willis realises that audio recordings that he had made with some of his patients also contain the voices of a large number of dead people.

Although the phenomenon has sprung into the public's attention over the last thirty years or so, its history goes back for almost a hundred years, almost to the beginning of the twentieth century, though some people would dispute this. We've already discovered that through things like the Spiritualist movement, the belief that we could communicate with the dead through the use of mediums was very popular, but as we entered into the 1900s and this new age of wonder and scientific achievement and were making astonishing advances in the field of communication technology, the theory that this same equipment could somehow also be used in the goal of contacting the spirit world started to come to the fore.

During a period in the 1920s, Thomas Edison, the man famous for inventing, among other things, the electric light, phonograph and the motion-picture camera, was also hard at work, along with his assistant Dr Miller Hutchinson, in an attempt to develop and manufacture a machine that he hoped would facilitate the user to communicate with the dead. It is believed that Edison first attempted to make contact with the dead via some type of phonograph device as early as the 1890s. When asked, Hutchinson stated that both Edison and himself were convinced that there were facts to be discovered in the field of psychic research that would prove to be of greater significance to the human race as a whole, far more so than all the inventions that they had made in the field of electricity. In a statement by the great man himself, Edison commented:

> If our personality does indeed truly survive after death, then it is strictly logical or scientific to assume that it retains memory, intellect, other faculties, and knowledge that we have acquired during our time on this Earth. Therefore . . . if we can evolve an instrument so delicate as to be affected by our personality as it survives in the next life, such an instrument, when made available, ought to record something.

But this wondrous machine was never to exist outside of the intellect of Thomas Edison as he subsequently died in 1931 leaving no plans, blueprints or sketches of the machine that he had envisaged for so long.

The theory of creating a machine to enable communication with the dead was taken up by many other famous inventors of the period. As well as Thomas Edison, Nikola Tesla and Guglielmo Marconi were active in the pursuit of creating this device.

To a great extent, the task was also undertaken by many mediums of the day, as they saw it as a way to further enhance their own communicative skills. One of the first people to try and record what he believed to be the voices of the dead was the American medium and photographer, Attila von Szalay. His early attempts in the 1930s and 1940s were using a 78 rpm record. In 1938, he said that he heard a tiny voice in the air in very close proximity to himself, which he believed was his dead son, attempting to speak with him for some unknown reason. He believed that he finally succeeded in his quest some years later, this time in 1956, but rather than the record that he had employed in earlier attempts, on this occasion he had elected to make use of a reel-to-reel tape-recorder deck. Szalay conducted a number of experimental recording sessions with custom-built equipment, usually consisting of some form of microphone, which in turn was wired up to the recording equipment along with a speaker. After reviewing the recordings, he reported that he had discovered many sounds on them that were not heard at the actual time that the recordings had taken place, both male and female voices were heard along with noises of whistles and rapping, a percentage of which were recorded when there was no living person within the vicinity of the microphone.

Contained on some of his first successful recordings were what he believed to be the voices of the spirits who were relaying some sort of message and contained such phrases as 'Merry Christmas and a Happy New Year to you all', 'This is G!' and 'Hot dog, Art'.

Marcello Bacci began making recordings of ghostly voices at his home in Grosseto, Italy, in 1949. He enlisted the use of an old vacuum-tube radio, and attracted a group of spirits that would communicate with him through the radio sounds. People from all around would visit him in his laboratory at home, and listen to the spirit communication and, very often, would receive messages from their dearly departed loved ones.

Another startling and puzzling example of the phenomenon happened again in Italy during the 1950s, and this time, it happened to two men of the cloth. Roman Catholic priests, Father Gemelli, who was the president of the Papal Academy, and Father Ernetti, who was a physicist, philosopher and an internationally renowned scientist, as well as a great lover of music, were conducting research into music together in 1952. During one session, they were attempting to record a series of Gregorian chants, but a wire on their magnetophone tended to break with an infuriating regularity. More than a tad fed up with this unfortunate series of events, Father Gemelli looked up to the heavens and asked for his father's help. To the complete and utter amazement of the two priests, Gemelli's own father's voice was recorded on the magnetophone saying 'Of course I will help you, I am always with you!' Obviously, to prove that they indeed did hear it correctly, they repeated the experiment, and this time a clear, humorous voice uttered, 'But Zucchini, it is clear, do you not know that it is I?' Shocked beyond words, Gemelli stared at the machine. Nobody, absolutely nobody, knew the taunting childhood name that his father used to call him. He was elated to be in contact with his father, but apprehensive at the same time, as what right had he to speak to the dead. Deeply troubled, the two were eventually granted an audience with Pope Pius XII at the Vatican in Rome. Father Gemelli, possibly fearing the worst, received another surprise when the Pope clasped him by the shoulder and said, 'My dear Father Gemelli, you really need not worry about this at all. The existence of this voice is strictly a scientific fact and has nothing whatsoever to do with spiritism. The recording machine is totally objective. It receives and records only sound waves from wherever they may come. This experiment may perhaps become the cornerstone for a building for scientific studies which will strengthen people's faith in a hereafter.' Somewhat relieved and reassured, the good Father still made sure that the recording was not made public knowledge until the latter years of his life, and it wasn't until 1990 that the details of this extraordinary event were released into the public domain.

In 1959, just a couple of years after the events in Italy, a Swedish film producer encountered voices on a tape recording that could not be accounted for, as he believed that he was completely alone when he had made the recordings. Friedrich Jurgenson was a man with many strings to his bow; he was a linguist, a singer and recording artist, a philosopher, an archaeologist, an accomplished artist (he was commissioned to do a painting for the Pope of the time, Pope Pius XII), and a documentary filmmaker. At the time of the event, he was out in the wilds of the countryside hoping to record various sounds of the natural world, primarily bird songs and calls, for a documentary project that he was currently working on. However, on later playing back the material that he had made earlier that day, he discovered what he believed to be the voice of his deceased father, along with the voice of his dead wife, which was apparently calling out his name. In addition to the voices of his nearest and dearest, he heard a male voice comment on something about "bird voices in the night". This was not the only occasion that this happened to Jurgenson as he made many more of these recordings, one of which he reported contained a message to him from his dearly departed mother, which stated, 'Friedrich, you are being watched. Friedel, my little Friedel, can you hear me?' Now, that's something you never come across with Bill Oddie on one of his many nature programmes, disembodied voices coming through on the transmission advising Bill what species of birds are about. But would this cause the diminutive naturalist to become lost for words for once? Perhaps not, as the poor spirit probably wouldn't be able to get a word in edgeways. No offence Bill, keep up the good work!

Jurgenson went on to publish two books about the subject, *Rosterna fran Rymden* ('Voices from Space') and *Sprechfunk mit Verstorbenen* ('Radio-link with the Dead'). One of these was read rather sceptically by the Latvian psychologist Konstantin Raudive. After consulting with Jurgenson, Raudive developed his own experimental recording techniques and went on to make more than 100,000 recordings during his experiments into the subject, some of which were made within the confines of a specially screened laboratory. Just like Jurgenson before him, Raudive heard his dead mother speaking to him, calling him by his childhood name. Many of the recordings contained readily identifiable words, and Raudive invited people to listen to the recordings and to interpret the material.

The work of Konstantin Raudive attracted a lot of attention worldwide, and in 1971, engineers from the Pye Record Company conducted a series of experiments in conjunction with the psychologist. Inviting him back to their sound laboratory, and using specially installed equipment to block out any pervasive radio and television signals, Raudive was not allowed to touch any of the equipment whatsoever, not even the microphone that he was to use to speak into for the duration of the experimental session. The engineers recorded him remotely for approximately eighteen minutes of continual speech, but no one listening at the time heard anything out of the ordinary. The engineers were less than impressed, and almost deemed the experiment an unmitigated failure right up until the point that they analysed the recording, on which they subsequently found over two hundred separate voices among the track of Raudive's voice. Raudive agreed to take part in more experiments, this time by a company that was employed by the British government to test the United Kingdom's most sophisticated defence equipment. Britain's leading electronic-suppression engineer led the experiments, and again specialist equipment and laboratories were used. An unused recording tape, which was to remain sealed until placed into the recorder for the experiment, was shipped directly from the factory to ensure that nothing could contaminate the contents of the tape. Such were the lengths to which the company went to eliminate any erroneous sounds, they even did one experiment where no microphone was used at all, but the voices still appeared on the recording to everyone's amazement. A. P. Hale, the engineer in charge, simply stated that he could not explain what had happened in any normal physical way. The research of Konstantin Raudive became so popular worldwide that the EVP is quite often known simply as 'Raudive Voices'. Raudive himself published a book in 1971 called *Breakthrough*; it contained much about his methods and experiences attained while researching the subject of EVPs.

Around the same time in the north of England, Raymond Cass had started to record a quantity of voices in his office based in Hull. After many years of constant research and recording, he amassed in excess of 2,000 individual examples of the EVP phenomena. Raymond Cass came to be regarded as the pioneer of EVP research in the British Isles.

A new invention, Spiricom, was unveiled to the world in 1980 and its creator, William O'Neal, claimed that it was an electronic audio device that enabled him to engage in a two-way conversation with the spirit world. O'Neal further claimed that he had received the specifications for the device from a scientist. Nothing so unusual in that really you may think, except for the fact that the scientist in question, George Mueller, had died in 1974, some six years earlier, and that the details were passed to O'Neal from the dead scientist by psychic means. Furthermore, O'Neal passed the specifications on to other researchers for them to construct and experiment with their own versions of the Spiricom device, though none of them managed to achieve the same results that O'Neal claimed to have obtained. The reason for this, according to O'Neal's business partner, was because he had medium-like abilities, and these helped the system work where all the replicated ones without this ability had failed miserably.

1982 saw the foundation of the American Association of Electronic Voice Phenomena (AA-EVP) by Sarah Estep. Set up in Severna Park, in Maryland, USA, its remit, as a non-profit-making organisation, was to increase awareness of the EVP phenomena and to establish and teach a standardised method of recording this elusive and enigmatic aspect of the supernatural. Sarah claimed to have received hundreds of messages from the time when she first began exploring the phenomena in 1976, from deceased relatives and friends, along with those from other spirit individuals. Some famous and unusual people were among those leaving messages on Sarah's recordings, including the famous German composer Ludwig van Beethoven and Konstantin Raudive himself, the psychologist having sadly passed away in 1974. Other messages were recorded by what Sarah claimed to be extraterrestrials.

As the years went by, more and more items of an electrical nature were being used in the exploration of EVP. Originally, recordings had been made on some form of audio recording device, but now things like televisions, computers and fax machines were being exploited in the search to enable communication between the living and the dead. The Germans being the efficient lot they are coined the term Instrumental Trans-Communication, which they thought was a more defining and accurate expression for the processes now being employed. One famous incident of ITC involved the EVP researcher Friedrich Jurgenson, who was said to have appeared on the television of one of his colleagues on the day of his own funeral. The fact that the television had been tuned in to a spare channel deliberately would suggest that this had been a prearranged experiment between the two in the event of Jurgenson's death. Friedrich Jurgenson died in 1987.

A German researcher into ITC, named Klaus Schreiber, employed a continuous loop to record images. He achieved this by setting up a video camera facing towards a television set. The video camera was then hooked up via its output socket and fed back into the television. Schreiber claimed some success by using this method, and in one session claimed to have caught the image of Austrian actress Romy Schneider.

So now you'll more than likely be wondering how it could be possible for you yourself to carry out an investigation into EVP and ITC. So far everything you have read in the history of these subjects has, on the whole, involved custom-built equipment and expensive sound laboratories and technologies, which may make you question just how the average person with access to no or little specialised equipment can hope to carry out this kind of experimental research . . .

Alternative Theories

Unlike most paranormal topics, EVP attracts quite a bit of scientific interest. This is partly due to the fact it is a purely instrument-based phenomenon, which lends itself more readily to the scientific method. However, EVP has attracted much criticism over the years, with sceptics pointing out that the results are very tenuous and are more likely to have a natural explanation than a supernatural one. The following is a round up of the most popular theories put forward to explain the strange voices that, although not heard at the time, mysteriously appear on audio recordings on playback.

Voices of the Dead?

The most popular notion is that these mysterious voices are messages from beyond the grave. This idea came about very early on in EVP research due to the fact that most of the early researchers claimed that the voices they were capturing belonged to their deceased relatives, colleagues or loved ones. Not only did the voices sound familiar, they also used specific phrases or modes of speech particular to the deceased individual and/or provided information that only they and the person making the recording could have known. Interestingly, many researchers observed that some of the voices they picked up tended to comment about things that were occurring at the time the recording was being made, almost as if the voice owner was occupying the same room in which the recording was taking place. The fact that almost everyone who undertakes long-term research into EVP comes up with the same conclusion is intriguing.

Radio Frequency (RF) Interference

Because EVP uses recording equipment, microphones, and sometimes, detuned radio receivers, several critics cite radio frequency interference and cross modulation as the source of the mysterious voices. The air around us is awash with billions of radio signals from many sources, ranging from TV and radio stations, Wi-Fi networks, mobile phones, Sat Navs and a whole host of other devices too numerous to mention. Sometimes stray radio signals can be picked up by devices that have poor earth connections or badly made components that are not adequately screened against radio frequency interference. This includes devices not originally designed to pick up radio frequency transmissions. One of the authors once possessed a portable record player that was capable of picking up the cockpit communications from passing aircraft!

When using a recording device, it is sometimes possible for stray RF signals to become amplified enough to be able to bleed into the actual recording, producing random noise and sometimes allowing fragments of speech to be mixed in with the input signal. Sceptics claim that these stray transmissions are responsible for all the voices picked up on EVP recordings. EVP researchers dismiss these claims on the grounds that they only pick up voices, not music, which you would expect to hear if the source of the EVP was a local radio station. Although there are a lot of voice-only transmissions broadcast over the airwaves that could be the source of the additional voices, such as taxis, emergency services, etc., researchers point out that the messages received appear to be aimed specifically at the person making the recording.

The experiments conducted in the labs of Pye and Belling & Lee in 1971 with Konstantin Raudive appear to completely discount the notion that EVP is all down to radio frequency interference. As previously discussed, voices still persisted to manifest themselves on tape in tests conducted in heavily screened laboratories. Ken Attwood, the chief engineer at Pye said, 'I have done everything in my power to break the mystery of the voices without success; the same applies to other experts. I suppose we must learn to accept them.' Peter Hale, the chief engineer of Belling & Lee, a physicist and electronics engineer who was considered to be the country's leading expert on electronic suppression, stated, 'In view of the tests carried out in a screened laboratory at my firm, I can not explain what happened in normal physical terms.'

More recent experiments, particularly those of former NASA speech researcher Alexander MacRae, not only verify the findings of the Pye and Belling labs but actually to go beyond them. In 2006, MacRae managed to obtain voices on recording equipment situated in a laboratory that was insulated against both radio and sound waves, clearly demonstrating that where EVP is concerned, something very strange appears to be going on.

Apophenia

Sceptics are keen to point out that most of the alleged voices captured are so indistinct that they could easily be random noise that is being misperceived as a human voice. Apophenia is the ability of the human mind to see or hear patterns that don't actually exist within random stimulus, such as the ability to see meaningful shapes in clouds. Sceptics are quick to point out that many of the EVP methods traditionally used by researchers, more often than not, introduce some form of background noise into the recording, which they claim gives us enough 'raw material' to be able to pick out anything we want to hear. A good example of this happening is when people are taking a shower and they mistakenly think that they have heard the phone ring. The noise produced by the running water forms a random sound backdrop from which the brain conjures up the sound of a ringing telephone.

Bleed-through from Old Tapes/Mechanism Noises

When EVP research started in earnest, the only devices available to use were tape recorders. Some of the effects that were claimed to be EVP were caused by researchers reusing tapes that had been recorded on and erased dozens of times previously. Sometimes when a tape is reused, the older recording can bleed through into the newer one, giving rise to extra sounds or voices that weren't audible at the time the tape was recorded.

In the early 90s, we worked on a suspected EVP case where a young girl had recorded herself singing a pop song. When the family played back the recording they were stunned to hear what sounded like an old man's voice accompanying her. Thinking that they had captured a ghost, they contacted a paranormal investigation team, who in turn came to us to ask us to conduct sound analysis on their behalf.

When we listened to the recording, we quickly discovered that the old man's voice only appeared on one channel of the tape (stereo tapes have two channels on each side, one for the left speaker and one for the right), and once this was isolated and sped up, it sounded identical to the young girl's voice. By conducting a spectrum analysis on both voices, it was possible to confirm that they both belonged to the young girl. We later discovered that she had recorded herself many times on the same cassette using two different tape machines. One of the machines was a karaoke device that had an adjustable record speed facility. This had been set to record at double speed, meaning that, once the recording was played back on a conventional tape player, it would make the girl's voice sound much slower and lower in pitch. The other tape machine's erase head (a device in the recorder that erases the tape just before a fresh recording is laid down) was out of alignment, meaning that when she rerecorded herself, only part of the original recording was erased. When the tape was played back, the 'old man' voice could be heard along with the girl's, forming a spooky duo.

Although tape recorders are seldom used nowadays, there are some EVP researchers who will use nothing else. They believe that digital technology is not capable of picking up anomalous voices, saying that there is something about the way sound is recorded onto analogue tape that lends itself to be easily manipulated by the 'spirit world', which apparently is something that can't be achieve on digital formats. Our personal opinion on this, based on our own successes with digital methods, is that you can achieve good results on either types of device. However, if you still wish to use analogue equipment it is important to use brand-new tapes every time you record to eliminate the possibility of a previous recording bleeding through. In addition, since tape recorders contain moving parts that can produce noise when operated, it is a good idea to use an external microphone so that you do not pick up the sound of the mechanisms on your recordings.

How to record EVP

The following methods are very simple ways in which to get you started in investigating EVP for yourself. Each method only requires basic equipment such as an audio recorder, a microphone and a source of white noise (hiss) or static (a radio receiver tuned between two stations). Each method has a few variations that can be explored.

Method 1: Capturing Passive EVP

What you will need:

Audio recorder
Microphone
Headphones
Notepad and pen
Watch

In modern paranormal investigation, EVP has now come to mean any anomalous sound that appears on a device, be it a voice, breathing, footsteps or any other noise that should not have been present during the recording. Anomalous sounds recorded in empty rooms are called passive EVPs, as they have occurred without the need for human presence. Passive EVPs are sounds that shouldn't occur naturally in the environment you are recording in, such as picking up a human voice in a room that you know is totally unoccupied, or picking up the sound of a ticking clock when there is no clock present.

This first method is typical of the sort of thing that is carried out on a ghost investigation. Find a quiet room in your house where you are least likely to be disturbed by other people, pets, etc., and stand there for few minutes with your eyes closed. Listen carefully to all the background sounds that you can hear, such as distant traffic noise, animals, birds, aircraft or sounds from other rooms in the house, such as from TVs, radios or stereos (ideally these should all be switched off while you are experimenting), and make a note of them all. Now that you know what sounds naturally occur in and around the room, you will be in a better position to identify anything anomalous that may appear on your recording.

Set up your recorder and microphone on a table or chair in the centre of the room, making sure that you place the microphone as far away from the recorder as you can. Make sure that the microphone is switched on and then start recording. Write down the time you start the recorder, exit and seal the room (if possible), and leave the recorder running for around thirty minutes.

Retire to a location where you can make sure that no people or animals can get into the room without you knowing and remain as quiet as possible for the duration of the experiment. If you hear any sounds from other parts of the house that you think could be picked up by the recorder, e.g., slamming doors, the telephone ringing, make a note of the sound heard and the time it occurred. This will be useful later when you come to review the recording.

Once thirty minutes have elapsed, return to the room and switch off the recorder and microphone. Rewind the recording (if necessary), and if your recorder has a counter or timer, reset it to zero. Plug in your headphones, make yourself comfortable and listen carefully to the recording. Make a note of anything you hear that you feel is anomalous, e.g., any knocks, bangs, sounds of movement, etc., and note down the counter or timer reading that they have occurred at. This will help you to locate them again quickly. Once you have reviewed your recording, compare the results with your notes to see if any of the sounds you have picked up are explainable.

If you haven't picked up anything unusual, don't despair. Experienced EVP researchers say that it sometimes takes a few attempts before you start to capture anything anomalous. However, if you feel you have recorded something significant, play the recording over a few times to make sure that you can't find a rational explanation, then let others hear the recording to see what they make of it. It is important that you do not give them any clue as to what you think you have heard, as this may colour their perception. Allow them to make up their own mind as to what they are hearing. If everyone is in agreement that what has been recorded is anomalous, you might have some interesting evidence on your hands.

Note: Make sure that you retain the original recording on its original media, as well as your notes. These will be required should you wish to send off your recording to be analysed.

Method 2: Capturing Interactive EVP

What you will need:

Audio recorder
Microphone
Notepad and pen
Camcorder and tripod
A friend or observer
Watch

One of the claims made by EVP researchers is that, for EVP to appear, people have to be present. In addition, the messages that appear are claimed to be specific to the person(s) making the recording. For this experiment, two people will need to stay in the room whilst recording.

As in method 1, listen carefully to the background sounds you can hear, paying particular attention to any natural voices that could be misconstrued as EVP, such as from TVs, radios or people walking past in the street talking.

Set up your recorder and microphone on a table or chair in the centre of the room, making sure that you place the microphone as far away from the recorder as possible. Set up the camcorder in a position where it can cover you, the observer and the recorder. Try to get as much of the room in shot as possible. The camcorder is present for two reasons. Firstly, it is there to eliminate the possibility of trickery (e.g., you or the observer whispering to fake an EVP). Secondly, it acts as a second audio recorder, for if you do pick up something on the sound recording, you can play back the appropriate portion of the video to see if the camcorder has also picked it up.

Start the camcorder.

Sit the observer in a spot where they can keep an eye on you and the recorder, and find a comfortable spot close to the microphone for you to sit. For the next few minutes, both you and the observer should relax and try to clear any thoughts from your minds. Being in a relaxed state of mind seems to be an important factor in helping anomalous phenomena to occur. Once relaxed, start the audio recorder. Make a note of the time you start recording. After a few seconds begin to ask questions such as: Is there anybody there? What is your name? Do you know me?

After each question, leave a long gap before asking the next question. This makes space for any EVP replies. Remain as silent as possible in these gaps. Throughout the whole experiment both you and the observer should be listening out for any stray voices that could be misconstrued as EVP. If you hear any, make a note of the time and where you thought the voice came from. Because the EVP responses are believed to be specific to the individual making the recording, try to ask a few questions that only you know the answer to, such as: What did I have for breakfast? What did I get for my eighteenth birthday? What is my middle name?

Again, leave long gaps between questions. Continue to ask questions for around fifteen minutes, stop the recording and stop the camcorder. When you are ready, play back the recording. If you do pick up anything, do not tell each other what you think it says. Instead, both you and the observer should write down what you think has been said. Once you have done this, compare notes. Are you in agreement? Again, if you do seem to have got a result, keep hold of the original sound and video recording in case they need analysing.

Method 3: White-noise Recording

What you will need:

Audio recorder
Microphone
White-noise source
Notepad and pen
Camcorder and tripod
A friend or observer
Watch

EVP experimenters often use a sound called 'white noise' whilst conducting their experiments. White noise is a sound constructed from all audible frequencies being played at once at the same volume. The resultant sound is a hissing or roaring noise that is often described as sounding like rushing water. Some EVP researchers have theorised that, for a voice to be able to 'come through', there needs to be some form of background sound that the 'spirit' or 'agency' can manipulate or modulate to produce an audible voice.

White-noise sound files can be found and downloaded for free on the internet, or purchased in CD format from online stockists. A handy white-noise generator is available for free download from the EVP Research Association UK. Although it is free, we urge you to donate some money to their research fund via their PayPal donation page: http://www.evpuk.com/evp_assistant_software.html.

Once you have obtained your white-noise source, set it up in the room you wish to experiment in and play it softly in the background, loud enough to be heard but not so loud as to drown out all conversation in the room. Set up and run the experiment as in method 2.

Sound Analysis

EVP researchers report other oddities peculiar to the voices they capture. The fragments of speech tend to have odd cadences (inflections in the voice, such as rising pitch at the beginnings or ends of words or unusual, rhythmic speech patterns) and sometimes the voices are found to be raised in pitch far beyond the normal frequency range for human voices. These characteristics make EVP all the more difficult to explain by conventional means. In order to investigate these properties, it is necessary to upload your recordings to a computer for detailed sound analysis. Unfortunately, any description of how you go about doing detailed sound analysis would take up the contents of another book and is, sadly, beyond the scope of this one. However, if you are keen to find out more about sound analysis, there is a free sound-editing software package called Audacity that will get you started. The American Association of EVP website has useful information on how to install and use the package and also displays a link from where you can download it: http://www.aaevp.com/techniques/techniques_evp_using_audacity.htm

We hope that we have sufficiently whetted your appetite for you to explore the mysterious world of EVP in greater depth, and that you will have many interesting hours investigating it.

Photographic Anomalies

Any sufficiently advanced technology
is indistinguishable from magic.

Arthur C. Clarke

A Brief History

For almost as long as photography has been around, strange and often puzzling images have been captured on film that purport to be physical proof of the reality of the paranormal. It is widely believed that the first ghost photograph ever taken was shot in 1860 by W. Campbell in New Jersey, who attempted to take a test picture of a chair in his photographic studio. However, when the picture was developed he found that he had captured more than he bargained for. In addition to the chair, Campbell had also caught the image of a young boy. Campbell claimed he was the only person present in the studio at the time.

The following year, Boston engraver and amateur photographer William Mumbler was experimenting with his camera by taking self-portraits. On one of the prints, his image was accompanied by the figure of a young woman that William recognised as one of his cousins who had tragically died twelve years earlier. Although this and hundreds of other pictures taken by Mumbler are now considered fakes, his pictures caught the public's imagination and ushered in the use of the camera in paranormal investigation. Spirit photography had arrived.

The first spirit pictures mostly consisted of poorly defined images of people or animals, which were either translucent or semi-formed. These were dubbed 'spirit extras', as they were not visible to the people taking the photographs, only appearing on the developed negatives and prints. One image, taken in 1891 by photographer Sybell Corbett, of the library room at Combermere Abbey in Cheshire, caught the unmistakable form of the body and arms of a person sitting in a large, leather armchair. The exposure time of the photograph was approximately one hour and the library was judged to have been vacant of people for the duration of the exposure. The man was identified as Lord Combermere, who at the time the photograph was taken was actually being buried. He had been killed five days beforehand in a tragic road accident. The picture was investigated by the Society for Psychical Research, who at first thought that, due to the photograph's long exposure time, the 'spirit extra' could have been one of the abbey's male servants who could have wandered in and sat down in the chair for a spell. However, it was soon pointed out that all the male staff in the house were in attendance at Lord Combermere's funeral. This photograph remains a mystery to this day.

Probably the most famous of all the ghost photographs that has ever been taken, dates back to the mid-1930s and is one of the many hundreds of ghostly activities that occur amid Britain's multitude of stately homes. The image was taken on 19 September 1936 by two photographers working on an article for *Country Life* magazine, and the whole event was published in the December edition of that year. Nestling in the quiet countryside of Norfolk, close to the town of Fakenham, lies the ancestral seat of the Townshend family, Raynham Hall. With part of the building said to have been designed by the architect Inigo Jones, Raynham Hall was to become famous for more than just its pleasing structural style. The photographers in question, Captain Provand and his assistant, Indre Shira, were to take a number of pictures of the beautiful building and at the time of the sighting were taking shots of the main staircase. After the first picture, Shira noticed a brown misty form descending the stairway in front of them and then a second subsequent picture was hurriedly taken. Although not witnessed by Provand at the time, on later developing the negative, the famous image was revealed for all to see. So certain was Shira of what he had seen that he enlisted the help of an independent witness to verify the events at the time the negative was developed so as to ensure that no trickery was taking place. But this was not the only time that the Brown Lady of Raynham Hall had been witnessed, the first recorded instance of the ghost happened at Christmas in 1835, and had subsequently been witnessed on numerous occasions prior to it being caught on film. On one of the ghostly encounters, a guest at the hall even attempted to shoot the spectre with his pistol, but the bullet passed through the head of the figure and lodged itself in a corridor wall. But possibly the most famous sighting of this apparition happened to the future King George IV, the then Prince Regent, who encountered her at his bedside watching over him as he slept. Completely perturbed, he woke the entire household during the night demanding to know who the little lady dressed all in brown was, and with no answer forthcoming to his liking, immediately left the premises never to return. Anyone who has awoken to find someone leaning over them can understand his reaction; it can be quite shocking, especially when, as in this case, you subsequently discover that the person leaning over you happens to be of the extinct persuasion. Since the photograph was taken however, there have been no subsequent reports of the ghost having appeared again, though there is a theory that she has now moved to a crossroads in the nearby vicinity, and she is also said to haunt nearby Houghton Hall. The lady in question is thought to be Lady Dorothy Townshend, who died in 1729 of smallpox at the rather young age of forty. She was the sister of Britain's first Prime Minister, Sir Robert Walpole.

A recreation of the famous
Brown Lady photograph.

Is this photograph of the Brown Lady of Raynham Hall the real deal or an elaborate example of photographic trickery? We may perhaps never know for certain one way or the other, but prior to the pictures publication, it was examined at length by experts at *Country Life*, and though puzzling, they deduced that the image was completely genuine and no alterations to the photograph had been made in any way.

In juxtaposition to the most famous ghost picture, we now have to contend with the most notorious faked series of images ever caught on film, a series of five photographs that caught the imagination of the British public as the First World War was drawing to a close. All the photographs were taken by two young cousins in a small Yorkshire village on the outskirts of Bradford. In 1917, the two girls, Elsie Wright, aged sixteen, and Frances Griffiths, aged ten, took the first two images of what became known as 'The Cottingley Fairies'. It wasn't until as late as 1981 that the two finally admitted that the images were indeed faked, but they still steadfastly defended their original statement that they had indeed witnessed the fairies for real.

The fairy photographs and the events surrounding them have been the subject of many documentaries and movies over the years. Elsie Wright took part in a TV interview for the series *Arthur C. Clarke's World of Strange Powers*, whilst the photographs themselves featured in an episode of the Doctor Who spin-off series *Torchwood*. In 1997, two major motion pictures were released based on the events in question: *Photographing Fairies* and *Fairy Tale: A True Story*, which starred Peter O'Toole and Harvey Keitel.

The first of the five photographs was taken at a place called Cottingley Beck, which was located at the rear of the home of the Wright family. Elsie had borrowed her father's camera to take the images, and in it, Frances can be seen gazing towards the camera whilst a troop of the fairy folk is joyously prancing about on the limb of a tree. Elsie's father developed the photograph, and upon discovering what the image contained, decided to dismiss it out of hand. But later, he developed more photographs and seeing the subject matter once again, he subsequently banned Elsie from using his camera. Kodak, the multi-national film-processing company declined to comment at the time about the authenticity of the series of images other than to say that there were many ways that these pictures could have been faked. However, many other photographers of the period did indeed examine them and deemed them all to be genuine. But other more eminent men were yet to investigate the circumstances surrounding the series of photographs.

Prints of the first two photographs came into the possession of Sir Arthur Conan Doyle, and in 1920, he was commissioned by *Strand* magazine to write an article about the two girls and the fairy folk photographs. Conan Doyle passed the prints onto various people for them to examine and decide on their authenticity, some of whom judged them to be faked, whilst others elected to take the opposite viewpoint. The article was published at the end of November, and copies sold out within five days. Conan Doyle, who was heavily into Spiritualism by this point, decided that the pictures did indeed contain the images of fairy folk. The article that he had written for *Strand* magazine had caused controversy and everyone was split as to the legitimacy of the images and the newspapers of the day reflected this: the *Truth* took an intolerant view saying, 'For the true explanation of these Fairy photographs what is required is not a knowledge of occult phenomena but rather a knowledge of children', while the *South Wales Argus* declared, 'The day we kill Santa Claus with our statistics we will have plunged our glorious world into the deepest darkness!' Perhaps Sir Arthur Conan Doyle should have stuck to the edict of his most beloved literary creation, Sherlock Holmes, when he said, 'If you eliminate the impossible, whatever remains, however improbable, must be the truth!'

Throughout the twentieth century, cameras became cheaper, smaller and easier to use. Recognisable 'spirit figures' were still appearing on prints and negatives, but were being joined by more amorphous forms such as blobs of light, light trails and eerie mists. However, a majority of these were caused by camera malfunctions or processing faults, especially on the popular cameras such as instamatics.

During the mid 1990s, cameras evolved yet again, and digital photography heralded a new type of anomaly: the orb. From around 1997 onwards, orbs have been appearing in ever-increasing numbers on pictures, and are currently the predominant photographic 'anomaly' of the twenty-first century. At the same time, 'spirit extras' have waned dramatically. Why this is so is a source of much debate, which we will cover later in this section.

Categories of Photographic Anomaly

After detailed investigation and analysis, allegedly paranormal photographs end up in one of four categories: fakes, faults, misidentifications/misperceptions and genuine anomalies. Let's briefly look at each in turn.

Fakes

There are many ways to create a fake photograph. With traditional film cameras the most commonly used technique was to create a double exposure, either by taking a picture and then winding the film back to take another shot on the same frame or by combining two separate negatives together in the dark room to make a composite picture. Either method could usually be detected by careful scrutiny of both prints and negatives. A lot of the early fakes created by the likes of William Mumbler were created in this way.

As well as double exposures, another popular method employed from time to time was the use of models and props. In particular, bedsheets or muslin gauze was used in Victorian séances to give the impression of the appearance of spirit guides or ectoplasm. Seen in the near dark, they appeared quite impressive, but when illuminated by the bright light of a camera flash the props look crude and unconvincing by modern standards. However, at the time, séance pictures were considered to be definite proof of the existence of ghosts or spirits. Modern day prop fakery is mostly confined to the UFO world, where hubcaps flung into the air are made out to depict spacecraft from another world, or tiny models suspended from trees with very thin wire are shot in such a way as to make them look like large objects at a distance. Another trick sometimes employed is to stick saucer/disc silhouette shapes onto a pane of glass and photograph it against the sky.

In the digital age, faking has become more of a problem, as there are now a lot of software packages available that can be used to manipulate or enhance digital photographs. With just a little bit of practice, almost anyone can produce fairly convincing fake pictures in minutes. The fact that digital photographs can be easily modified, coupled with the ever increasing power and sophistication of photo editing software, has made some investigators dismiss everything that is offered as evidence. However, there are several ways to help you determine if a digital picture might have been tampered with.

Spotting fakes

EXIF Information

When a digital camera takes a picture it not only stores the image data but also information about the camera and the settings used (such as exposure time, shutter speed and aperture) at the time the image was taken. This information is embedded within the image itself as an EXIF (Exchangeable Image File Format) file, which can be extracted by using EXIF-reader software. The most recent image editors and picture viewers contain EXIF readers as standard. If you do not currently have the capability of looking at EXIF data there are several free EXIF readers available for download on the internet.

The EXIF file contains a wealth of information that is massively useful for photographic analysis. One of the most important pieces of information it can contain is the name and version of the last piece of software used to view or edit the photograph. Since the EXIF information is imbedded in the actual image, once the picture is uploaded into a software package, the name of the software is automatically added to the EXIF file. Therefore, if the package last used to 'view' the picture is an image editor (e.g., Photoshop), the chances are that the image has been altered in some

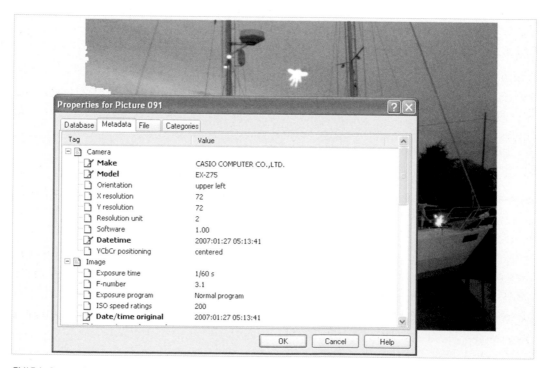

EXIF information.

way. Pictures straight from the camera or memory card should display something along the lines of: Software: 1.0. If anything else appears under the 'Software' tag, chances are that you have a fake on your hands. As well as the software tag, other useful EXIF data elements include:

The make and model of the camera used – This is useful for checking out the camera's functions, i.e., does it have the capability of making double exposures (there are a few rare models, such as the Pentax Optio 450 and 500, that do have this capability) or are there any 'issues' with the camera's reliability. The make and model tags helped us to identify the work of a serial hoaxer who submitted a series of 'UFO' photographs to us and other groups in the UK over a period of two years. Although his digital image manipulation skills improved over time, his (fairly unique) camera make and model EXIF tags helped us to identify anything he sent in.

Time and date – Knowing the exact time and date that an image has been taken is massively useful, especially if the witness has only estimated either. However, the time and date setting on the EXIF file is only as accurate as the time/date displayed on the camera, so it is essential to compare what the camera is displaying with the current time. If you are having difficulty reading the current time/date off the camera, ask the owner to fire off a picture while you are interviewing them and compare the current time and date with what the picture data displays. However, even if the time and date are correct, do not forget to make allowances for time zone differences or daylight saving if applicable.

Flash fired (on/off) – This has proved useful to determine if the illumination seen in some images shot in low light conditions was caused by light emanating from an object or reflected light from the camera's flash.

Shutter speed – If there is any blurring seen on the picture, has it been caused by a long exposure or by an object moving at high speed? This is particularly useful for analysing UFO pictures shot in low light.

Newer cameras are now capable of recording the exact location where a picture has been taken by storing the GPS (Global Positioning System) coordinates in the EXIF file. Once this facility becomes more widespread, it will be a very useful tool in determining exact locations out of doors or to help with witness cross-examination if you suspect someone isn't telling the whole truth.

However, EXIF information is not without its problems. For instance, it can easily be lost. If the image file is uploaded onto a computer and renamed (some image uploaders will do this automatically), the EXIF information can be partially or wholly erased. If you are presented with a picture that contains no EXIF information, this could be another indicator to show that the picture may have been tampered with. To retain the EXIF information, it is essential to take a copy of the image directly from the camera or memory card. This needs to be done by manually copying the file (using file manager) straight from its source without using a photo uploader. Although EXIF data is very useful as a tool to quickly identify files that may have been manipulated, it is important to note that it is possible (although not easy) to rewrite EXIF information to make it look as though the image has not been touched. Therefore, checking that the tags appear to be unchanged should not be your soul means of determining if an image has been faked.

Light Reflections and Shadow Angles

Another useful way to spot faking is by carefully scrutinising every element in the photograph. Most digital fakes are created by adding elements of one photograph to another and then making the new elements blend into the original by adjusting their scale, brightness, contrast and softening or blurring their edges. However, since the original picture and the one that the additional elements have come from are usually not taken under the same lighting conditions, discrepancies between original elements and added items can sometimes be detected. The angle that light is being reflected off every element in the photograph and in which direction any shadows fall are two of the main indicators to help detect any image manipulation.

Pixilation Halos

Yet another tell-tale sign of trickery is to check to see if any of the elements in the photograph have pixilation halos surrounding them. These are unusual colours or excessively dark or bright outlines (depending on the background) that can be seen around elements that have been cut and pasted into a photograph. In order to spot these, you will have to load the image into photo-editing or -viewing software and zoom in until you can see the individual pixels. However, most cameras can produce pixilation halos around objects that are shot against a bright background, so if this is the case, compare the element under scrutiny with other elements in the picture to see if the halos are consistent before declaring that something has been faked.

Edge Detection and Embossing

If you have a good photo-editing package, using the Edge Detection tool can help you to see hidden wires (as used to suspend UFO models from trees) or you can use the

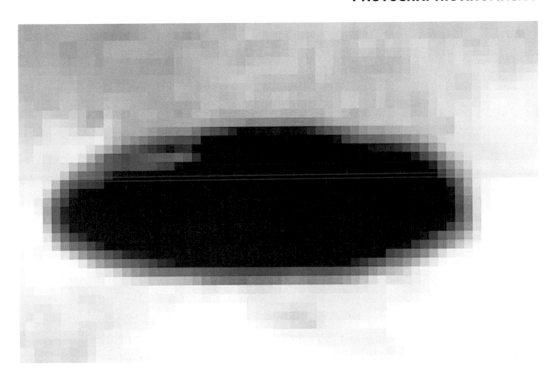

Above: Pixilation halo. Elements that have been cut and pasted into a photograph tend to show an odd-coloured halo or ring around them.

Right: By embossing this picture, it is easy to tell that the 'UFO' has been added later. Notice the difference between the edges of the buildings and the edge of the 'UFO'.

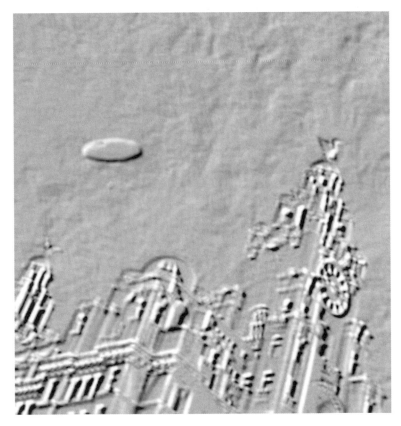

Emboss tool to detect objects that are two-dimensional. Anything that is added to a photograph after it was taken will, more often than not, stick out like a sore thumb once the picture has been embossed.

Faults

Both film and digital cameras can develop faults that can produce anomalous-looking artefacts on pictures, but film cameras have more potential to develop a fault than their digital counterparts because they contain more moving parts. The greater the number of moving parts, the bigger the potential for the camera to develop some form of mechanical failure that can add strange effects to photographs. The most common mechanical failure to plague film cameras is when the camera fails to wind on the film fully to the next frame, producing a double exposure. Another fairly common problem is light leakage. If the back of the camera is accidentally opened, stray light hitting the film inside can lead to the appearance of mists/fogs or dark blobs on photographs once the film has been processed. The authors have seen many examples of light leakage on photographs that have been thought to represent ghostly apparitions.

It is not uncommon for digital cameras to develop faults, but unlike their film counterparts most of the malfunctions that can plague a digital camera do not usually result in producing ghost-like effects on images. However, on digital SLR cameras, mechanical problems with their internal mirrors can lead to parts of pictures appearing completely dark. Although not technically a camera fault, another fairly common effect can occur when taking pictures in low light conditions without a flash. On cheaper models (mostly digital compacts), individual pixels within a picture can appear oddly coloured compared to their immediate neighbours; on occasion, these have been interpreted as tiny, hovering spirit manifestations.

It is important to note that double exposures are not possible on most digital cameras, but there are a few rare models, such as the Pentax Optio 450 and 500, that do have this capability, so if you are presented with a digital photograph that looks as though it has been double exposed, remember to check the camera specifications before getting too excited.

Misidentifications/Misperceptions

When looking at photographs, our perception of what they contain is not simply a case of taking in what our eyes can see, but also how our brain interprets what we see. Depending upon our own memories and experiences, our brain picks out details that interest us and disregards others that do not. To illustrate this, imagine that you have taken a photograph of a goat standing on a rocky outcrop. You show the picture to two friends, a biologist and a geologist. The geologist will pay more attention to the outcrop, the geological processes that shaped it and the type of rock being pictured. The biologist will pay more attention to the goat, its breed and the flora and fauna that is in the picture. Although both people saw the same picture, their individual interpretations of what it contains are entirely different. Our ability to zoom in on certain aspects of photos and disregard others can lead us to entirely misperceive or misidentify what we are seeing. In addition, the circumstances surrounding the taking of the picture, e.g., photographing an eerie graveyard or spooky dungeon, can make our expectations so high that we almost *will* ourselves to spot something out of the ordinary in the photograph. This can lead us to misinterpret ordinary things such as random patterns of light and shadow as ghost-like figures or faces. In particular, where picking out faces is concerned, psychological studies of baby perception seem to suggest that we are conditioned from a very early age to pay close attention to faces and face shapes, notably the arrangement and relationship between the main facial elements (eyes, nose, mouth). Because of this, we are all highly capable of misinterpreting random elements within photographs as faces. You can experiment with this yourself. Simply stare at a blank wall and see how long it is before you can pick out something resembling a face! If you are presented with a picture where someone has to point out the 'anomaly' to you, show it to different people without giving them clues to see if they can also spot the same thing. Chances are that a whole range of 'anomalies' will be pointed out, indicating that there is a high chance that what has been captured is nothing out of the ordinary.

The second most common type of misperception to occur is when an object or a person wanders into shot unseen by the photographer just as the picture is being taken. When the picture is later reviewed the extra objects or people suddenly become 'very mysterious' purely because they were not seen at the time. When 'unexpected' people appear on pictures they are often referred to as 'spirit extras'. Sometimes, depending on the camera's setting, people who get caught in frame as they are walking past can take on a more spooky appearance, especially if the picture is being taken at night with a long exposure time. One setting in particular, called 'night shot' on most digital cameras, holds the shutter open for several seconds after the flash has fired to allow details in the background to also appear on the photograph. Anyone or anything moving around whilst the shutter is still open will appear as a translucent blur. Although it is a common occurrence for people to wander into shot unexpectedly, this type of misidentification is on the decrease because of the move from traditional film cameras to digital. Whereas a roll of film has to be finished, developed and printed before the photographer sees the results, digital images can be reviewed a few seconds after they were taken. This has meant that the occasional passer-by who gets accidentally caught in shot is easier to spot and dismiss seconds after the picture was taken.

On the UFO side of things, small birds flying into shot are the main cause of UFO misidentifications. When flying past the camera, birds tend to get caught at odd angles or in odd postures, which makes them look very unusual and un-birdlike. A majority of them tend to take on a more lenticular or saucer-like shape, as in the following example, taken in Cheshire, England, in 2008.

Small birds caught in shot are often mistaken for UFOs.

There are other sub-categories of photographic anomalies that, like all the above, are not seen at the time pictures are taken, but are so common nowadays that they have been given their own descriptive names, such as Mist Forms, Vortexes, Light Trails and Orbs. In order to understand what these objects really are, it is important for us to do a little historical research into their humble origins and their rise in popularity in the paranormal world. Let us start with the most widely known of them: the Orb.

Orbs

Although it is difficult to say with any certainty when the first Orb was captured on camera, the general consensus is that they started to appear on pictures in large numbers from around 1997 onwards, although our research has unearthed some Orbs on pictures taken as far back as the mid-1980s. Since 1997, the number of Orbs captured on cameras has increased steadily, reaching epidemic proportions in recent years.

Opinion is divided as to what Orbs represent. To believers they are considered to be 'the first manifestation of a ghost or a spirit', whereas sceptics see them as something else more ordinary, such as camera malfunctions or atmospheric contamination. In order to unravel the truth about Orbs, it is important to ask a few pertinent questions.

Orbs caught outside. (*Photo Credit: Fiona Campbell*)

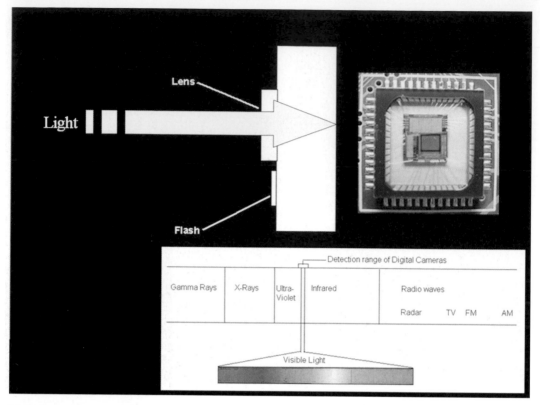

Gamma Rays	X-Rays	Ultra-Violet	Infrared	Radio waves		
				Radar	TV FM	AM

Detection range of Digital Cameras

Visible Light

Digital cameras are capable of detecting ultraviolet and infrared light, both of which are invisible to the human eye.

If Orbs *are* the first manifestation of a ghost or a spirit, why have they not appeared on photos in greater numbers before 1997?

Some believers are of the opinion that Orbs are on the increase because they believe the boundaries between the spirit world and our world are breaking down. This, they say, accounts for the dramatic increase in Orbs captured on camera since 1997. However, other believers think that the dramatic increase in Orb pictures is due to the move from traditional cameras to digital. They claim that, although Orbs are not visible to the naked eye, digital cameras can 'see' things that humans can't.

Here is how a digital camera works: light enters the camera through the lens and then hits a special chip called a CCD or Charged Coupled Device; the CCD converts the light entering the camera into an electrical signal.

Unlike conventional film cameras, the CCD can pick up not only visible light, but also a portion of ultraviolet (UV) and some infrared (IR). It is important to note that both UV and IR are not normally visible to the human eye. Could it be that orbs are only visible in either UV or IR? This is highly unlikely. UV light is blocked by glass,

Orbs caught on a traditional 35 mm camera.

therefore, the lens in the camera won't let it pass through. As for IR – this is a better possibility, although, as we shall see next, it is also unlikely.

Sceptics agree that new technology is to blame for the rise of the Orb, but they plump for more down-to-earth explanations to explain the increase in Orbs on photos. One idea is that Orbs are in fact digital glitches caused by the way that a digital camera processes its image data, which manifest as circular translucent blobs in pictures. However, both this idea and the notion that Orbs can only be seen in infrared are negated by the fact that Orbs also appear, albeit rarely, on pictures taken by some traditional film cameras, which do not have CCDs and therefore are not IR sensitive.

Because Orbs also occur on some traditional film cameras, which do not have CCDs and are not sensitive to UV or IR light, we now have to ask: what do all orb pictures have in common?

No matter if an Orb is photographed by using a traditional film or digital camera, there are two things that are universally true for both: the Orbs are not seen by the people present whilst the photograph is being taken; Orbs are only captured when the camera's flash is fired or if there is a strong light source either in front of or behind the camera.

But what do these statements tell us? So far we have ascertained that Orbs are not digital glitches, therefore must represent something real that is external to the camera. We have also eliminated the possibility that Orbs are things that are invisible to the human eye. The fact that Orbs can be captured on traditional and digital cameras, coupled with the yearly increase in Orb pictures, made us wonder if there was something else about cameras that has made Orb detection suddenly possible. We decided to look at what else, apart from a move from traditional to digital, happened to cameras around 1997 that could account for the rise in Orb pictures.

The move from mechanical (film) to electronic (digital) technology eliminated the need for a lightproof chamber and winding mechanism to accommodate a traditional camera's film. This made it possible to make cameras much smaller than they could have previously been. As the technology improved, cameras started to shrink dramatically. The smaller cameras became, the better they appeared to be at capturing Orbs.

So what has a reduced size got to do with a camera's ability to detect Orbs? The smaller the camera becomes, the closer the flash gets situated near the lens. This means that, when the flash fires, any small particles (dust, pollen, fine rain and insects) that are close to the lens will get illuminated by the flash. Anything that appears within

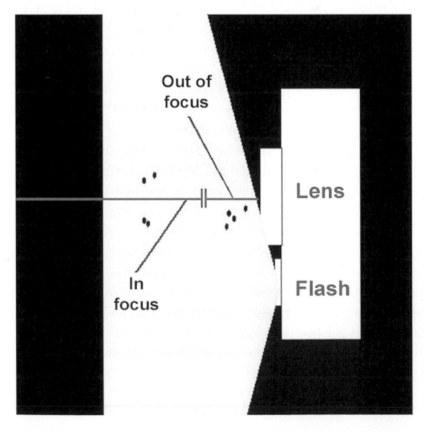

Out of focus

Lens

In focus

Flash

Small particles close to the lens get illuminated by the camera's flash. Because they are so close to the lens, they will appear out of focus, making them appear magnified, round and translucent.

the first 10 centimetres (4 inches) or so in front of a lens will appear out of focus, translucent and much larger than its actual size. Furthermore, small particles that are out of focus assume a more rounded shape. Since most of the Orbs seen on cameras are dust particles that are extremely close to the lens, it is not surprising that they are not seen at the time the picture was taken. As a further proving point, not all cameras are good at capturing Orbs. Digital SLR cameras, by virtue of their larger size, have their flash mounted further away from the lens, and therefore do not capture as many Orbs on their photos. Digital compact cameras are veritable Orb magnets.

You can experiment with this yourself. Simply get a duster and load it up with some dust. Next, shake the duster into the air and wait a few seconds. Turn on your digital camera and take a picture, making sure that the flash is on. The resultant photograph should be full of Orbs. Finally, compare your picture with Orb pictures that have been deemed by some to be paranormal in origin (a quick search on the internet will provide you with thousands of examples). We are confident that you will agree that they will be uncannily like the pictures you have taken. Mystery solved? We think so!

Although it galls us to say this, when believers look at Orb pictures and say 'I see dead people', they are partially correct. As you are probably aware, dust (the main particles which appear as Orbs in pictures) is mostly composed of dead skin cells – which means that the believers aren't strictly seeing 'dead people', but rather 'dead bits' of people. We are happy to conclude that Orbs are not the first manifestation of a ghost or a spirit, but more like the first manifestation of the need to do some housework.

Mist Forms

Over the many years that we have been investigating, we have often been presented with pictures that show strange mists hanging in the air. In some of these, the photographers have seen 'spirit-like shapes' that they have interpreted as a ghost in the process of materialising. Like Orbs, Mist photos have a few common factors: the Mist was not visible at the time the picture was being taken; the pictures were taken at night in the dark; the camera flash was fired; the temperature was cold at the time the picture was taken.

It will be no surprise that, when conditions are cold, your breath condenses in the cold air forming mist. This invariably gets illuminated by the flash and is captured in the picture. A variation of this is when someone close to the camera is smoking. The shapes seen in the mists are all down to the imagination and interpretation of the people viewing the picture.

Here is a picture of a 'mist form' taken on an investigation. In this case, cigarette smoke is the cause.

Vortexes

In paranormal terms, a vortex is a field of energy of some sort that is said to represent a doorway between the spirit world and ours, which allows spirits to manifest at specific locations. It is unclear where this notion first came from, or what tangible evidence exists to support their existence. In recent years, many people claim to have captured vortexes in photographs, which usually appear as thin, opaque or glittering columns of light, usually found towards the sides of photographs. Like Orbs, these manifestations are not seen by the photographer at the time the picture is taken.

Every single picture we have examined to date that is claimed to be a vortex has turned out to be nothing more than a camera strap that has fallen in front of the camera's lens. Like Orbs, the smaller the camera, the better chance of stray objects right in front of the lens getting illuminated by the cameras flash. The 'glittering' effect is usually caused by the material that the strap is made of: usually braided nylon that is quite reflective. If you are confronted with a picture that you suspect to be a camera strap in front of the lens, check which side of the camera the strap is attached to and compare it against the side that the 'vortex' appears. Sometimes the 'vortex' will also

Camera straps dangling in front of the lens cause some people to think they have captured something anomalous on camera. *Left:* A picture submitted to us. *Right:* One of our own recreations.

cast a shadow on adjacent walls, so it is worth looking at the photo carefully to see if you can spot anything. In addition, if the owner is willing, get them to take a test shot with the strap in front of the lens and compare this against their original picture.

Top Tip: If your camera is equipped with a wrist strap, put it over your wrist. Not only will it eliminate the possibility of it getting in the way of your photographs, it also protects your camera from harm if you accidentally drop it.

Light Trails

Paranormal Light Trails are photographs that are thought to show fast-moving Orbs or ribbons of energy that are considered by some as evidence of ghosts attempting to manifest themselves. Like Orbs, Light Trails are not seen by the photographer at the time the picture is taken. Light trails are mostly caused by two factors: strands of hair or fibres straying in front of the camera lens or people walking past the camera quickly with light sources, i.e. torches, while the picture is being taken.

The latter can even occur if the camera flash is fired, due to the fact that, although a flash fires quickly, measured in thousandths of a second, the camera's shutter is much slower, usually around 1/60th of a second. This is enough time for a stray torch beam to leave its trail on a photograph.

However, there are some intriguing photographs that show Light Trails that are not so easy to explain, especially knowing the circumstances in which they were taken.

Hairs and fibres close to the lens take on the appearance of light whooshing past the camera. *Left:* A strand of fibre deliberately held close to the camera. *Right:* Strands of the photographer's hair accidentally getting in shot.

When a camera is set to 'night shot', the shutter stays open for a few fractions of a second after the flash has fired. Anyone walking past with a torch at the time will leave a light trail. Note that only the torch beam is visible in shot whilst the person holding the torch has not appeared at all!

This light trail was caught on camera in an empty room without the use of a flash. Notice that the trail goes over the window frame, proving that this is a small object inside the room. A genuine anomaly? (*Photo: Maureen Kidd*)

The following example, taken on an investigation of an allegedly haunted property in Penny Lane, Liverpool, by Maureen Kidd, shows a Light Trail that was shot from a doorway looking into an empty storeroom.

For some reason, the camera's flash did not fire, and when the picture was later reviewed a small Light Trail was clearly visible in the centre of the room. It is important to note that no one was in the room at the time the photo was taken. Since the flash did not fire, the only source of illumination was from the anomaly itself. By adjusting the picture's contrast, it is clear that the Light Trail is inside the room, as the trail clearly overlaps a window frame in the background. This light was not seen at the time the photograph was taken.

Genuine Anomalies

On the whole, around 95 per cent of all photos submitted for investigation turn out to be explainable. The remaining 5 per cent show us that there are genuine mysteries out there that are worthy of further study. The following examples are from our own case files of investigations that we have taken part in, which we believe illustrate that there are things out there that are currently unexplainable by conventional means.

Chingle Fireball

The following photograph was shot by Robert Bethell during one of our investigations at Chingle Hall, in Cheshire, regarded by many as one of the most haunted locations in England. Since the immediate surroundings outside of the hall are reputedly as active as inside (several sightings of phantom monks, cavaliers and a horse have all been reported in the grounds over the years), Robert decided to go for a wander, armed with a camera. After walking around the adjacent car park, he located a fairly dark spot and proceeded to take a series of nine photographs, turning around to capture a 360-degree panorama. Eight out of the nine pictures showed nothing out of the ordinary, but the middle picture (below) contained an amazing Light Trail or fireball effect. At first, we presumed that this was another example of an Orb-like effect, in other words, something small and close to the camera lens being illuminated by the camera flash, but on closer inspection it appears that whatever has been captured is much larger, and at considerable distance from the camera, as portions of the trail appear to be illuminating parts of the tree's branches. We have subsequently discovered that a similar image was captured several years earlier by another team, but this time within the hall itself, although we have yet to see this picture for ourselves.

Valle Crucis Apparition

The following photograph was taken by a lady called Carol Hughes who was out sightseeing in North Wales in October 2005 when she spotted the abbey ruins whist driving through the countryside. Being a keen fan of old castles and sites of antiquity, she decided to have a closer look. Since it was off season, and because of bad weather, she had the place completely to herself, and spent a good half hour wandering around the site. At the back of the ruins, she took two photographs with her new digital camera in order to test it out. Because the rain was now coming down much more heavily, she decided to put the camera away. While she was walking round, she got the feeling that there was something odd about the place, but on the whole, nothing out of the ordinary occurred while she was there. At first, she spotted nothing unusual on the pictures. A few months later, she posted the pictures to a keen-eyed friend who spotted something odd in one of the abbey's windows. Zooming into the first picture, her friend was amazed to discover what looked like the head and upper torso of a figure looking out towards the camera. The second picture, taken about thirty seconds later, showed nothing.

This is not a trick of the light. The picture, without question, shows a human figure. Carol is adamant that she was the only person present at the site when the picture was

Chingle Fireball. This blazing light trail was not visible at the time the picture was taken. *Left:* The original picture. *Right:* When enhanced and enlarged, more detail in the background can be seen. The trail appears to have illuminated some of the tree branches, suggesting that it was at a fair distance from the camera, so therefore not a stray hair or fibre close to the lens.

Valle Crucis Abbey face. Although no one else was present at the time, the photographer managed to capture this figure looking out of one of the abbey windows. There have been numerous sightings of a similar figure all around the site. (*Photo: Carol Hughes*)

taken. Normally, pictures like this have to be discounted because of the likelihood that the figure could be just another visitor who inadvertently got into one of the shots. The fact that it was off season and that the weather was particularly bad that day make the chances of this being just another visitor a bit slimmer. But the fact that no one else appeared to be present at the time doesn't discount the possibility altogether. The real clincher for us was when we decided to look into the history of the site.

Established in 1201, the abbey was home to a community of Cistercian monks who lived there for more than 300 years. Over the centuries, the abbey was ravaged by fire, black plague and civil wars, but despite all of this, it stood the test of time until finally being dissolved in 1537, whereupon it fell into disrepair and eventual ruin. Usually, when an area is blighted by tragedy and hardship, it is not uncommon for it to be a hotspot for alleged paranormal activity. This area proved to be no exception.

When Carol returned to the abbey a year later, this time in season, she met up with the abbey's caretaker and showed him her picture. He told her that he had received many reports of people seeing a figure that matched the one she had managed to photograph. In addition, there have been countless reports of sightings of hooded monks wandering around the ruins, some of which have allegedly been seen to dematerialise, and many people have reported hearing sounds of choral singing coming from the ruins in the dead of night.

Carol decided to post her picture on a Welsh forum on the internet and was surprised by the number of people who replied saying that they too had experienced all manner of spooky goings on at the abbey. Again, all of this is not concrete proof that what Carol has captured is a genuine anomaly, but the weight of supporting evidence suggests that she may have indeed captured something out of the ordinary in her picture.

Bidston Hill Apparition

The following photograph was taken by Niamh Rimmer at Bidson Hill on Friday 6 June 2008 at around 8.30 p.m.

Niamh and her friend Jen were out on the hill taking an evening stroll, when suddenly Niamh caught sight of a small, child-sized, shadowy apparition moving around near the base of the windmill located at the hill's summit. Acting quickly, she took out her digital camera, called to her friend and managed to take a single picture before the apparition disappeared.

Although her friend didn't see the apparition herself, the photo shows Jen trying to get out of the way of the camera, closely followed by a shadow-like form directly behind her. Niamh sent the picture to a paranormal group called Northwest Spirits, who in turn asked for our assistance in helping them to investigate the incident.

Bidston Hill apparition. Whilst out for a stroll, Niamh Rimmer saw a small shadow-like figure approach her friend. Is this picture proof that something paranormal is taking place on Bidston Hill? (*Photo: Niamh Rimmer*)

After carefully examining the photo, we did not find any obvious signs of hoaxing (digital manipulation), but we did wonder if the shadow-like effect could have been caused by the camera itself. We thought this unlikely, due to the fact that Niamh had claimed to have seen the apparition with her own eyes, but we needed to check out the possibility in order to eliminate it from our investigation. The EXIF file from the image told us that the camera had been set in 'Creative Mode' whilst the shot was being taken. Since we did not know what the camera did in creative mode (the manual gave us no real clues), we decided to ask Niamh if we could try to recreate the photograph with her camera. We took photos using every setting on her camera and none of them recreated the shadow-like anomaly. Next we checked the sun's position at the time of the incident to see if the shadow-like effect could have been a real shadow, but found that any shadows cast (and it was mostly cloudy that day anyway) would have pointed in a completely different direction than the one shown on the picture.

Again, like Valle Crucis Abbey, Bidston Hill has a history of paranormal activity being witnessed over the years. At the spot where Niamh captured the apparition, a

Chingle Hall apparition. Although not seen at the time, this picture appears to have captured an anomalous figure standing by the front door of the hall. Apparition or trick of the light?

miller tragically lost his life when he walked out of the wrong door of the windmill and was struck by one of its sails. An apparition, dubbed the Angry Miller has been seen on the spot regularly ever since. Could this be what Niamh has captured on camera? Or could she have captured one of the other frequently experienced apparitions on the hill, a Victorian child who has been seen regularly in the vicinity of the nearby farm?

At the time of writing, this photograph is still undergoing extensive analysis by independent teams, but the initial results returned so far seem to indicate that this picture will turn out to be a puzzling anomaly.

Chingle Hall Apparition

On our last visit to Chingle Hall, it was decided that, since Rob had been successful in capturing something anomalous in the grounds, someone should try the experiment again. At around 1 a.m. Mark ventured outside along with Rob, and the pair did a circuit of the hall, taking pictures as they went. At the time, nothing unusual was seen on the pictures, but upon review back home, Jebby spotted a dark shape near the hall's front door that he thought looked unusual.

Once the picture's brightness and contrast had been enhanced, a figure could be clearly seen at the door. Rob and Mark were the only people from the team outside when the pictures were being taken, as is attested to by the investigation log sheets, as everyone else was busy monitoring other parts of the hall. In addition, the mysterious figure does not resemble anyone who was present that night. The fact that this picture was the last one taken outside, coupled with the fact that Rob and Mark then immediately went inside, makes it impossible for anyone else (e.g., an unexpected visitor to the hall) to have slipped past them unnoticed. It is interesting to note that the area around the front door has been one of the main spots where apparitions of monks have been seen by many people. Could this be the much sought-after proof of the reality of the phenomena witnessed at Chingle?

The hall is now closed to visitors and investigators, and the current owners request that they are left to enjoy their home in peace. We trust that you will respect their wishes.

Cryptozoology

'What is now proved
was once only imagined'

William Blake

A Brief History

The pure definition of the word cryptozoology is the science of hidden animals, yet the creatures that come under this banner, whether they are reclusive or not, have captured the imagination, fear and wonder of the human race for hundreds of generations. Cryptozoology research can be broken down into two categories; firstly, it is the search for living examples of animals that have been previously identified through fossil records and are currently believed to be extinct, and secondly, it is the search for creatures for the existence of which we have no absolute record, where the only evidence is in the form of undocumented sightings, myths and legends. These creatures have been a stable part of the mythologies of nearly all cultures throughout the history of the world, and yet, even in today's modern societies, there continue to be hundreds of reports from right across the globe of various examples of them every single year. But what exactly are we talking about here? Yeti, Chupacabra, the Loch Ness Monster, Sea Serpents . . . are you getting the idea now?

Different regions of the world seem to have their own particular example of a cryptozoological species and many appear to be, judging by the many sightings and reports received, of a fairly similar nature. For example, in the Himalayas, there is the Yeti or Abominable Snowman, while in North America, it's Bigfoot or Sasquatch, while the wilds of Australia is said to be the home of the Yowie. But sightings of this kind of creature aren't limited to countries with vast areas of wilderness; a number of reports have come in from a small, heavily inhabited country; a nation whose landscape has many pockets of unspoilt countryside amid urban sprawl and industry, but none to equal the size of those of the countries already mentioned. The country in question . . . the United Kingdom. From the Scottish Highlands to Snowdonia and down through to England's White Cliffs, reports of these Yeti-like creatures have come in from a variety of sources with alarming regularity.

All of these hairy man-ape-type creatures bear remarkable similarities to each other in descriptions of their appearance, so is it possible that what the legions of people are witnessing is some form of unknown species of large, furry, bipedal creature that, if not identical to each other, are to some extent a related species, or variations on a theme? Could these creatures, which have remained elusive for so long, really be such a globally widespread phenomenon?

The Yeti is home in the mountainous region of Nepal and Tibet, right in the heart of the Himalayas and has been part of the indigenous people's myth and folklore for hundreds of years, though the creature didn't come into prominence in the West until the late nineteenth century, and the alternate name of the 'Abominable Snowman' wasn't used until the 1920s. It was during the 1800s that the Westerners were exploring much of the Himalayan region, and some of the earliest reports of the Yeti were purely anecdotal, basically relaying stories that their guides (or Sherpas) had told them. Some discovered footprints and made erratic speculation as to what had caused them. Some said they were caused by exceedingly large wolves, while one even stated that the prints were those of an Orangutan, but on each occasion, the Sherpas stated that it was the Wild Man of the Snows, or Yeti. However, in the twentieth century, when people started to scale the various mountains in the area, the number of reports increased. These people were setting out on a great adventure at the roof of the world, and some of these intrepid individuals got a lot more than they bargained for. In 1925, a member of the Royal Geographical Society witnessed something at around 15,000 feet above sea level in the region of the Zemu Glacier. His description says he witnessed what he thought to be a creature at about 200-300 yards away; it stood upright like a man and wore no clothing that he could see. A short time later, he and his party happened across a set of footprints which they presumed were from the creature that they had witnessed earlier that day. In 1951, a number of pictures were taken of a set of footprints, which some people believe to be the most convincing evidence of the existence of the Yeti that has come to light so far. However, the sceptics merely believe that the footprints in question are of an animal common to that region, and the distorted shape and size are simply caused by the melting of the snow into which the prints had been made. The highest mountain on the planet was conquered in 1953 by Sir Edmund Hillary and Sherpa Tenzing Norgay, and they too reported seeing a number of large footprints on their ascent of Mount Everest.

But footprints are not the only evidence that people have witnessed of the Yeti. Some people even claim to have Yeti body parts and even Yeti faeces. The Pangboche monastery is said to be the location of a remnant of a Yeti scalp, and specimen hairs from the scalp have been the subjects of experimental research since the mid-1950s. However, nothing conclusive has come from these experiments. The famous Hollywood actor James Stewart is reported to have smuggled a Yeti hand in his luggage while travelling from India to London in 1959. That was half a century ago, yet people are still witnessing the creature and are also stumbling upon the footprints to this day. In December 2007, the American TV show presenter Josh Gates reported discovering a set of prints possibly belonging to the Yeti whilst filming in Nepal. Casts were made of the footprints, and these along with photographic evidence, were taken to be examined at Idaho State University, which judged them to be neither faked nor man-made, as the prints were too accurate in morphological terms and they also bore a remarkable resemblance to a set of prints reported to belong to the American equivalent of the Yeti, the Bigfoot. Even more recently, in October 2008, a set of footprints was photographed by a team of Japanese explorers in the Himalayan region.

Probably as famous as its Himalayan counterpart is the Sasquatch, or Bigfoot as it's more commonly known. This tall, hairy, humanoid creature is home predominantly on the north-western seaboard of the United States, though reports have come in from various other areas around the country, and like the Yeti, it is the stuff of native folklore. It has also had more than its share of publicity, due to fake video footage, etc. Reports of the creature include the size of its footprints, some measuring as large as 24 inches long by 8 inches wide. This would make the prints over twice the length of the average human being's. Now you can understand why it is called Bigfoot. Along with the foot size, reports include that the creature gives off an unpleasant smell, while the height is given as anything up to 10 feet tall.

Stories of the creatures have been passed down through many generations of Native Americans, with different tribes giving it different names, one of which is 'sésquac' meaning 'wild man', from which we get the name Sasquatch. In 1924, a small group of miners were allegedly attacked by what was described as 'ape men'; a young mother and her children were approached near their log cabin in 1941 by a 7½-foot tall Sasquatch; but it was in the 1950s that the Bigfoot phenomenon took off, when a gentleman called Eric Shipton photographed what he described as a collection of Yeti footprints. These photographs were subsequently published and rapidly gained vast public attention. In 1958, a plaster cast was made of a set of enormous footprints that was discovered near Bluff Creek in California, and then, nine years later, again at Bluff Creek, came the first proper video footage of what was thought to be a Bigfoot. The film was made by Roger Pattison and Robert Gimlin. This piece of footage shows a hairy creature walking upright on two legs along the course of a river bed, and is believed by many to be the best evidence that has ever come forward for the existence of this creature. However, many years later, a man by the name of Bob Heironimus came forward to state that this footage was faked, and that he himself, dressed in an ape suit, had played the part of the lone, perambulating beast. Today, most people acknowledge this footage to be fraudulent, but still some people adhere to the notion that it is legitimate and the actual fake is Bob Heironimus himself. A much more recent fake occurred in 2008, when a video was posted on the internet supposedly showing the dead body of a Sasquatch that had been discovered in some woodland in Georgia, USA. The story was picked up by many of the world's news networks, including the BBC and CNN, and the two individuals responsible for the footage agreed to a press conference. After the press conference had concluded, the body was brought out for all to see, encased in a block of ice. Unfortunately for the duo, the prank was discovered for what it was. As the ice melted it became apparent that the head of the creature was hollow, the fur was not fur at all and the infamous large feet were constructed from a rubber material.

Moving east across the Atlantic Ocean from the United States, we arrive in Scotland at a large, murky body of water, stretching some 24 miles in length and running over 700 feet deep in places. It sits in a natural geological fault-line at the base of windswept mountains and spans the fault from near Inverness to its north-east and almost down to Fort William to its south-west. It is a lake so vast that it holds more fresh water than all the lakes of England and Wales combined, a place with ancient castles and arguably the most famous cryptid (cryptozoological creature) of all, *Nessiteras rhombopteryx*, better known to you and me, along with the rest of the world, as Nessie, the Kelpie or the Loch Ness Monster. This lake monster has been the subject of public speculation since the early twentieth century, but its legend stretches back into the mists of history for a far longer period, and during its time, the creature has had to contend with all manner of visitors, from submarines to saints and everything in between.

Probably the earliest reported account of the Loch Ness Monster is one of the very few, if not the only report where the lake monster is said to have actually attacked someone. It happened in 565 AD, and Nessie is said to have been in conflict with one of the locals. Although the identity of the local is very much in question, it is popularly believed to have been a monk. Whoever it was, the story goes that the person was swimming in the loch in order to retrieve a boat that had come adrift on the waters, but part way to it, Nessie emerged from the depths and charged at the helpless swimmer. The Irish saint, Saint Columba, was stood on the shoreline watching the proceedings along with some of the locals and called out to the creature 'Go no further, do not touch or harm the man! Go back!' At this challenge by the holy man, the creature is said to have turned away and sank back into the loch, and the man continued on his mission to retrieve the boat and return it safely back to the shore, where hopefully, the group of onlookers would have supplied him with a hot toddy and a change of underwear. Since then there have been many other sightings of the creature. In fact, as the population of mankind has increased and our exploration has made the planet an almost, but not quite, a completely explored place, we, as a species, have managed to make our home in some of the more rugged, desolate, remote and inhospitable parts of the world, so the chances of mankind coming into contact with any of the reclusive cryptids worldwide has increased exponentially, and subsequently, so have the reported sightings.

Our interest in the creature from the Scottish loch probably stems from the spate of sightings that occurred throughout the whole of the twentieth century. In July 1933, Mr and Mrs Spicer were travelling in their car along a road that runs next to the loch when a large creature crossed in front of them some distance ahead. From their report of the incident, the creature is described as being some 25 feet in length, with a long neck, possibly up to 12 feet long, and the creature lurched across the road towards the loch some twenty yards away. The following year, a photograph was taken of the Beastie, and though the picture is generally regarded in this day and age as being faked, the image itself is probably the one that most people picture in their mind's eye when the subject of the Loch Ness Monster is mentioned. Supposedly taken in 1934 by a London gynaecologist, Robert Kenneth Wilson, it became known as the 'Surgeon's Photograph' due to the reluctance of Wilson to have his name attributed to the picture. There have been many theories as to what the image displays if not the real Nessie; some say it is an otter or perhaps a diving bird, both of which are relatively plausible given the surrounding natural environment, but a more unusual explanation came forward, which is probably more outlandish than if it was Nessie itself, and that was the suggestion that what is seen in the photograph is a submerged elephant with its trunk raised above the level of the water. The generally accepted explanation is that the faked image was made by the deployment of a toy submersible with the head and neck of the creature grafted onto it, which was made in someone's garage or shed somewhere.

Something large was picked up on sonar some twenty years later by a fishing boat on the loch. The crew of the vessel, *Rival III*, encountered a strange sonar signature that seemed to be keeping speed with them, but the object was nearly 500 feet below them under the surface of the loch and maintained this position for half a mile before the sonar contact was lost. The sheer quantity of sightings over the years led to the creation of the Loch Ness Investigation Bureau in 1963. Its job was to monitor the loch via self-funded volunteers armed with video cameras in the hope of capturing the creature on film. They conducted their own sonar study in 1967-68, and though nothing conclusive was discovered, they did, over the course of the study, amass a number of sightings of a large creature or creatures swimming in the loch, sometimes swimming at over 10 knots. However, the bureau was fairly short-lived and ceased to function after 1972.

There have been many studies carried out on Loch Ness in the hope of finding the elusive creature, and each one seems to employ more and more sophisticated gadgetry from various forms of sonar to submersibles. On one such expedition in 1970, a number of photographs were taken, the contents of which seemed to represent the shape of a flipper or fin, and on the back of this evidence the British naturalist and founder of the Wildfowl and Wetland Trust Sir Peter Scott gave the name *Nessiteras*

Sir Peter Scott, naturalist, 1909-1982. Along with setting up the Wildfowl and Wetland Trust, he was one of the founding members of the Loch Ness Investigation Bureau. (*Photo: Dave Owen*)

rhombopteryx, which in translation means 'the Ness monster with diamond-shaped fin'. Sir Peter Scott was the son of the ill-fated Antarctic explorer Robert Falcon Scott and the godson of Peter Pan author J. M. Barrie, and, as well as being a renowned naturalist, Peter Scott was a founding member of the Loch Ness Investigation Bureau. But the 'flipper' photograph has been highly retouched and enhanced, and the Latin name given to the creature by Sir Peter works out to be an anagram which reads 'monster hoax by Sir Peter S'.

The deep, dark and murky waters of Loch Ness are not the only habitat in which lake monsters are said to dwell, in fact there are many reports of creatures not just in other lochs in the Scottish Highlands (twenty other lochs in Scotland apart from Loch Ness are reputed to host such a creature), but in lakes, rivers and waterways globally. In British Columbia in Canada, the Okanagan Lake is said to be the home of a creature called 'Ogopogo', Lake Victoria in Kenya has the 'Lukwata', there is the Lake Labynkyr Monster in Russia, the 'Peiste' near Connemara in Ireland and Australia has the 'Bunyip', these being just a few examples of the 300 plus lake and river monsters reported worldwide. But if there is the possibility that creatures such as these can exist in the inland bodies of water, what could be lurking in the depths of the open ocean, an environment totally alien to us? We have scaled the highest peak on Earth at 29,000 feet above sea level, but we live on a planet whose total surface area is more than 70 per cent covered by oceans, the deepest part of which is almost 36,000 feet below the surface, which is far beyond the limits that we are capable of reaching. We know more about outer space than we do about the oceanic environment, so what may live in places where we as a species have yet to discover and explore?

Since mankind first took to the world's oceans in boats in the name of exploration, there has existed the notion of sea serpents and sea monsters, and the mythologies of the world are littered with them. Such was the belief in these creatures that many of the vessels of antiquity were constructed with carvings of these creatures incorporated into the ship's design. The Vikings that terrorised much of Northern Europe travelled the seas in their longships, the prow of which was fashioned to resemble a 'sea dragon'; perhaps this was due to superstition or for luck, or just to evoke fear into their enemies. From the home of these Scandinavian raiders comes a Norwegian word that for centuries struck fear into the hearts of every person that sailed the seas: 'Kraken'. If, for some reason, you have missed the most recent Hollywood portrayal of the beast in the *Pirates of the Caribbean* movies, it is best described as a giant octopus on steroids with a very serious attitude problem. The Kraken is said to be a many-tentacled creature of such a gigantic size that it was possible for it to reach the top of the masts of sailing ships, and from a distance, it was said to resemble a small island, causing the mariners of old to stop at this supposed landmass, go ashore and set up camp. This would awaken the monster, which would then promptly dive causing the ship and crew to be drawn down into the wake of the sinking creature. Many seafaring stories tell of the Kraken attacking ships, devouring the crew and then dragging the stricken vessels down into the depths of the ocean.

Even over the course of the last century, the number of reports of sea monsters is staggering, with the crews of everything from private yachts to submarines coming forward with tales of some fantastic creature that they had witnessed or were even attacked by on the open ocean. A German submarine crew was captured by the British towards the end of the First World War; their submarine, the UB-85, had been caught on the surface and had been fired upon and destroyed by a British Navy ship. Upon questioning, the German officer in charge stated that the only reason that they were on the surface was because their vessel had been attacked by some gigantic creature from the depths of the ocean, and the damage caused to the submarine was sufficient to make diving impossible. Captain Krech, the submarine commander, described the creature to have large eyes set into a small head but with large teeth that were clearly visible even though the attack had occurred during the twilight hours. It was so large that it had caused the submarine to list violently making the German officer fear that it would push the open hatches of the submarine beneath the ocean's surface causing it to sink. The crew of the submarine opened fire on the creature with their sidearms, and after what seemed an eternity, the creature relinquished its hold and returned to the deep. In 1937, a nurse aboard a British troopship in the China Sea noticed a large creature keeping pace with the ship. Originally thinking it was a tree or large log that was adrift in the waters, she soon realised that, far from just being a large bit of driftwood, the object was actually manoeuvring under its own power. This fact caused the nurse to observe it in more detail, and she subsequently managed to get a better look at it. What the nurse described was a creature with a grey and black body, some 25 feet in length, with a giraffe-shaped head. But these creatures aren't just restricted to the open ocean, many have appeared close to coastlines, in fact, Falmouth Bay, in the picturesque English county of Cornwall, has had many reported sightings of a sea monster that has become known locally as Morgawr.

But all of these creatures so far, whether it is the Abominable Snowman or Nessie, are all quite old examples of cryptozoology, ones with a history possibly dating back hundreds of years, if not longer. How about one whose legend is much shorter, with a history going back only twenty or so years, the modern man's cryptid . . . the Chupacabra!

Since the early 1990s, reports of this creature have gained it a fearsome reputation due to the sheer volume of reported attacks on livestock that have been attributed to it. Possibly the first of these attacks occurred in Puerto Rico in around 1992 with the discovery of the mutilated carcasses of horses, goats and birds. Initially the killings were attributed to some form of satanic practice. But the slaughter continued and many farms with livestock were targeted. Soon the phenomenon became more widespread with the same things happening in Mexico, Argentina, Bolivia, Chile, El Salvador, Brazil, the Dominican Republic and the United States, with similar reports from as far afield as Russia. In each country, the attacked animals bore the same set of distinguishing marks, two small, circular puncture wounds around the area of the neck with many of the victims also being completely drained of blood.

The name Chupacabra is Spanish and its literal translation means 'goat-sucker'. From being dog-like in appearance to almost reptilian, the descriptions of the creature's physical appearance vary considerably, as do the theories surrounding the origins of this enigmatic cryptid, with some people believing that it is extraterrestrial, whilst one particular school of thought adheres to the notion that the Chupacabra is a result of top-secret US military experiments. The most popular description is of a creature that stands upright on two legs, maybe up to four feet tall, with grey or green scaly skin, the mouth having pronounced fangs with some reports giving it a long, forked tongue. A row of sharp quills is said to run down the entire length of its back. Some reports state that on occasion the eyes glow red, and quite often it is described as having a small pair of wings, much like the type of leathery looking ones that bats possess. A less common description is of a hairless, wild dog-like breed of animal, again with a pronounced ridge on its back, along with pronounced eye sockets, with large fangs and long claws.

For years the residents of Maine in the USA had reported encounters with a strange beast that coincided with a number of pet dogs being savagely mauled. Then, in 2006, a carcass was found alongside the edge of a road, presumably it had been hit by a vehicle. The local residents were almost unanimous in the description of the animal; it was an evil-looking thing, vaguely rodent-like in appearance with large fangs. Photographs taken at the scene show the creature to be of possible canine origin, but unlike anything that lived within the surrounding environment. Unfortunately, before it could be examined by experts, the unidentified body was said to have been set upon by vultures and the carcass picked clean. In 2008, in DeWitt County in Texas, a deputy sheriff recorded an animal using the video camera mounted on the dashboard of his police car. Running along a remote road, the beast was canine in appearance, about the size of a large dog; the body was hairless with short front legs and long back ones. The deputy was at a loss to identify the creature, but his superiors judged it to be some sort of coyote with an exceedingly bad case of mange.

Film footage of all these forms of cryptozoological specimens is in short supply, but this hasn't stopped Hollywood and the TV companies making their own renditions of the creatures. Public interest in these 'what if' animals has never waned, hence their inclusion in so many aspects of the entertainment industry. The Yeti has appeared in many films, including the 2008 blockbuster *The Mummy: Tomb of the Dragon Emperor*, and has even graced theme-park rides such as Walt Disney's *Expedition Everest*, while Bigfoot took centre stage in a couple of episodes of the 70s series *The Six Million Dollar Man*. Nessie, for its part, has also been the subject of Hollywood-made movies, featuring in the imaginatively titled *Loch Ness* starring Ted Danson. Not to be outdone, Chupacabra, as well as being the subject of many a documentary and magazine article, was the basis for an episode of *The X-Files*. But are all these creatures purely based in our own imaginations or in the work of a special-effects crew? Perhaps not! Up until the beginning of the twentieth century, stories of the Mountain Gorilla were just that: stories. Although listed as an endangered species, they are now known to exist. How can something that resembles a dinosaur, as the Loch Ness Monster is popularly perceived to be, exist through the ages and be currently resident in a lake in Scotland? In 1938, a Coelacanth was discovered in fishing nets off the coast of South Africa. This creature is from an order of fish believed to have been extinct for the past 65 million years, and yet, there it was. Could this not be the same story for others of these fantastic creatures? Science tells us no, but history has shown us that this is not always the case. The name of the game is EVIDENCE!

Alternative Theories

The first fossilised remains of a prehistoric primate species, which became known as *Gigantopithecus*, were first discovered in an apothecary shop somewhere in China during the 1930s. This species of primate is judged to have roamed the Earth between 1,000,000 years and 300,000 years ago. Of the fossils collected thus far, it seems there were various sub-species, one of which, *Gigantopithecus blacki,* is believed to have been a little less than 10 feet tall according to measurements carried out on the fossil remains. Some people believe that the discovery of this creature was the basis for the movie *King Kong.* Is it also possible that what people are reporting as Yetis, etc., could be the modern-day descendant of this once massive ape?

Just because a Coelacanth was discovered off the shore of Africa, does that necessarily mean that no fossils were ever found prior to its discovery and that we were completely unaware that this species had ever existed? No, some fossils were recovered, and bearing in mind where the fish was discovered, the sheer lack of remains could be entirely due to the environment in which it lived. What we have to remember is that an exception does not necessarily prove the rule, and each individual case should be taken on its own merits. By all means use the value of historical sightings, but investigate the current sightings entirely separately, at least initially. Once you have gathered all the information you can, then you can compare it with any history that you have discovered in your research and assess any correlations between the two. Remember that what we are dealing with here is an animal in the wild, and as well as its own territory where it would normally roam and gather food, environmental conditions may force it to behave erratically. For instance, during extreme weather conditions, such as a harsh winter, the food source may diminish causing the animal to venture further afield in search of prey. In 1914, in Italy, packs of wolves forced out of the Apennine Mountains by heavy snows descended into Abruzzi Province, and went close to the outskirts of Rome itself in the search for food.

In the case of the Loch Ness Monster, there have been many proposed explanations as to what the many sightings could actually be. The general consensus of opinion is that if the creature is real, it is possible that it is a plesiosaur or an evolutionary derivative of that long-dead dinosaur. But, to survive through the millennia, there would have to be more than one: possibly as many as ten individuals at any one time are needed to maintain the species, according to some experts. Could the lake monsters, along with the others reported globally, be capable of migration or are they entirely resident in their own particular body of water? Would this account for the numerous sightings in other lakes throughout Scotland?

Lake monster or something more commonplace? Many sightings of the Loch Ness Monster are down to the misidentification of some sort of local wildlife. In this case, a dolphin.

But if not some form of cryptid, what could Nessie actually be? One explanation is that it is a sturgeon, which is a species of fish that can grow in excess of nine feet long, with some examples growing anything up to eighteen feet in length. Could it be that what is actually being witnessed is merely floating logs or debris, or simply just the motion of waves causing a visual effect which leads to erroneous identification.

Without hard evidence, no one can say for definite whether this planet is home to creatures that defy history and our own imaginations. Is everything that is witnessed around the world merely misidentification or the effects of an over-active imagination? Without exploration and investigation, human ignorance is set to win the day and none of us will be any the wiser and probably will be the poorer for it.

How to Investigate a Cryptozoological Species

As we have stated, each case should be evaluated and investigated on its own merit. For the sake of this example, we are going to use a phenomenon which has grown in recent years, especially in the United Kingdom where reports come in annually from right across the length and breadth of the country. ABCs or Alien Big Cats is a growing element within cryptozoological circles, but don't be fooled by the name as it has nothing whatsoever to do with spaceships, little green men or visitors from distant galaxies, it simply relates to the fact that the big cat of the title is not indigenous to the area concerned, and in the case of Britain, there are no truly big cats native to the British Isles. Since the 1960s and '70s sightings of what are reported to be leopards and panthers have escalated dramatically. Some are given names that are quite Sherlock-esque such as the Beast of Bodmin, the Fenland Tiger and the Buchan Beast of Banffshire.

There are two possible reasons for the emergence of these sightings. One is that they are offspring from animals that escaped from travelling circuses and the like, and the one most commonly citied is the 1976 Government Act, which basically banned the private ownership of dangerous wild animals without a licence. Prior to this act, the ownership of these big cats had almost become a fashion statement. The Act was set up to ensure the welfare of these wonderful animals, and because of the conditions laid down within the Act many people decided it would be simpler just to release them into the British countryside, and up until the year 1981, this course of action was entirely legal.

Year on year, there are constant reports of sightings of these exotic and elusive felines, in point of fact, two of this book's authors have had dealings of some sort with sightings of a big cat species. Mark's encounter happened in the run-up to the Christmas holidays in 1991. Mark relates the experience like this:

> It was around 6.30 p.m. on a cold, dark, December evening in 1991. I had ordered a taxi to take me to a work Christmas party. The taxi dutifully arrived, and as I got in the cab I couldn't fail to notice the driver, who was as white as a sheet and shaking like a leaf.
>
> I asked him if he was OK, and he replied that as he was turning his cab around after dropping off a fare in a location very near to Runcorn Town Park in Cheshire, his lights shone on a big cat that was sitting in the undergrowth at the side of the road. He described it as being jet black, like a panther or puma, and said that it was huge and looked incredibly powerful.
>
> It also did not seem to be frightened of him at first, and stood there defiantly for what seemed like an age, before eventually turning and slinking off deeper into the undergrowth. The driver was visibly shaken by the experience, and he begged me to get in touch with the police to report it, as he thought the authorities wouldn't believe him and take his licence off him if he reported it himself, but at the same time he was fearful that someone would fall victim to it.

Mark concludes the testimony by stating that he believed the driver to be entirely sincere, and as the event had occurred a matter of only ten minutes prior to their meeting, the details would have been exceedingly fresh and prominent in the mind of the taxi driver. In the case of Rob's encounter, the experience was entirely more personal and perhaps too close for comfort.

I was on holiday in North West Wales a couple of years ago, and was staying in a cabin. I was getting ready to go out on one occasion and was looking out of the window admiring the scenery, and as it was February, I was thinking how quiet and peaceful it was, when my attention was drawn to one of the cabins opposite ours, about thirty yards away.

I saw a movement, and then saw what I at first took to be a dog, as it appeared to be the same colour and roughly the same size as a Labrador. But this didn't seem right somehow. One of the rules of the site was that no dogs were allowed to roam the site off the lead and unattended; this being due to the sheep close by in fields adjacent to the camp.

The animal moved, and as it did, I realised that what I was looking at was not a dog; it was very feline in its movement.

Unfortunately I also realised that my camera was still in the boot of my car! Nevertheless, I continued to watch it as it turned in a sideways position to me, and because of this, I got a good look at its tail, and also noted that it had quite a small head that looked out of proportion to the size of its body.

The arrow indicates the location that the feline witnessed by Rob left his field of view. Although, even after vast encouragement from his partner, Rob, through a sense of self-preservation, decided not to follow for a closer look.

I excitedly called to my girlfriend to come and look. By this time the animal was heading towards the back of the cabin and she only got to see its hindquarters disappearing out of sight. Once I had calmed down a little, my girlfriend suggested that maybe I should go out and try to look for the animal, but I didn't think this to be a good plan as I may just bump into it coming back around the cabin, or perhaps that was what she was hoping for.

I know that some people may suggest that it was, in fact, a dog which had maybe slipped its lead or even a domestic cat, but I have to say that neither of these would describe what I saw that day. The animal moved with feline grace and raw power so it couldn't have been a dog. This is also ruled out by the size of the thing, which I would estimate to be around 2½ feet tall, because as it moved around the cabin, it passed one of those big, wooden picnic benches and it looked to be just under the height of that. Its body length I would estimate to be around three feet but that isn't counting the tail. The whole encounter probably lasted less than a minute, but I'll never forget it!

Evidence Assessment

Reports of these creatures could come from a variety of sources, whether it is a story in a local newspaper or radio programme, word of mouth, or you know of someone who claims to have witnessed one of these large felines. It is then a case of trying to qualify the testimony to see how genuine the sightings actually are.

Is there more than a single sighting of the creature, and if so, do the facts back each other up, i.e., size, colour, behaviour, movement, sounds, locations, etc.?

Is the witness a credible source? Could they have mistaken the creature for some form of indigenous wildlife, such as a feral cat, a fox or even a pet dog? A lot of the reported sightings fall victim to these misidentifications for many reasons.

Are there any photographs or video footage to go along with the testimony? If so, do they give you any sort of reference point on which you can judge the size of the animal? Look at buildings, trees or other natural features that appear in the picture and try to work out how far away they are as this may give you a basis on which to estimate the size of the animal in relation to these features.

If you are familiar with the location in which the sighting of the animal supposedly occurred, think about the type of environment it contains. Could a wild animal survive in this? If the area is unfamiliar to you, drag out a map of the area concerned, or look on the internet as there are many sites where you can look at maps, many of which give satellite imagery of the area in question, such as Google Earth and the like. This kind of image is invaluable if you aren't that used to working with maps and the information they contain, as what may be portrayed on a map as a green shape, on a satellite image, that suddenly becomes an area of open space, or an area of woodland. It gives you more of a sense of what the location actually contains. You may think that it would be impossible for a wild animal to live in the area in question without being seen on a regular basis, but just consider for a moment . . . how many times have you actually seen a hedgehog, badger or a fox whilst out in the countryside? There are herds of deer roaming the British countryside, but how many times have you seen the carcass of one whilst out walking in the wilds?

Investigation

So you now have judged that the sightings warrant further investigation and have decided to visit the area in which they took place; but what are you actually looking for?

The area that these animals cover can be quite vast, and actually discovering some form of evidence can be the proverbial needle in a haystack. But if you don't look, you'll never find, and you may just be lucky and stumble upon the evidence that you are searching for. Generally, you are looking for things like tracks, claw marks or maybe even carcasses of animals that have been used by the cats for food.

As you move around the area looking for these tell-tale signs you may come across people who use the site regularly: dog walkers, joggers, horse riders, etc. Speak to them, ask them if they have noticed anything untoward lately: have the dogs or horses behaved erratically? Have they shied away from certain areas? You may feel awkward approaching someone with this type of query; some people are uncomfortable doing so and others have no problem with it whatsoever, and it may turn into a dead end, but it is surprising the amount of times you question someone who says that they haven't witnessed anything personally but they know a man whose wife is related to so and so, and her cousin's friend is the uncle of the bloke who works on that farm over there, and they said they saw . . . OK, it might not be hard, reliable evidence, but it could just lead to another piece of the puzzle. This type of thing will happen a lot during your time investigating various facets of the paranormal.

When walking down a track in search of the elusive paw print, don't just roar down it in an effort to cover as much ground as possible, take your time, remember the saying 'slowly, slowly, catchy monkey!' If there are a couple of you, spread out across the track and look a few paces in front of you as you move along, and also look towards the edge of the track to see if there is any path that comes in from surrounding thickets of vegetation. If searching alone, criss-cross the track at regular intervals; take a few paces down one side then cross to the other, take a few paces and then cross back and so on. Check out any soft ground, as these areas present the best chance of revealing an identifiable print, and can give you an idea of the size of an animal.

The soft ground idea, or soil trap, is a good tool to use on an area that you think a big cat may travel along. If you have located such a place, shortly before dusk sweep this area with a branch or similar to smooth out the surface and remove any traces

Look closely at the trunk of this tree. The picture was taken in Belize and the marks visible are the claw marks from an adult jaguar. (*Photo courtesy of Paul Howse, with thanks to Clare Rooney.*)

of animal and human footprints already *in situ*. In the morning, revisit this site and see what prints have turned up during the course of the night. The same effect can be achieved by using sand. If you are fortunate and think that you may have discovered a big-cat track, make sure you take photographs of the print, and remember to give it some form of reference that can be used to judge the size of it. This can be done simply by laying a ruler next to the print. If possible, a plaster cast could be made in the indentations of the footprint; this again would prove invaluable in the correct identification of the species. The making of this cast is a fairly simple thing to do and requires no specialised equipment, the plaster of Paris is easily obtained from a myriad of places, but one thing we would suggest is to also take with you a couple of shopping carrier bags or the plastic containers that you get with a takeaway meal, these can be used to protect the print from the elements prior to making the cast. To make the cast, firstly clear away any stray twigs, leaves, etc., to leave the bare print. Around the print itself, you need to construct some form of shield, this acts as the edge for when you pour in the wet plaster and is easily done with cardboard placed edge first into the ground, or if you have a takeaway container large enough you could use this too. Next, mix the plaster, it shouldn't be too runny if at all possible, imagine the consistency of

This print is from an adult jaguar. Notice how the track has been measured, tagged and photographed. This is how to mark and record any prints that you discover, whether they belong to a big cat or the Yeti. (*Photo courtesy of Paul Howse, with thanks to Clare Rooney.*)

This print has been left by a fox (*Vulpes vulpes*), which had wandered into a small holding in search of food. It could be an initial foray, but after interviewing the owner, it was established that this is a regular occurrence.

a really thick gravy or milkshake, that's what you're aiming for, and then pour it into the cast. The plastic bag/container that you used to protect the print originally can now be used in the same role again, to cover the plaster while it dries but this time place over the edge of the shield and not directly onto the plaster. Wait for the plaster to dry, and then ever so carefully remove the cast from the ground. If you have a pet dog or cat, you can practice using their prints at home in the garden, plus if you have small children, get them involved with helping you and this will keep them amused for an hour or two also.

Alongside the use of the soil trap, you could install a trail-monitor camera to help cover the area during the night-time hours. This is a device that can be strapped to a tree, for instance, which then monitors the area concerned via an infrared beam; when the beam is broken by an animal moving past it takes a photograph. The resulting picture can then be downloaded to a computer and provides another invaluable source of evidence to accompany any prints that are left in the soil. During the hours of daylight, the alternative would be to set up a hide or observation post that you could man yourself. The amount of time that you spend in this position is entirely up to you, there are no hard-and-fast rules concerning this. It may well prove worth the effort to schedule a return visit, and then you will be able to spend as much time as possible in the hide. This observation post can be manned alone, though this can prove exceptionally tiring; you will also have to counter the effects of boredom, and you will get bored – very, very bored indeed! It is best done with a partner or two, but we would say no more than three people. The position of the observation post should provide you with adequate cover to enable you not to be readily visible, but not so much that your window of observation is hindered, and as you are going to be in this position for a lengthy period of time, you need to be protected from the elements too. The hide should be big enough for you to place any equipment in that you intend to use, such as binoculars, spotting scopes, camera and video camera, and also provide enough room for the people who aren't actually monitoring the area at the time. Think of your creature comforts: hot drinks, food, etc., need to be brought in with you, and it may be prudent to take along a sleeping bag or two as you can wrap yourself in it if the weather becomes chilly, and if nothing else, you can use it rolled up to sit on. Personal discipline is the order of the day in these situations; it's pointless going all Rambo only for your friend's mobile phone to start belting out the theme to *Close Encounters* when they receive a text message.

If you happen to discover a paw print, does it have four toes and a pad print to the rear? If the answer is yes, you could be onto something. Now look more closely, are there claw marks in front of the toes? If there are, calm down, what you have got is probably the print from a dog or a fox.

The two headless birds are the result of an attack by a fox. The fox in this case is not necessarily hungry, but the instinct is so strong, the animal is driven to kill anyway. (*Photo courtesy of Tracy Brown.*)

Dog prints tend to be oval in shape and usually show the marks of claws, but not always, it depends on the ground and the movement of the dog at the time; similarly with the fox, though these tend to be slimmer and longer than dog prints and quite often fur marks show up in between the pads. Cats have claws too, but they tend to be retracted unless they are using them on prey or climbing trees, which apart from the likes of a lion, they are quite adept at doing. So another thing to look out for is claw marks on the bark of trees.

If you happen to stumble across a carcass, try to work out how the animal was killed. Big cats tend to attack the area of the throat and neck, so look closely, as this is a good indication of a big-cat kill. You may also come across faeces left behind by a variety of animals; **DO NOT TOUCH UNDER ANY CIRCUMSTANCE** as they can contain diseases that are extremely harmful to humans.

Fieldcraft

It is all very well and good being in the great outdoors on the track of that elusive big cat, but as we have seen, the chances of actually witnessing one are remote. The way we conduct ourselves whilst in the wild could actually reduce these odds and may provide us with the opportunity of witnessing these creatures first hand.

As we have said, don't go rampaging your way through the countryside; take your time. Stop every now and again and take fifteen minutes out just to sit and listen to the world around you, become accustomed to the sounds of the environment, as this will enable you to detect anything out of the ordinary when it occurs. If you hear a sound that you cannot locate, stand still, open your mouth slightly and cup your hands to your ears, moving your head slowly from left to right. This will enable you to improve your chances of hearing any sound better and help to determine from which direction the sound is emanating.

If at all possible, try to melt into the background. Don't stand on the edge of woods when observing a potential sighting as they are more than likely to spot you, instead stand a few paces back into the tree line, you'll still be able to see them, but the chances of you being witnessed are greatly reduced. The last thing you want is to happen upon some creature only for it to bolt because it saw you first. Use the shadows to the same effect, and try never to peer over any cover that you are using, as your silhouette will give you away almost as quickly, try to look through or peer around whatever you are hiding behind.

Noise is a big one for giving the game away; the jangling of keys, sounds from a mobile phone, all these will do their very best to betray your presence, and usually at the most inopportune moment. Clothing too makes noise, a lot of these modern waterproof fabrics rustle when they are being worn, so just keep that in mind. Colours of clothing can prove an unfortunate choice too; it is best to opt for dark, natural colours. This doesn't mean that you have to go out looking like a special forces sniper, but at the same time, turning up dressed like you've just come from auditions of *Joseph and his Technicolor Dream Coat* will do you no favours at all. Also, consider reflection, especially when using optics like binoculars, as sunlight can reflect on the lenses causing the same effect as a signalling mirror. The way to counter this is to hold the binoculars so that your hands are half off the end of the lenses; your hands, in effect, become a sunscreen. Also with binoculars, if you do happen to spot something, bring the binoculars up to your eyes while keeping a visual fix on whatever you are observing, don't look down to find your binoculars, chances are they will be around your neck anyway. As soon as you look down to find them, what normally happens is, in that split second or two, your quarry will have made like the Pimpernel and done a vanishing act.

Last light and first light are potentially the best times to spot these animals, but don't stay out in search of these creatures once night has fallen. Apart from the fact that any noise you make will be amplified during this period, the danger to yourself is increased, as most people find moving around at night in an unfamiliar location difficult as well as being potentially hazardous. Plus, the use of torches to find your way will simply alert the animals to your presence even more.

Be mindful of the country code in your travels. If you use a gate ensure that you close it once you're through. Never leave rubbish in the countryside; apart from it being unsightly, it can prove to be a danger to the wildlife and also the natural environment. You should come away from any site without having left any remnants to show that you were there in the first place.

When working outdoors in any countryside-type setting, it is essential that you are aware of your surroundings and this means that you have in your possession a map of some description. Go for one with as much detail as possible; a 1:25,000-scale map is ideal in these situations. It is always a good idea to keep your map in some kind of map case too; not only does this protect it from the elements, but the clear plastic panels enable you to mark various locations that you need to note on the map without having to mark the face of the map itself. If you are unfamiliar with the symbols used on the maps, refer to the key or legend that comes attached with all maps, this will help familiarise you with what the map actually contains, and they will also help you locate your position on the ground.

If you don't understand how to read a map already, they can appear quite daunting. In the case of Ordnance Survey map coverage, the grid squares represent a 1 km square on the ground, so from line to line, both horizontally and vertically, represents a distance of 1 km, and from corner to corner diagonally, it is a distance of about 1.5 km. A typical grid position is usually shown as 6 numbers, such as 321654; most of the time, this six-figure grid reference is prefixed by two letters, such as SJ. If your map employs this two-letter prefix, make sure that any grid references you record have the same prefix, as this is specific to that particular area in question. But how do the six numbers relate to where you are on the map? If you look at a map, you will see a sequence of numbers running both horizontally and vertically along the sheet.

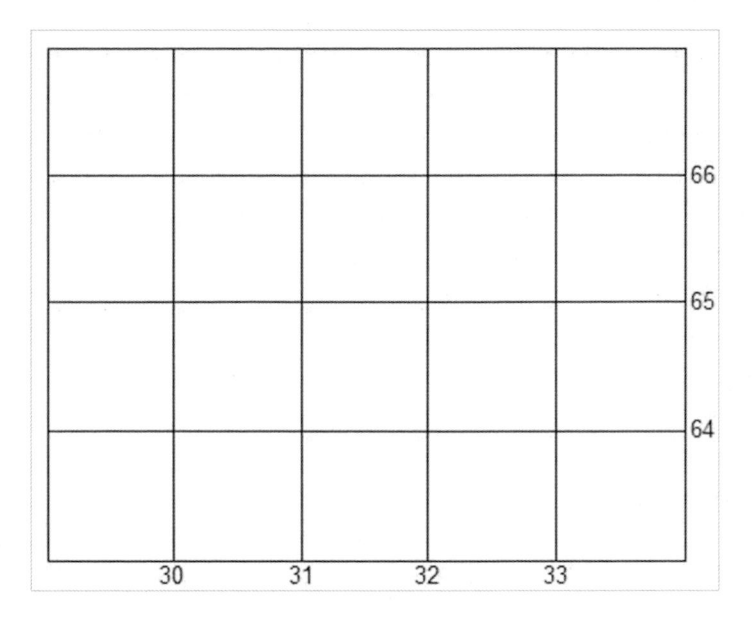

Always work out the sequence starting at the bottom left corner, moving across the box, then upwards. Split the grid reference into two parts, 321 and 654. The first two numbers in each sequence represent a square on the map, so 32 and 65 working horizontally and then vertically would give us the following grid square.

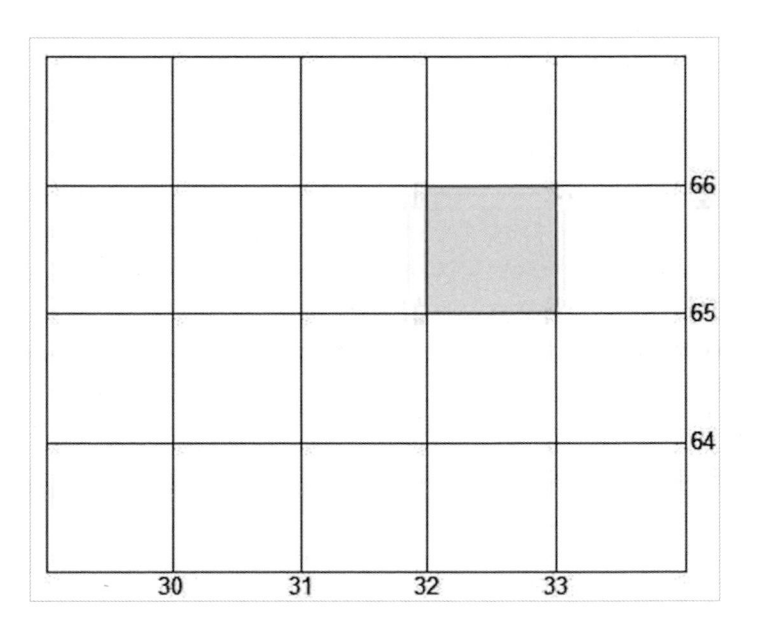

Now divide this square mentally into ten equal parts, again both horizontally and vertically. The last number in each of the sequences is how many tenths along the square you are; in this case, one tenth horizontally and four tenths vertically.

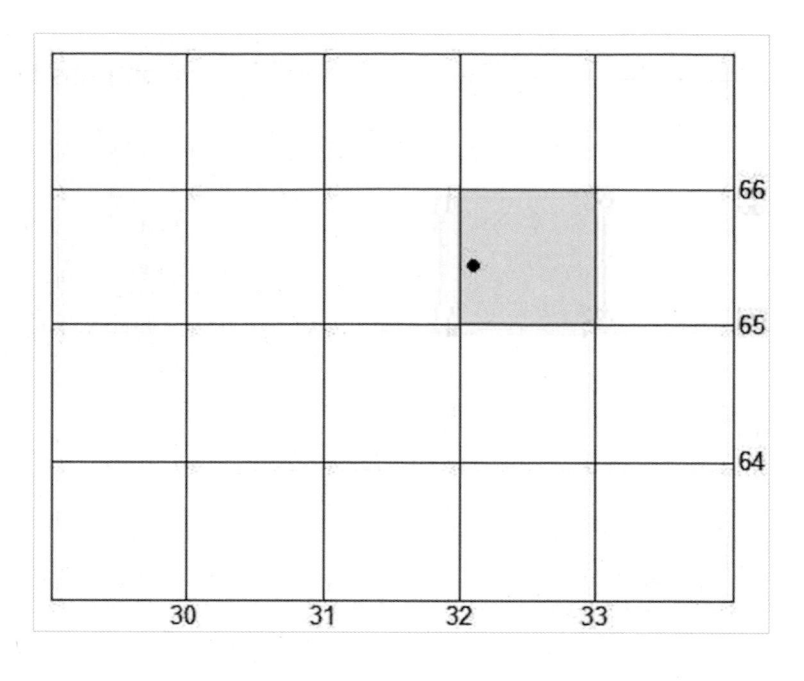

So now you have the grid reference 321654 located on your map. Just practise – it's a lot easier than you think. A lot of compasses now come with a roamer scale etched onto the side in both 1:25,000 and 1:50,000 scale. This is to aid you in plotting accurately those ten divisions. A point to note is that with all commercial maps, like the Ordnance Survey variety, the top of the map is always north; in this case, it is called grid north. A magnetic compass will show magnetic north, and although there is a slight variable between the two norths, it is not essential, at this stage, to compensate for this. In featureless terrain, the use of a compass will help in orientating your map to what you can actually see on the ground.

The needle in the centre that swings as you turn the compass is the part that shows you the direction of north. On the dial in which the needle is housed is a red pointer with a red N at its extremity. Around the outside of the dial you'll notice a series of numbers usually marked up in increments of twenty, these represent the 360 degrees of a circle and are used to take a bearing. Also on the dial, you can see a white line that doesn't move when the dial is turned; this is aligned with a direction arrow permanently marked on the base plate of the compass. These two things are used along with the degree markings to take a bearing.

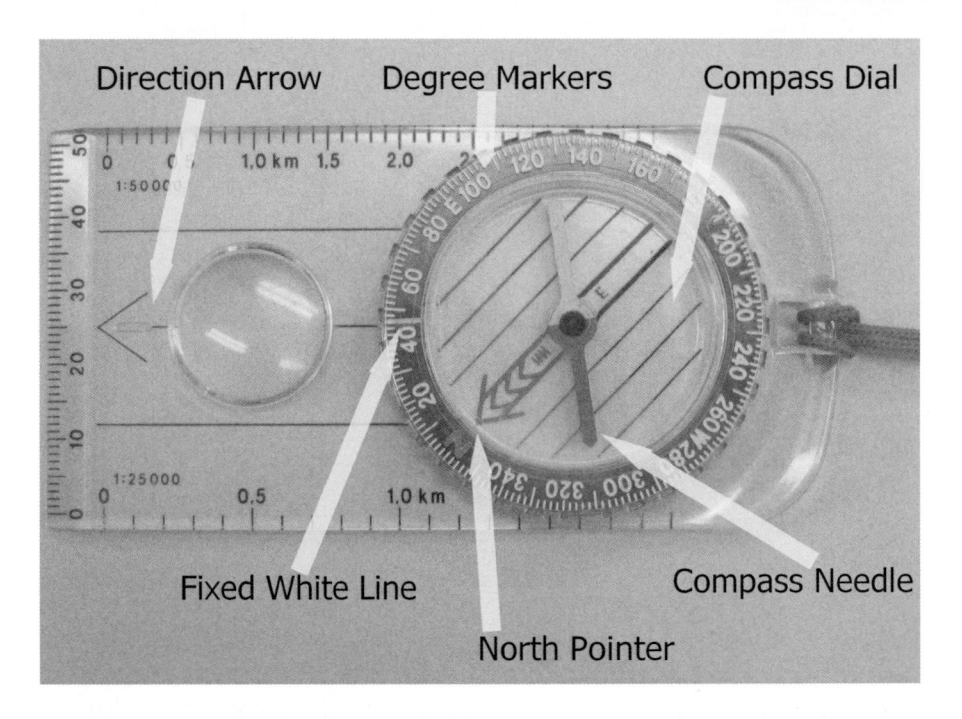

Direction Arrow   Degree Markers   Compass Dial

Fixed White Line   Compass Needle

North Pointer

To find north on the compass, rotate the dial until the red needle is over the red arrow on the dial, it is now set to north.

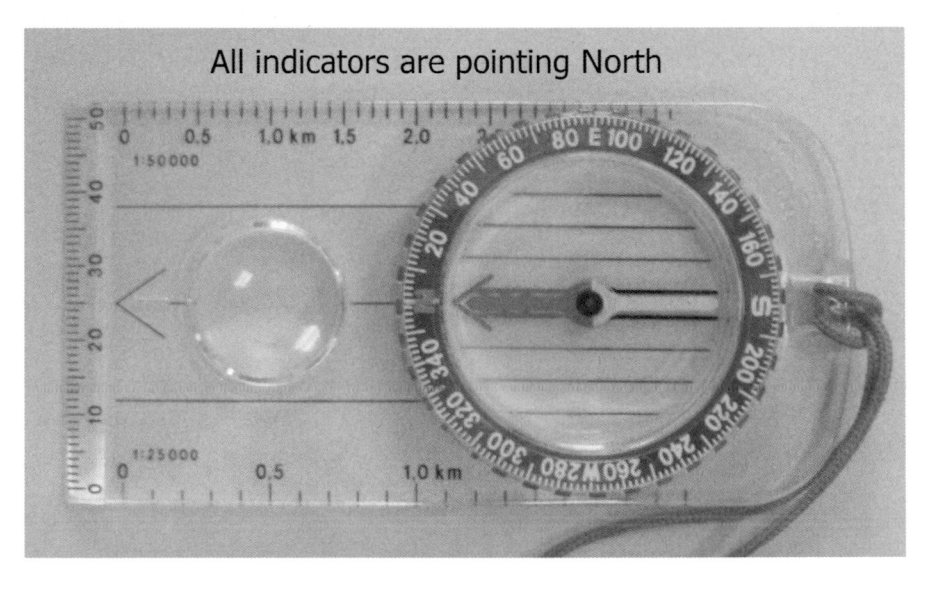

All indicators are pointing North

Why do you need to take a bearing? This is to show the direction of an object in relation to where you currently are, the object in question could be something you can see in the distance such as a church spire, lake or a mountain peak, or it could be where you just saw that elusive big cat or UFO. The act of taking a bearing isn't difficult at all, and as with anything else, the more you practise, the more it will become second nature to you. The procedure is simple. Firstly, point the direction arrow on the base plate at whatever you are looking at. Next, keeping the base plate as still as possible, rotate the dial to find north as described above. Finally, read off the number that is now showing over the fixed white line on the dial, in this case 290 degrees; this is your bearing! You should always do this procedure twice to check the figure.

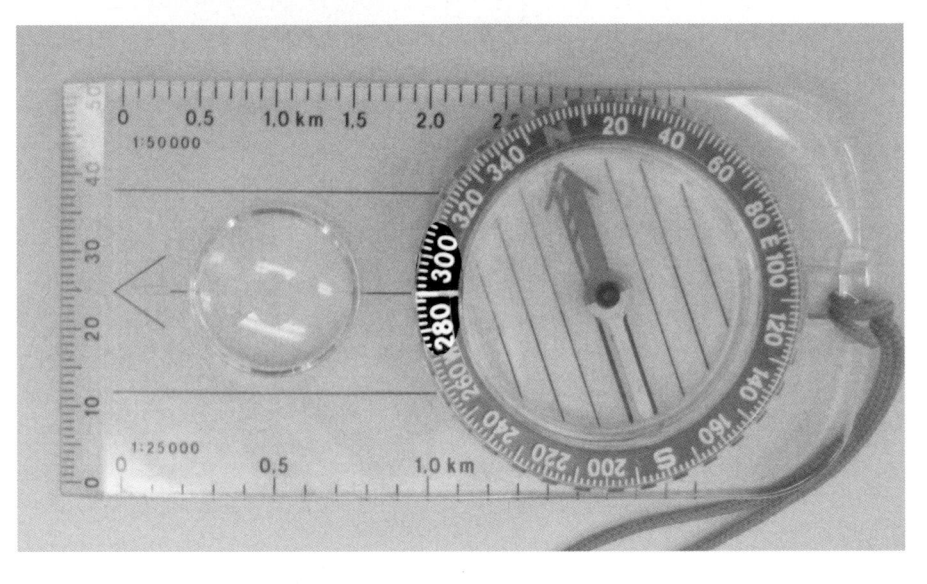

If for some reason you are out without being in possession of a compass, there is a way of finding north by the use of an analogue watch in conjunction with the sun. What you need to do is to hold the watch horizontally and rotate the watch so that the hour hand points toward the sun.

Now imagine a line running through the middle of the space between the hour hand and the number twelve position. This line will run north to south.

This little trick only works when in the northern hemisphere. For the southern hemisphere, it is slightly different though the procedure is the same; in this case, point the number twelve position at the sun and then split the angle to the hour hand. When trying this, please remember to rotate the watch and not pull out the crown and rotate the hands as recently happened when trying to show someone how to carry out this method.

Mother Nature herself gives us little clues as to where north lies in relation to our current position. In the northern hemisphere the sun is always in a due south position at midday, plants and trees tend to grow towards the sun, trees tend to have more branches on the southern side with these branches going more horizontal as though reaching out towards the sun, while the branches on the northern side grow more vertically as if attempting to reach over the top to find the sunshine. But there are no hard and fast rules in nature, so these little clues and tips are not guaranteed, as Mother Nature has a habit of biting you in the seat of your pants when you least expect it, so carry a compass to be sure!

Equipment

The list of equipment that can be used during a cryptozoological investigation is nowhere near as extensive as the equipment used for investigations into other paranormal phenomena, nor is the majority intended solely for this purpose; they may be used in a different way but can be used on investigations into other elements of the paranormal too, especially UFOs, as once again, you will be dealing with the great outdoors.

Listed here are a number of items that you could possibly employ during this type of investigation. Certain environmental conditions may limit what you can actually use, so don't think that everything listed needs to be taken. You will soon get a feel for what needs to be used where and when.

Camera, camcorder, audio recorder, spotting scope, compass, maps, GPS, trail-monitor camera, watch, pen and paper, torch, basic first-aid kit, spare batteries, walkie-talkies, food/drink, clothing and footwear suitable for the location you are visiting (also taking into account weather conditions).

Investigation Analysis

Chances are that 99 times out of 100 nothing significant is going to turn up in your investigation. You have failed to witness anything and your soil trap and any camera and video footage have not captured any sign of the elusive feline. But what if it has? What if you have been fortunate enough to witness one of these animals moving around the British countryside and have been successful in capturing it on film? Is the feline on the screen really a big cat or one of a more domestic variety? It can be very hard to distinguish, and unless you yourself are sure of what you've caught, you will be understandably hesitant in putting your evidence forward to be examined by experts.

Apart from sifting through hours of documentaries on TV looking for footage of these big cats in their native environment, you could treat yourself and go and spend some time at your nearest zoo or safari park. Here you will be able to take pictures and footage of the animals to your heart's content without the constraints of foliage, etc. getting in the way. Spend some time watching them, how they move, the way the tail moves in relation to the body when walking, etc.; get a feel for the shape of the animal. Any pictures or recordings you make can be taken home and used in comparison against the ones you made in the investigation.

Once you are happy that what you have recorded is a big cat, it's time for your evidence to be put forward to the experts. Be of stout heart – at worst you will have evidence relating to an indigenous species, at best you and the rest of the world will have proof positive that big cats are officially roaming the wilds of the British Isles.

Unidentified Flying Objects

If you look into the sky in the early morning
you can watch them playing tag between the stars!

Muhammad Ali

A Brief History

In April 1961, the human race took its first steps beyond our own planet when Yuri Alexeyevich Gagarin became the first human in space, but it took another eight years for us to set foot on another astral body. On 20 July 1969, Neil Armstrong became the first man to walk on the moon, and along with the other members of the crew of Apollo 11, Buzz Aldrin and Michael Collins, they brought the exploration of space out of the realms of science fiction and right into the here and now via a live television broadcast from the moon's surface. But as yet, that is as far as man has got into the vastness of space, we have sent out deep space probes and had missions to Mars but these have all involved unmanned exploration. The moon for now appears to be our limit. But what about traffic coming in the opposite direction? We have taken our first tentative steps towards the exploration of space, but what about life out there, is it possible for life to exist in the depths of the cosmos, and if so, could they be more advanced than us? If it is possible that life does exist elsewhere, it is then equally possible that their exploration of space has taken them far beyond their own world and maybe even brought them to ours.

We have all heard the stories about UFO sightings and visitations by alien life-forms, the supposed crash of an alien vehicle at Roswell in New Mexico, etc., but does the history of this phenomena only go back as far as the history of our own 'space race'? This would appear not to be the case as history is littered with reports of strange occurrences involving unknown aerial phenomena that go back long before the events of Roswell; from events that are happening seemingly almost as a daily occurrence, to the Second World War and back through time to our earliest civilisations.

Many of the texts of our most ancient peoples contain details about encounters with unusual beings and strange sky ships. The ancient Indian texts, the *Mahabharata* and the *Ramayana*, describe mythical flying machines called 'vimanas', while in the Christian religion, various parts of the Bible describe encounters with what could be described as visitations by alien craft. One such story occurs in the Book of Ezekiel where a craft that looked metallic on the ground and was shaped as 'a wheel within a wheel', containing four occupants, rises into the sky where it is further described as a fiery storm. But these stories are not the only basis for the belief in historical UFO encounters, as around the world, pictures and other graphic representations of what some people believe are a visual record of contact with beings and ships from beyond our planet have been discovered. Cave paintings, such as the ones at Val Camonica in Italy, have been suggested to represent the images of visitors from another world, as some of the figures depicted in these pictographs appear to be wearing domes on their heads, which could, after a fashion, be judged to be similar to the headgear that our current astronauts employ. These images are judged to be between 8,000 and 10,000 years old. Similar figures have been found in North Africa, the Sahara Desert and the Sego Canyon in Utah, but as well as these cave paintings, strange images have been carved into the landscapes, often in gigantic proportions, such as the collection of geoglyphs that are located near the small Peruvian town of Nazca. The earliest of these ground-based pictures are believed to date back to 200 BC, and even today the exact purpose of the Nazca Lines remains a mystery. As well as simple lines and designs, animals, birds and insects are depicted and theories abound as to their intended use: perhaps as some sort of astronomical map, maybe they were used in religious ceremonies, or as some people would have us believe, they might represent some kind of way-marker or beacon to visiting alien beings or possibly even an alien landing strip. The reasoning behind this theory is that some of the images are so large that they are only easily visible from the air and are practically indistinguishable from ground level. Similar geoglyphs have been discovered in the Mojave Desert in the United States, but these are not on the same vast scale as the Nazca Lines of Peru.

A great proponent of the ancient astronaut theory is Erich von Däniken. A former Swiss hotelier, von Däniken is the controversial author of books such as *Chariots of the Gods.* As well as members of alien civilisations visiting our own, he puts forward the notion that some of our more ancient monuments, such as the giant heads or Maui of Rapa Nui (Easter Island) and Stonehenge in Wiltshire, along with the Nazca Lines, were constructed at a time when the human race did not have the sufficient knowledge or the capabilities to carry out these feats of engineering. Possibly these constructions were done by the aliens themselves or they imparted the necessary knowledge to the people in order that they could build them. Another claim of his is that our current human evolution is part due to genetic engineering carried out by these extraterrestrials.

As we move forward through the centuries the quantity of reports of supposed extraterrestrial encounters does not diminish in the slightest. In 329 BC, one of the most successful military commanders of all time had an encounter with two UFOs. Alexander the Great witnessed the two objects continuously diving at his army causing them to abandon a river crossing that they were attempting. Described as flying, silver shields, they spat fire at his army as they swooped across the massed ranks of his forces, sending men, horses and elephants scattering to seek cover from the aerial onslaught. Another account of a similar nature happened in 1235, when on 24 September, a number of strange lights hovered above the troops of the Japanese commander General Yoritsumi. The terrified troops believed that they were being attacked from the sea by dragons.

Nuremberg in Germany saw what appeared to be a battle between UFOs in the skies in April 1561, where two large cylindrical objects spewed forth dozens of smaller red, blue and black objects, which then proceeded to beat the hell out of each other. The onlookers below reported that the battle raged for over an hour with many of the damaged objects crashing outside the city. A similar thing happened in the skies over another European city just five years later. A local newspaper from Basel in Switzerland tells an account of a multiple UFO sighting in August 1566. It happened at sunrise and was witnessed by many of the local townsfolk. A quantity of black spheres were witnessed in what appeared to be aerial combat as the spheres were attacking each other and on impact some turned flaming red and promptly died out.

On 8 July 1853, Commander Matthew Perry recorded details of an encounter with what he described as a strange meteor. The reason for him calling it strange was the fact that the 'meteor' changed course repeatedly and illuminated his ship in an eerie, blue light before plunging into the sea off the coast of Japan. A group of astronomers at the Radcliffe Observatory in Oxford witnessed a luminous object in the sky in 1868. Travelling fast and changing direction repeatedly. At one point, it stopped and hovered for a number of minutes before moving off at speed in a northerly direction.

The sightings are legendary, and along with Alexander the Great, many of the witnesses are famous figures from history. The famous Portuguese explorer and sailor Christopher Columbus witnessed a bright light that danced in the sky, disappearing and appearing again during the course of one night whilst aboard the Santa Maria in 1492. Columbus later took this occurrence as some sort of portent, as four hours after the sighting, the landfall of the New World was spotted. Edmund Halley, the discoverer of Halley's Comet is said to have witnessed two UFOs during his lifetime. The first in 1676, when he described an object apparently bigger than the moon, which after some careful observation, he estimated was some forty miles above him and travelling at around 9,600 mph. Author and occultist Aleister Crowley witnessed what he believed were two small alien beings while he was out walking in the mountains in Arolla, Switzerland in 1896. More contemporary figures to have had some sort of encounter or witnessed UFOs or aliens include round the world yachtsman Sir Francis Chichester, former US presidents Jimmy Carter and Ronald Reagan, boxing legend Muhammad Ali, singers Jimi Hendrix, Mick Jagger, Robbie Williams and David Bowie, former President of Uganda General Idi Amin Dada, actors Jackie Gleason of 'Smokey and the Bandit' fame, Will Smith, Dan Aykroyd and the captain of the USS Enterprise, James Tiberius Kirk himself, William Shatner.

Another famous music celebrity is said to have witnessed a UFO during the summer of 1974. Former Beatle and peace activist John Lennon is reported to have watched the UFO along with his companion May Pang from the balcony of his apartment in New York City. He even included the event in one of his songs: 'There's a UFO over New York and I ain't too surprised/ Nobody told me there would be days like these,/ Strange days indeed . . .' Indeed, but perhaps no more strange than any of the other UFO related events that occurred throughout the duration of the twentieth century.

As the nineteenth century was drawing to a close and giving rise to the formative years of the 1900s, a spate of unusual sightings occurred on both sides of the Atlantic Ocean that caused consternation amongst the populations of both the United States and Great Britain, and sparked the start of the modern UFO era.

From November 1896 and through to April of the following year, the United States witnessed a number of unusual sightings of mysterious airships. Mainly described as being of the shape of a luminous, elongated cigar with some claims that the craft also had some form of wing assembly, the descriptions were relatively similar from the various witnesses of these phantom airships. The mayors of both San Francisco and Oakland openly admitted to having seen these craft themselves, as did many residents of California, and soon reports were spreading across the country, and then the rest of the world, with reports coming in from as far away as New Zealand.

During the sighting frenzy in America someone coined the phrase 'Scareships' and this name was to prove rather apt when a number of sightings of these craft happened over the British Isles. The bulk of the sightings appear to have been over Wales, East Anglia and the south-east coast, and many people put the aerial phenomenon down to some sort of spying mission being carried out by the Germans, which, given that the country was rapidly approaching the start of the First World War, would seem quite a reasonable assumption, and did subsequently happen once the war had commenced. The year was 1909, and on 25 July, Louis Bleriot became the first man to fly across the English Channel in a heavier-than-air craft. The Bleriot XI was a monoplane, and it carried its creator into the history books, but earlier in the spring of that year in the night skies over Britain, some form or airship was witnessed performing manoeuvres that could not be achieved by any airship or aircraft of the time. Germany did indeed have airships, the Zeppelins, but these were not thought to have been capable of traversing the distance, especially at

This is an artistic representation of an aerial dogfight that is said to have taken place in the skies over Belgium during the First World War, in which the Red Baron is said to have engaged and shot down a UFO.

night, and yet, people reported witnessing these phantom airships across the land, with 'stars' of light emitting from both ends of the craft and searching the ground far below.

It was close to the end of the First World War that this next report is supposed to have occurred, and it happened to the most famous pilot of the war, the Red Baron. Baron Manfred von Richthofen is said, according to one of his command, to have shot down a UFO sometime during the hostilities in 1917 in the skies over Belgium. On an early morning sortie in their Fokker Triplanes, the pair of them witnessed what appeared to be some sort of craft with pulsating orange lights, with a diameter in excess of 130 feet. The day was bright and clear and the object could be clearly seen manoeuvring around the sky. The Red Baron fearing it was some sort of new aircraft employed by the Americans who had only recently entered the war; he set off with guns blazing in pursuit of the object. The craft was severely hit by the machine-gun fire and crashed into a patch of woodland, where two small beings were witnessed escaping into the countryside. Obviously, Snoopy wasn't flying this one!

Baron von Richthofen was not the only military aviator to encounter unusual things in the sky during times of war. A phenomenon known as 'Foo Fighters' were witnessed for much of the duration of the Second World War, and reports of these swift and acrobatic lights came from all sides involved in the conflict, with each side thinking it was some secret experimental aircraft belonging to the opposition, the British thought it was the Germans, the Germans blamed the Russians, the Americans thought they were the Japanese and so on and so forth. Also known as 'Kraut Fireballs', British flight crews first reported the phenomena in September 1941 and immediately suspected them to be some sort of Nazi secret weapon, but in all the encounters reported throughout the war, not once did these mysterious aerial craft behave in an aggressive manner. The same could not be said of the aircraft reporting the incidents, as many of them tried to engage the craft in combat, and all unsuccessfully. Many were the reports that cited 'large, glowing orbs' or 'silvery discs' that travelled at high speed and performed astounding aerial acrobatics. Sometimes they followed the aircraft and often manoeuvred through the flight formations, which caused some of the flight crews to take evasive action, at which time, the Foo Fighters duly copied before zooming away again at high speed, or just simply vanishing. The vast majority of these sightings tended to occur during the night-time flying missions.

During 1942, a battle occurred that you will not find in any of the contemporary history books about the Second World War, and it happened in the skies over the American city of Los Angeles. Were the Germans or the Japanese attempting to invade hometown America? The events in question would prove to be nothing so mundane. This battle occurred on the evening of 24 February and lasted for many hours through the night to the following morning as the defending American military forces sent barrage after barrage of artillery and anti-aircraft fire into the sky attempting to hit … a swarm of UFOs. Less than three months earlier, the Japanese had attacked and caused mass devastation to the American fleet at Pearl Harbour, so the sight of these unidentified craft over the suburbs of a large American city set alarm bells ringing, and the military reacted with everything it could muster, both ground troops and aircraft. During the ensuing blackout, many witnesses could clearly see the objects in the sky, and some reported that they witnessed many of these craft being hit time and time again from the barrage of fire. One witness of the events said that he could see nine of the mysterious aircraft in the beams of the anti-aircraft searchlights at any one time. A few reports stated that the artillery fire had managed to shoot down one or more of the aircraft, but no wreckage of the downed vehicles was ever found. The next morning, after the shooting had ceased, some 1,440 artillery and anti-aircraft shells had been spent on the barrage and the only casualties from the Battle of Los Angeles were the deaths of three luckless civilians plus damage to a lot of the city's buildings.

1947 proved to be a very telling year as far as the subject of UFOs is concerned. Mount Rainier in Washington State is an active volcano and sits amid its own national park. The area is a Mecca for outdoor enthusiasts with hiking, camping, mountaineering and winter sports available for anyone willing to brave the highly changeable weather conditions. On 24 June 1947, the weather was clear and bright with only mild wind conditions, and businessman Kenneth Arnold was piloting his plane over the area on a business trip. Flying at around an altitude of 9,000 feet, he noticed a bright glint in the sky off to one side, then moments later he noticed it again. At first, he put the sighting down to a skein of geese, as the objects he was witnessing appeared to be flying in an extended line formation, but due to the altitude and speed of flight, he quickly dismissed this idea. He counted a total of nine objects that remained in formation for the duration of his sighting, but they flipped around the sky en masse, weaving through valleys and around the peaks of the mountains appearing dark against the snowy peaks yet glistening blindingly when their erratic flight caught the sun. Arnold made careful note of the flight path of the objects in relation to the time on his watch and the geographical features around him, and later, when he landed, he was able to calculate the distance of the objects from his own position, along with their rate of travel, which he conservatively estimated to be around 1,200 mph and at times as fast as 1,700 mph. In his report, he described the objects as being a disc shape and flying erratically, resembling 'a saucer being skipped across water'. This eventually led to the term 'flying saucer'. Later, he changed the description slightly saying that the point or lead object was of a crescent-shape.

Just a couple of weeks later in the arid environment of New Mexico, another event occurred which has become the mainstay of all UFO/ET incidents worldwide. Sheep farmer Mack Brazel discovered a mass of material that was scattered over the grazing lands of his animals. Upon discovery of this find, and being the good citizen that he was, Mack Brazel reported it to his local county sheriff, who in turn, passed it on to the military at the Roswell Army Air Field, which then promptly dispatched two officers to investigate. The officers in question, Major Jesse Marcel and Captain Sheridan Cavitt, spent much of that day and the following night inspecting, collating and collecting the mass of debris. Some of the material from the wreckage appeared to be metallic, and looked very much like tin foil, except that when it was crumpled up and then spread out again, it showed no signs of creasing whatsoever. Major Marcel even tried hitting it with a sledgehammer, but this made no impression on the material either. The following day, they returned to their base with the debris in tow. What happened next has caused consternation and given rise to a vast plethora of conspiracy theories ever since. Shortly after the return of the two officers, a press release was issued from the office of the commander of the Air Force base, Colonel William Blanchard, which stated that a 'flying disc' had been recovered. Within hours of this astonishing statement, a press conference was held at Fort Worth in Texas, but the person giving the statement this time was Blanchard's superior, General Ramey. In the conference, General Ramey basically refuted the earlier statement given by Blanchard and stated that the wreckage in question was from nothing more than a weather balloon, and not from a downed flying saucer.

It wasn't until thirty years later, during an interview with Stanton T. Friedman, that Jesse Marcel expressed his opinion that what had really happened was that the military had indeed performed a cover-up of a crashed alien spacecraft. Since this time, the world has been awash with supposed witnesses and proposed theories of what really happened in the desert during the summer of 1947. Many of these theories put forward the premise that as well as recovering a crashed alien ship, the aliens themselves were recovered. The statements and reports say that three bodies were recovered from the crash site, while others state that a fourth alien creature was discovered alive and removed to the military base at Roswell, though some propose that the survivor, along with the dead bodies of his crewmates, were shipped nearly 900 miles to the facility known as Area 51. It is more probable to assume that they were taken to the Roswell facility for initial examination prior to be shipped elsewhere for in-depth investigation. It is at the time that the creatures were at Roswell that the infamous 'Alien Autopsy' is said to have occurred.

In 1995, footage was released to the world's media that appeared to show the autopsy of one of the dead aliens from the Roswell crash. The black and white footage shows an alien entity lying on a gurney inside some sort of medical facility, which is believed to have been housed within the Roswell military complex. The creature then undergoes a medical procedure where parts of the body and internal organs are examined and removed. The footage caused a sensation worldwide upon its release, and almost immediately, many people, as is often the case in these things, came out to question the authenticity of the film. The footage had been released by a film producer based in London, Ray Santilli, who had bought the footage for £100,000 from a man who claimed to have been the actual military cameraman at the autopsy. Santilli originally saw the footage in 1992 but it took him another couple of years to raise the money to buy it, and in the intervening period, the condition of the footage had degraded greatly, leaving only the odd snippet that could be used. To fill in the rest of the footage, Santilli arranged a reconstruction based on the footage that he had originally witnessed, or so he stated when he eventually came clean about the whole affair in 2006. Which segments of the film contain the genuine footage, if any, Santilli has never divulged.

Area 51 is surrounded by as much speculation as the Roswell crash itself. Also known as Groom Lake, Dreamland, The Box and Paradise Ranch, Area 51 lies within the Nellis Air Force complex, deep in the heart of the Nevada desert. It has, over the years, been pivotal in the development and testing of some of America's most secret aircraft, including the SR-71 Blackbird, U-2 Spyplane, F-117 Stealth Fighter, B-2 Stealth Bomber and the RQ-1 Predator. The secret nature of the base completely lends itself to the notion that, among the secret programs to develop the aircraft by the United States, it also is the centre of reverse engineering of alien spacecraft, and this includes the one that supposedly crashed at Roswell. The part of the complex that deals with such things is designated as S-4, and physicist Bob Lazar claims to have been employed there during the years 1988 and 1989. His job involved the investigation of the propulsion systems of the alien craft, of which he says there were a total of nine. He also stated that one of the alien vehicles was test-flown on a regular basis, usually on a Wednesday evening. But Lazar made the mistake of taking his family and some friends to watch one of the alien test flights from a vantage point overlooking the complex and was subsequently caught and sacked. In November 1989, Lazar gave a television interview and divulged everything he had witnessed and learned while working at S-4. Some people investigated his claims and were unable to find evidence of him having worked for the military or the government, and were unable to even trace his college and university attendance records. To date, Bob Lazar still claims to have worked on these extraterrestrial vehicles.

In 1980, an event occurred in the United Kingdom that earned it the nickname of 'The British Roswell'. It occurred in Suffolk at a vast area of pine woodland known as Rendlesham Forest, and it sat between RAF Bentwaters and RAF Woodbridge, which at the time, were both used by units from the United States Air Force. The incident started in the early hours of 26 December, when the guards on duty at the east gate of RAF Woodbridge witnessed a craft flying low overhead. Initially thinking it was an aeroplane about to crash, they were stunned when the craft suddenly descended vertically into the woods. Obviously, the two guards immediately reported the incident, and Sergeant Jim Penniston was tasked to investigate. Along with the two guards, Penniston went into the forest and witnessed the lights of the craft flickering through the trees. He described the vehicle as being around the size of a small car but conical in shape and appeared to be floating on beams of light about twelve inches from the ground. The other witnesses claim to have seen landing legs. As the three tried to get closer to the object, they found it difficult to make any headway and described the effort as similar to trying to walk through treacle. A similar description was given on the second night by another member of the security detail, Larry Warren, who described everything happening as if played at half speed, almost dream-like. Suddenly, the craft emitted a bright flash of light and shot upwards into the night sky. Investigations during daylight the following morning revealed three indentations in the frozen forest floor in the location in which the craft was reported to have landed; also many trees surrounding that area had broken tops.

The craft returned that evening and a security team from the base was dispatched to the forest under the command of the base's deputy commander, Commander Charles Halt. Lights had been witnessed floating above the trees of the forest an hour earlier, but on arrival of the team, they were nowhere to be seen. Floodlights brought out by the team started to malfunction and the radios were experiencing a lot of static interference, but the team carried on and took samples of the soil and trees and made careful observations of the site and transmitted them via the radios back to the base. A Geiger counter was also employed to scan the area for radiation, and throughout the night, Halt had been making a record of the event into a dictaphone. The object reappeared shortly before 2 a.m. and was tracked through the forest for over an hour by the security team, before disappearing again back into the sky. Hundreds of base personnel along with local civilians witnessed the lights in the sky on that night.

Apart from witnessing UFOs, many people claim to have travelled in them or made contact with their occupants. Others claim to have been abducted or experimented on.

George Adamski was a Polish-born American who claimed to have spotted many UFOs through his telescope during the late 1940s. In 1952, while on a UFO-spotting trip in the desert, he not only witnessed a UFO but made contact with one of the craft's occupants. Conversing with a mixture of English and telepathy, Adamski went on to describe the alien as being of human form, with blonde hair, and originated from the planet Venus. The alien informed him that our solar system consisted of twelve planets and all contained some form of enlightened beings. In all future references to these races Adamski referred to them as 'Space Brothers'. The recent testing of the atomic bomb had caused the alien races concern, as they feared that the ensuing radiation would escape our atmosphere and pollute their own habitats throughout space.

Over the years, Adamski's continuing relationship with the Space Brothers inspired him to write a series of books, and he published a number of photographs that he claimed showed the image of many different craft from beyond our planet, and these, along with lectures, raised his popularity and gained him cult status. Many famous people of the day wanted to be associated with him, and he himself claimed to have met many of the world's leaders to pass on the message from the Space Brothers. He met Queen Juliana of the Netherlands and is rumoured to have had secret audiences with John F. Kennedy and Pope John XXIII of which the Vatican denies all knowledge. The Pope could not add any credence to this statement as, at the time of the alleged meeting, he was suffering from cancer and subsequently died four days later.

In his books, he not only described his encounters with the extraterrestrials but told of travelling in their ships to the planets of Mars, Saturn and Venus and even to our own moon; he went on to explain that the moon was inhabited and he witnessed its citizens strolling along the streets in a lunar town, and among the landscape he saw trees, waterways and mountains covered in snow. Obviously this occurred before the time of the Apollo moon landings. Though generally regarded as a hoaxer today, certain parts of his photographic records, both stills and cine-film, are still being investigated.

During the 1960s, a husband and wife from Portsmouth, New Hampshire, came forward with the statement that they had been witness to an encounter with a UFO. On the evening of 19 September 1961, Betty and Barney Hill were driving home after their holiday in Canada, when each of them noticed a bright star that seemed to follow them for many miles. During the journey, Barney decided to take a break from driving and pulled the car over, allowing him to rest for a short period while Betty exercised their dog and allowed it to do what dogs do. Barney decided to use his binoculars to get a better look at the star and was stunned to discover that the star was in fact a UFO, and to astonish him even more, the inhabitants of the spaceship were staring back at him through a series of windows. In a mix of shock and fear, Barney hurriedly told his wife to get back into their car and they then sped away home as quickly as possible.

After only travelling a short distance, they both heard a beeping noise that seemed to emanate from the rear of the vehicle. A second beep was heard, rapidly followed by a bang and then nothing more for the rest of their journey home. The following morning Barney went out to unload the rest of their belongings from the car and noticed that it had parts of the paintwork stripped down to the bare metal. On further examination, he discovered that these scuffs were heavily magnetised; holding a compass over the exposed areas caused the pointer to veer wildly from the north indicator. Along with this, he noticed that the shoes that he had worn the previous evening were in a similar state, with scuff marks to the toes. To make matters worse, for some reason his back was causing him extreme discomfort too. Perplexed by the events of the night before, the couple decided to report the event to the nearest Air Force base and to a national UFO research group.

Towards the end of September, Betty had a string of nightmare dreams in which she saw small humanoid creatures that possessed eyes like those of a cat. For some reason, she got the impression that these creatures wanted to kidnap her husband and herself.

During October, an investigation was started by astronomer and UFOlogist Walter Webb. During the course of his investigation, it became apparent that there was a period of two hours and a distance of some 35 miles that could not be accounted for by the couple. Over the course of the next six months, the dreams and the anxiety did not subside, and in an attempt to remedy the situation, they were both referred to a psychiatrist who persuaded them to undergo regressive hypnotherapy. Even though Betty and Barney were regressed separately, their accounts of the events of that night were uncannily alike.

During the sessions, the couple came forward with the description of the craft along with a lot of disturbing information. The spaceship, they said, had landed by the side of the road; small, pale-skinned creatures had emerged and placed the couple under a type of suspended animation, at which point they were taken aboard the ship and subjected to medical experiments. At some point during the proceedings, Betty was shown a celestial map and one of the creatures indicated to her their point of origin; from within a star system called Zeta Reticuli. After the regression had finished, Betty could accurately reproduce this part of the star map, and she pointed out its location on a map belonging to Webb. Unfortunately, there was nothing in this part of his star chart, at least not until six years later when the star system of Zeta Reticuli was discovered by astronomers in exactly the same place that Betty had indicated.

In a case very similar to that of Betty and Barney Hill, author Whitley Strieber, in his book *Communion*, tells of his experiences as an abductee during which he is subjected to periods of lost time and bizarre medical procedures. Throughout the book, Strieber never refers to the creatures as being of extraterrestrial origin; he simply calls them 'visitors'. During a Christmas vacation in 1985, Strieber awoke on hearing a strange noise and witnessed a being standing alone in his bedroom. The next thing that he was consciously aware of was sitting in the woods surrounding the cabin where his family was staying. Under hypnotic regression he tells of being carried from the cabin to a UFO where a number of different creatures carried out procedures on his body; these included a blood sample being taken from his finger, and a long needle being inserted into his brain.

Communion was later made into a film with Christopher Walken playing the part of Strieber. However, as we have discovered through this short history, not all the beings encountered are as sinister as the ones portrayed in *Communion*; we have also come across the benevolent kind too, the type of alien that Hollywood has portrayed in movies like *Close Encounters of the Third Kind*. But which one do we take as being the real McCoy? Do we have to believe there are aliens at all, and do they have to be from outer space? The truth, as they say, is out there . . . somewhere.

Alternative theories

As is the case with ghosts, UFOs appear to represent not just one, but a whole range of phenomena. Some sightings seem to suggest that we are having close encounters with physical craft, which may be extraterrestrial in origin. Others imply that UFOs may be man-made devices, such as secret military technology. Some sightings appear to indicate that more 'down-to-earth' causes, such as ball lightning or some hitherto undiscovered natural phenomena might be the solution. The following is a list of most of the current theories that have been put forward to explain what people have reported seeing in the skies around the world.

Alien Visitation

The most popular theory is that UFOs are alien spacecraft from other worlds visiting Earth for a variety of reasons, some benevolent, others more sinister. This has been a popular belief since the birth of modern era UFOlogy, when Kenneth Arnold reported seeing unusual craft flying over Mount Rainier, Washington, in 1947. Fuelled by the paranoia of the Cold War between East and West, the belief that the strange things seen in the skies were spacecraft from other worlds flourished and took root in popular culture.

Over sixty years of intensive research and investigation has not offered any real proof that UFOs are extraterrestrial in origin, but some claim that this is due to a massive worldwide cover-up orchestrated by world governments to stop us from knowing 'the truth' – that we are not alone in the universe. The claims and counter-claims of the extraterrestrial hypothesis (ETH) supporters versus the sceptics are far too complex and convoluted to discuss here, but it is important to note that there are a lot of people convinced that Earth is under the watchful eyes of alien visitors. Is the evidence in support of the ETH strong enough to come to a firm conclusion? In our minds, no; but it is an interesting idea.

All in the Mind/Hallucinations

Some people believe that some sightings are hallucinations created by witnesses going into altered states of consciousness caused by fatigue, drugs, or environmental factors – such as exposure to intense electromagnetic fields, both natural and man-made.

Fatigue can cause people to have hallucinations that can sometimes be difficult to separate from reality. As we grow tired and approach the edge of sleep, we slip into a state somewhere between being fully alert/awake and unconsciousness. It is at this point that people can experience hypnagogic hallucinations that seem very real due to the fact that the person experiencing them believes that they are still fully awake. In this state, they are capable of seeing literally anything. This might be a plausible explanation for situations where there is only one witness, but it cannot be applied to multiple-witness cases, where independent witnesses report seeing the same thing.

Another effect that can cause hallucinations is exposure to electromagnetic fields. Natural electromagnetic fields are generated by thunderstorms, which according to some researchers, are capable of causing people who suffer from electrical hypersensitivity (people who experience effects such as nausea or headaches when they are near electrical devices) to enter into a trance, in which they see UFOs. It has been noted in laboratory tests that exposing certain parts of the brain to electromagnetic fields can cause people to experience a wide range of strange sensations from seeing people/objects that are not there to experiencing feelings of floating or flying. There are many sources of intense man-made electromagnetic fields scattered around the environment, such as high-energy power lines and mobile-phone masts, that some people believe to be the source of UFO experiences, and may also constitute a health risk.

Natural Phenomena

Could UFOs be hitherto undiscovered or poorly understood natural phenomena? Some researchers believe this may be the case. Many ideas have been put forward to explain away some UFO sightings, from huge living organisms that some believe populate the upper reaches of the atmosphere to patches of marsh gas that form luminous amorphous clouds that people mistake for vehicles from another world.

Of all the possible natural explanations for UFOs, there are two phenomena that are only just being acknowledged by the scientific community as being real phenomena in their own right. These are ball lightning and earthquake lights (or earthlights).

Ball lightning is still very controversial, with many scientists still refusing to believe it exists. However, the weight of evidence has convinced quite a few academics that there is something here worthy of further scientific study. Ball lightning appears to be composed of layers of electrically charged air that forms into plasmas – glowing spheres which can range in size anywhere from a few centimetres (half an inch) to several metres (6-8 feet) in diameter. These balls of light have been observed to hover, zig-zag, materialise, dematerialise, and in some rare cases, have been reported to cause vehicles to stall. Because they are highly electrically charged, some researchers have speculated that ball lightning may give off intense electromagnetic fields, which could even cause witnesses to experience hallucinations, which again brings electrical hypersensitivity to the fore.

Earthlights are another hotly debated phenomenon that appears to have gained credibility in recent years. These lights appear to be created by energy released near fault lines in the Earth's crust during times of geologic stress, such as earth tremors or earthquakes. This energy forms balls of light that can appear in many different colours ranging from blue to orange, and whole groups of lights have been seen to move around in formation.

In Hessdalen, eastern Norway, a long-term scientific study of earthlights was mounted to investigate the regular sightings of strange balls of light seen travelling around the upper mountain ranges. These lights have been seen to pulse, blink on and off, travel around in formation and appear in all manner of shapes ranging from spheres to weird filament-type structures that have remained on view for up to an hour at a time. In some rare cases, the lights have appeared to be attached to darker, solid-looking objects. Many hours of footage of the lights have been captured by the scientists over the years.

The behaviour exhibited by both ball lightning and earthlights do in some cases resemble some of the characteristics reported in UFO cases, which seems to lend support to the idea that some, if not all, UFO sightings may be eventually found to be natural phenomena that we do not yet understand.

Misidentifications

There is a school of thought that suggests that all UFO sightings are misidentifications of perfectly normal things in the sky, such as aircraft seen at odd angles or under unusual weather conditions, stars and planets, artificial satellites or the International Space Station (ISS).

It is true that around 95 per cent of all UFO sightings turn out to be identifiable once investigated thoroughly, and of the 5 per cent that remain, 4 per cent of those stay unidentified only because there is insufficient information to determine a satisfactory explanation. The last 1 per cent, however, remain unidentified because they exhibit behaviour that defies any rational explanation. It is this 1 per cent that UFO investigators are most interested in. Since misidentifications form such a large part of UFO investigation, we will cover the subject in more detail later on.

Hoaxes

Some people think that the cases that cannot be explained away as misidentifications are nothing more than hoaxes perpetrated by people for a variety of reasons. Hoaxing is a real problem within UFO investigation, and it requires a lot of painstaking work to detect and eliminate. However, hoaxing cannot explain every exotic case that is reported. There is a growing body of reliable evidence, usually from multiple-witness cases, backed up by physical evidence such as video footage, ground traces or radar contact, which prove that some sightings are far from hoaxes.

In 1996, we took part in an investigation of a UFO case from Southport, Merseyside, where a family of four were woken from their sleep by fierce, low-frequency vibrations that were literally shaking their house to bits. One of the children looked out of his bedroom window and saw what he described as a huge, black, triangular-shaped object hovering over a piece of wasteland about thirty metres from the house. As the triangle began to move, the shaking ceased and the family watched in amazement as the 'craft' shot off skywards faster than their eyes could follow.

Because the house they lived in was in the centre of a row of houses, we checked with their neighbours (after asking for permission) to see if they had also felt the shaking or seen the UFO. The neighbours hadn't seen or heard anything. This was deeply puzzling, as low-frequency sound has very long wavelengths that are impossible to channel in a specific direction, making it very strange that the adjacent houses were not also affected. From this, we concluded that the family had encountered something that had seemingly defied the laws of physics.

The family were incredibly sincere, and had absolutely nothing to gain except ridicule in coming forward. Luckily they were not the only people to see the 'craft', for two independent witnesses later came forward to say that they had also witnessed the same triangular UFO at the same spot, but had not felt any 'terrifying' vibrations. Since the witnesses did not know one another before the incident, hoaxing becomes a far less credible explanation for this case.

Time Travellers from the Future/Interdimensional Beings

There is a growing body of people who are firmly convinced that UFOs are not visitors from other worlds, but they are visitors from other times or other dimensions. They claim that this theory easily explains some of the more exotic behaviour exhibited by UFOs, such as their ability to instantly materialise or dematerialise into thin air, or the ability of the 'occupants' to manipulate time during abduction cases.

Time travel theorists believe that we are being studied by scientists from the far future who may want to chart the development of us as a species, or observe first hand key points in history. They also suggest that the beings that are described as aliens are, in actual fact, the next evolutionary step of the human race, where we eventually develop larger brains and smaller bodies.

The interdimensional theorists believe that UFOs and their occupants are beings from parallel worlds that have developed the ability and technology to jump from dimension to dimension. These ideas do not have much credibility within the UFO investigation fraternity, mainly due to a complete lack of substantial evidence, but they are two of the many theories 'out there' to explain what UFOs are all about.

Hollow Earth Theory

There is also a fringe element of people who believe that UFOs come from within the Earth itself. Advocates of this theory believe that the Earth is hollow and inhabited by an ancient race of humans who possess technology far in advance of our own. It is claimed that the UFOs we see in our skies emerge from holes located at both the north and south poles. Belief in a hollow Earth goes back many centuries, but belief in an inhabited hollow Earth appears to have come from the pen of Richard Sharpe Shaver, a writer who had a string of hollow Earth stories published in the magazine *Amazing Stories* between the years 1945 and '49. The Shaver mysteries, as they came to be known, were written as fiction but were claimed to contain factual information garnered from Shaver's own research. They caught the imagination of the public for a time, raising the profile of the hollow Earth theory in the process. Nowadays, Shaver's theories of subterranean super civilisations are regarded as just fanciful ideas, but there are still a few people who firmly believe it to be true. Again, like the time travel and interdimensional theories, the evidence is lacking.

Military Technology

Many researchers are convinced that a majority of the UFOs reported around the world are not sightings of spaceships, but sightings of man-made technology in the shape of experimental aircraft and weaponry that is being developed and tested in secret for the military.

The fact that some sightings appear to defy our current understanding of the laws of physics doesn't surprise the military technology advocates. A conservative estimate puts military scientific know-how at least twenty to twenty-five years ahead of where we are in civilian terms. But does this explain everything? Some UFOs have exhibited fantastic capabilities, such as phenomenal acceleration that would create G-forces so high that it would be impossible for a human being to survive or amazing manoeuvrability that defy the laws of aerodynamics. Could our technology be as far in advance as all this? Some say yes. New materials are being developed constantly that are making us think again about our understanding of the world around us. For instance, a new meta-material has been developed and tested that has the remarkable property of having a negative refractive index, meaning that it bends light away from itself, making anything you place behind it completely invisible. Who knows what the military could develop with their twenty-year lead on conventional technology. Although military testing will possibly account for a number of sightings, we feel that there are others that even advanced technology could not explain.

How to Investigate UFOs

As pointed out earlier in this section, it is important to note that, after investigation, most UFO sightings will turn out to be something normal that has been misidentified. When a rational explanation can be found, a UFO becomes an Identified Flying Object, or IFO for short.

All manner of natural things have been reported as UFOs throughout the decades, ranging from aircraft to stars and planets. All told, there are around 200 common objects or sights in the sky that often get reported as UFOs. This is due in part to the fact that many people do not take much notice of the sky and the things that can be seen in it. To make matters worse, depending on pressure, humidity and temperature, the air around us can play tricks with light, making normal objects in the sky look very unusual. A good example of this happening was told to us by a UFO investigator from Yorkshire (who wishes to remain anonymous) who received a phone call early one morning from two witnesses who told him that they were 'looking at a UFO' as they were speaking. The investigator grabbed his camera and equipment case and drove to the scene as fast as he could. As soon as he pulled up, the witnesses hurried him out of his car and over to their vantage point and pointed excitedly at the mystery object. The

Investigation Life Cycle

Initial Contact
Witness Interview
Background Research
Initial Location Reconnaissance
Planning the Site Investigation
Pre Brief
Running the Investigation
Analysis
Writing Up Your Findings
Making Your Findings Public

investigator took one look, paused for a few seconds and then delicately broke the news to them. They had mistaken the sun emerging from early morning mist as a UFO.

The principle job of a UFO investigator is to carefully analyse sighting reports in great detail to see if a rational explanation can be found. If, after thorough investigation, you still can't find a satisfactory explanation, chances are that you have a genuine anomaly on your hands. Unlike ghost investigations, UFO sightings need to be investigated as soon as possible after the event, because assessing the sighting for possible causes becomes much harder the longer you leave it. Information such as weather data, aircraft movements and information about special local activity, such as people using illuminated advertising balloons or 'laser' light shows becomes more difficult to track down even after only a few days have elapsed.

As with ghost investigations, our preferred method of investigation is to methodically go through all the stages in the Investigation Life Cycle. Although we have already covered the first two stages, initial contact and witness interviews in the Core

Concepts and Skills section, we would like to revisit them again to show how both these stages are treated a little differently when investigating UFOs.

Report Forms

One of the common procedures used by most serious investigators is to send the witness a UFO report form for them to complete. We have abandoned this practice for two reasons. On the whole, people do not like filling in forms. We found that 9 out of 10 forms we sent out did not come back, and we never heard from the witness again. This we felt was a waste of time, stamps and trees. The forms that did come back often came back weeks after the event, resulting in a delay that made it much harder to investigate the case.

Although we do not recommend that you send report forms out for witnesses to complete, a report form is still useful as an aide-mémoire at both the initial contact and the witness interview stages so that you remember to ask all the important questions and gather as much information about the incident as possible. We have included several forms for use at the back of this book, which are also available for you to download from our website at www.para-projects.com

Initial Contact (UFOs)

As soon as you receive an initial contact about a UFO case, it is vital that you gather some basic information to help you to do some preliminary checking. This is because, as already stated, a majority of sighting reports you will receive will turn out to be misidentifications, and can usually be resolved with just a quick check. In order to do this you should obtain the following information from the witness as soon as possible after the sighting:

Time and date of sighting
Exact location where they witnessed it
Brief description of what they saw
Weather conditions (cloudy or clear)
Direction they were looking in (north, south, east, west)
Elevation (how high up in degrees was the sighting from the horizon? – see diagram)
Duration of the sighting

Armed with just the above information you will be able to do some basic checking. Misidentifications usually break down into three main categories: astronomical objects – stars, planets, meteors; man-made objects – aircraft, helicopters, balloons, satellites; weather related – clouds, mock suns (parhelia), northern lights. Below are the most common explanations for most sightings.

Daytime:

Stationary objects – tethered balloon, hovering helicopter.
Moving object – aircraft, helicopter.
Stationary lights – Venus (early morning and evening).
Bright moving lights – sunlight reflecting off high-flying aircraft, child helium balloons, Iridium flares (see satellites).

Night-time:
Stationary light – star, planet, hovering helicopter.
Moving light – aircraft, helicopter, fire balloon (also known as Chinese lanterns), meteor, satellite, effects lights.

Using the information you gathered from the initial contact, you will be able to work through these basic possibilities and do some quick checks. We will cover how and where to find information regarding the various possibilities in more detail later. If, after a basic check, you feel that a witness interview is needed, arrange one with the witness as soon as possible. Remember that time is of the essence where UFO investigation is concerned.

Witness Interview (UFOs)

As well as covering all the points raised in the witness interview stage discussed in the Core Concepts and Skills section, it is important to also gather more specific UFO-related information from the witness.

Familiarity with the Sky

Find out how familiar the witness is with the sky – both day and night. More often than not, the witness will tell you if they have any hobbies that involve skywatching, such as astronomy, aircraft spotting or amateur weather forecasting, but if not, don't be afraid to ask. If the witness is a trained observer (such as military or police personnel), chances are that you will have more of a mystery on your hands.

Drawings or Sketches

Get the witness to sketch out a drawing of what they saw. It doesn't matter if they say they are not an artist – any diagram is useful, as you will be able to use it to clarify what the witness has described, and also to help tease out more detail about the sighting without putting words into the witness's mouth.

If the object the witness saw was moving, get the witness to draw out the path of the object's motion in the sky; for example, did it travel from left to right, move up or down? Both the sketch and movement diagram will be useful when you come to do your research on the sighting.

Questions to Ask the Witness

The questions we have included here are intended to extract as much detail about the incident as possible from the witness. For your convenience, we have included a form at the back of this book for you to use as an aide-mémoire. Copies are also available for you to download from our website at www.para-projects.com

Date, time and duration of sighting – These are very important questions, so make sure that the witness is sure that they are giving you accurate information. In particular, ask the witness how they knew what time it was. Did they look at their watch? Was it an estimate? If it was an estimate, get the witness to evaluate their estimate by thinking about the whole evening, before, during and after their sighting. Where had they come from? What were they doing at the time? Where were they going? In one investigation we conducted, we worked out the accurate time from a witness who remembered hearing TV news theme music blasting out of a nearby house, which helped us to pinpoint exactly when the sighting took place.

When trying to assess how long (duration) they saw the UFO for, get the witness to imagine they are observing it again, and get them to trace the movement (if any) in the air with their finger. This will also give you a good estimate of how high up (elevation) the witness saw the object and also its speed if it was moving.

Gathering accurate time information is essential when it comes to checking details like locations of stars or planets or aircraft movements at the time of the sighting.

Location, direction and elevation – Knowing where the witness was at the time of their sighting and which direction they were looking in is also essential in any UFO investigation. One of the methods we use is to bring along an area map and get the witness to pinpoint where they were. If they are unable to do this from the map, another possibility (if the case merits it) is to arrange for the witness to take you to the location to show you where they were positioned and in which direction they were looking.

Elevation is how high up in the sky (in degrees) the object was observed. Imagine that your arm is outstretched straight ahead. This is zero degrees. If you point directly up towards the ceiling this is 90 degrees. The point halfway between the two is 45 degrees. By using these three points as guides it is possible to get a fair estimate

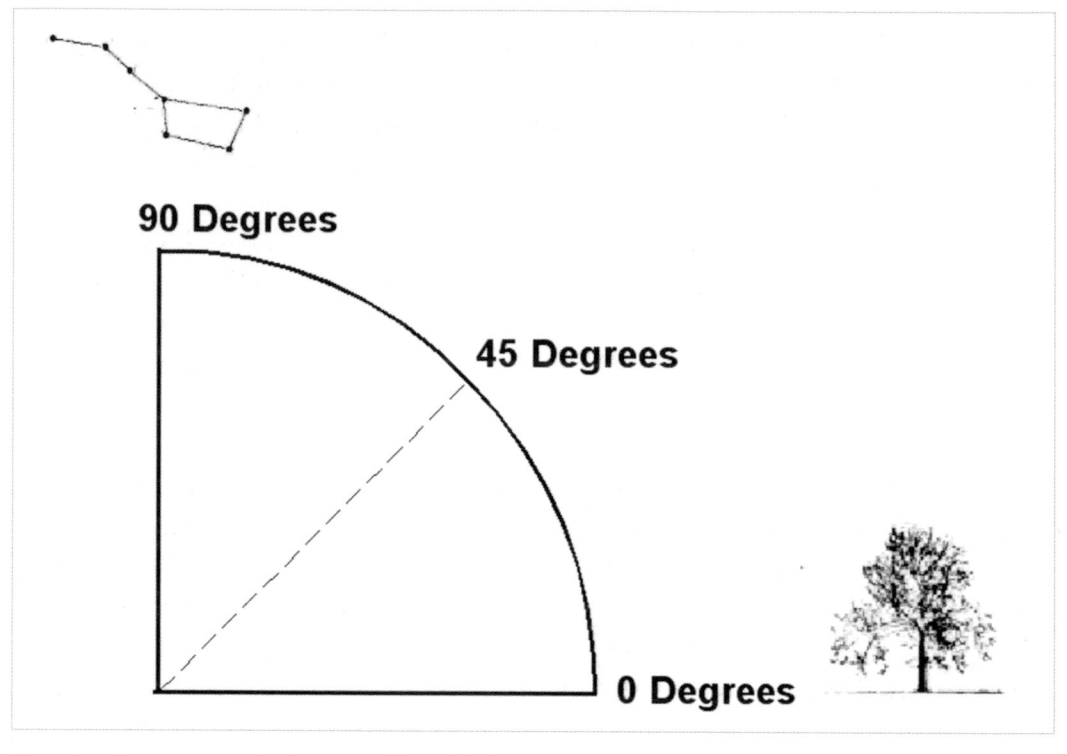

Elevation is a measure in degrees of how high up in the sky an object is seen.

of how many degrees up the object was. Get the witness to imagine that they are observing the object again and get them to point at where it was in the sky. This will give you a good idea about the object's elevation. When combined with time information, location and direction, elevation can be used to check out the positions of stars, planets, aircraft and other IFOs in relation to the position of the UFO at the time of the sighting.

Weather conditions – Weather conditions are important when trying to work out what the witness has observed. For instance, if the sighting took place at night but the sky was heavily overcast, this completely rules out anything astronomical as being the cause of the sighting. Similarly, if it is daytime and the sun is shining, a bright, moving light could easily be sunlight reflecting off the surface of an aircraft or a child's helium balloon. There are four main questions about the weather that are important to know.

Clouds –Was the sky clear? If not, was the cloud cover hazy, scattered or thick? If the sighting occurred at night, this might be difficult for the witness to judge correctly. In one investigation we conducted, the witness reported seeing lights spinning around in the sky. From the description the witness gave, we suspected that what had been seen was special-effects lighting (misleadingly referred to as 'laser light shows', even though lasers are seldom used) but for these type of lights to be seen in the sky some form of cloud cover is required for them to project onto. The witness was adamant that the sky was clear, but upon checking, we discovered that there was thin cloud cover present overhead, which made the light show visible up to 18 km (12 miles) away from the source.

Wind – Was there any wind? If so, how strong was it? Gentle breeze? Strong wind? If there was a wind during the sighting, which direction was it blowing in? If the object was moving, was it moving with or against the wind? If it was moving with, could the UFO have been a balloon or an unusual cloud? If it was moving against the wind, could it have been an aircraft?

Precipitation – Was the atmosphere dry or was it foggy, misty or raining? Atmospheric vapour can cause a number of weird effects that make natural things in the sky look strange, such as producing halos around aircraft landing lights or creating fake suns (parhelia) where airborne ice crystals form bright patches of light either side of the sun.

Temperature – What was the temperature like at the time of the sighting? Was it cold, warm or hot? Hot weather conditions could lead to atmospheric effects such as mirages or heat hazes that distort the light from distant objects. Cooler conditions may be indicative of ice crystals being present in the sky, which are capable of scattering light, causing effects like halos.

Object size and distance – The object's size and distance from the witness are two of the most difficult things to estimate, especially if the sighting has occurred in the dark. Before we look at ways of helping to determine them more accurately, let us look at how our normal perceptions of both are formed.

Distance perception – People use a combination of visual clues and memory to determine an object's distance, such as:

Relative size – When we look at an assortment of different-sized objects, for instance, whilst looking at the view out of a window, we tend to assume that the smaller objects we see are further away from us than the larger ones. In addition, if we look at objects that we are more familiar with, such as a car or a house, our knowledge of how large or small these things usually are also helps us to gauge how far away they are from us, which in turn helps us to estimate how far away other objects are in relation to them.

Relative brightness – We perceive brighter objects as being nearer than dimmer ones. Brightness also affects our perception of object size (see Size perception).

Aerial perspective – The further away an object is, the less defined it will look. Its edges will appear to be fuzzier and its detail and colour will be less distinct. This is caused by the light from the object being scattered by the atmosphere. The further away an object is, the more atmosphere there is between you and it, which causes more scattering. Think of how a distant mountain range looks compared to objects that are closer to you.

Motion parallax – An important part of our distance perception comes from looking at moving objects, or their apparent movement in relation to us. We perceive distant objects as moving more slowly than ones that are nearer to us. A good example of this is when you are the passenger of a car looking out of the side window as you travel. Objects close to the roadside, such as lampposts or bushes tend to whizz by, but more distant objects, such as buildings and trees, remain in view for far longer.

Retinal disparity – Because our eyes are around six centimetres apart, each eye will see a slightly different view from the other when looking at the same scene. When the two separate images are superimposed in the brain, the differences give us visual clues as to how far away something is in relation to us. The further away something is, the less disparity you will see. You can demonstrate this yourself by closing each eye in turn and seeing the differences in each eye for both near and far objects.

There are a few other ways in which we gauge distance, but the above provide the main clues that we use to gauge how far away something is to us.

Size perception – People use a combination of visual clues and memory to determine an objects size, such as:

Size comparison – Again, like distance, we tend to judge the size of an object by comparing it to other objects in view at the time. Say, for instance, we see an unusual shape low on the horizon that appears to be close to a distant tree. Since we are familiar with the sizes of trees, we are then able to estimate roughly how big the object is by comparing its relative size to the tree.

Relative brightness – Usually, the brighter an object is, the nearer it is to us. This is down to the fact that the light from distant objects is more scattered by the atmosphere, making them appear dimmer than nearer objects. However, very bright objects can appear to be much bigger than they actually are. The apparent size of the full moon is a good example of this, as we will see next.

Now we know how our brains estimate size and distance, let us consider how our estimations will be far less accurate when observing unusual objects in the dark. Firstly, when looking at an object in the night sky, we lose vital perspective information, such as being able to compare the object against the surrounding backdrop as easily as in daylight. In addition, since the object is unknown to us, we have no real way of gauging its true size, even if we have nearby objects to compare it to. Therefore, when confronted with something never seen before, the chances are that the average observer will not be able to determine either size or distance with any accuracy.

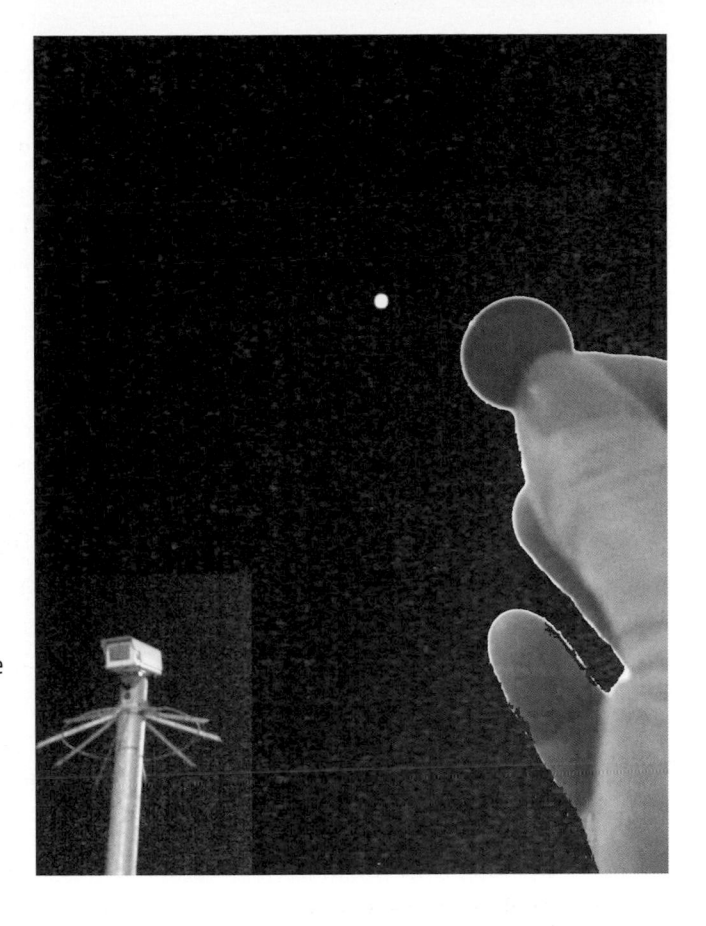

Angular size. When asked what size object held at arms length would just cover the full moon, many would say something the size of a small coin like a 10p piece. Even a 5p piece (17 mm in diameter), as shown here, is around four times larger.

The traditional method used for many years on UFO investigations was to ask witnesses to compare the size of the object they saw against common objects held at arm's length, such as a pin head, a small coin, a dinner plate, etc. This method determined the UFOs true size by comparing its angular size (the apparent width of an object, measured in degrees) against a known object. However, in tests, we have found that this method is unreliable due to people's perceptions being different. For example, when asking witnesses what size object held at arm's length would just cover the full moon, many people chose a 10p piece.

As you can see from this picture, even a 5p piece held at arms length is far too big. The actual size of an object that would just cover the moon needs only to have a diameter of around four millimetres!

The best method we have found is to inform the witness of the apparent size of the full moon (i.e., a circle with a diameter of around four millimetres) and then get them to compare the UFO against the size of the full moon in the sky. This gives more realistic estimates.

Physical effects and evidence – In some UFO encounters, witnesses have described a number of effects that have seemingly been caused by the UFO's presence, such as cars stalling or radio reception being reduced to meaningless static. In more dramatic encounters, UFOs have been reported to leave physical traces, such as indentations on the ground or singed/scorched earth. At the interview, it is important to ask the witness to think carefully about anything they experienced that might have been associated with the sighting. A good tip is to ask the witness to work through their five senses – sight, sound, smell, taste, touch – to see if they can relate anything to each. In our UFO investigations, this line of questioning has brought out extra details, such as feeling static electricity in the air, odd smells like electrical burning or ozone, displacement of air, animals behaving erratically, metallic taste in the mouth and so on.

If the witness has reported that the UFO left physical traces, such as ground markings, it is important to arrange to visit the scene as soon as possible in order to record and preserve the evidence, as ground traces have provided some of the best evidence to date in support of the existence of UFOs. We will cover ground trace analysis in more detail later.

Was the UFO photographed or filmed? – If so, ask the witness if they can supply a copy of the picture/footage. If the picture/footage was taken on a digital device, ask the witness to supply you with a copy direct from the memory or memory card as images that are loaded onto computer via certain 'helper' applications, such as picture-managing software, have a tendency to lose vital imbedded information in the picture/footage file. For more information about this, see Section 4: Photographic Anomalies.

Were there any other witnesses? – Ask the witness if there were other people present at the time of the sighting, including bystanders. If the witness was with friends or family, get their contact details and arrange a separate interview for them. If the witness remembers any bystanders present at the time of the sighting, e.g., someone walking their dog, it may be possible to find out who they are by placing a request in a local newspaper or visiting the location around the same time as the original sighting, as the additional people that were present at the time of the sighting may routinely walk past the spot..

Other experiences – The final question you should ask is if the witness has experienced any other unusual experiences in their life, such as ghost sightings, premonitions, out of body experiences, etc. We have found that people who experience UFOs tend to have experienced other unusual things in their life prior to their sightings. Sometimes their answers can lead to other investigations. In one UFO case, we found out that the witness was also experiencing ghost activity in their home, which we also got to investigate.

Account Write-up

Once the interview has been wound up, it is important to get the details written up as soon as possible and for the witness to read the write-up to check that what you have written is an accurate and full account of what they experienced. Once they are happy with it, get them to sign and date the copy as proof to others that this is the case.

Research

Now that you have a full account of what the witness has experienced, it is vital to start doing in-depth research into the sighting as soon as possible. Since most UFO reports turn out to be misidentifications of conventional sky-borne objects or atmospheric phenomena, we have prepared two handy charts that will hopefully help you to check out all the most likely conventional explanations for what the witness has seen.

Using the appropriate chart (day or night), select whether the sky was cloudy or clear. Next, select if the object was moving or stationary. As you move down the branches of the chart, it should narrow down the IFO possibilities enough for you to do more in-depth checking into the likeliest scenario.

Astronomical Objects

There are a lot of different astronomical objects that get reported as UFOs. Here is a brief run-down of the more common ones and some handy sources of information to help you check out each possibility.

Stars and planets – Stars and planets are by far the most common objects that get misidentified as UFOs. In particular the planets Venus, Mars, Jupiter and Saturn, and the stars Sirius, Arcturus and Vega are the common culprits. In addition, the moon has had its fair share of misidentifications over the years, especially if seen behind thin ice-crystal-laden clouds.

Although stars and planets slowly change their position in the sky over the course of an evening (due to the rotation of the Earth), they appear more or less stationary in the sky to observers. If you suspect that the witness has seen a bright star, a planet or the moon, there are a number of resources available to you in order to do some checking.

Astronomy software – There are a few pieces of free software available on the internet that can show you the location of stars and planets at any given time from any location. Two pieces of software that we highly recommend are Home Planet and Stellarium, which are both available for free download.

Home Planet: http://www.fourmilab.ch/homeplanet/

Stellarium: www.stellarium.org

They are very easy to install and use. Because Home Planet only takes up 14 Mb and Stellarium only takes up 62 Mb of memory space, and both work independently of the internet, they are ideal to load onto a laptop computer to use on field investigations.

One of the best features of both software packages is that they both have a horizon view setting, which makes it very user-friendly for people who are not too familiar with using star charts. All you have to do is put in the location's longitude and latitude (which you can find from resources such as Google Earth or select off the world map on Home Planet), input the date and time of the sighting and then select Horizon View. You can then look at the positions of the bright stars and planets in the direction that the witness was looking in to see if there are any likely candidates to account for the 'UFO'.

Online resources – There are many online sites that also provide astronomical information. One of the best we have come across is a site called 'Heavens Above', which not only charts the positions of stars and planets, but also provides information on asteroids and comets. It can be found at: http://www.heavens-above.com.

Heavens Above is also a useful resource for finding out your precise latitude and longitude. If you wish to use this site regularly, it is a good idea to register for membership, so that you don't have to re-input your location every time you use it. Registration and use of the site is free.

Magazines – Another good source of astronomy information can be found in magazines such as *Sky at Night*, *Astronomy Now* or *Sky and Telescope*, which feature monthly star charts, planet positions and special astronomical activity such as comets and meteor showers.

Meteors and fireball meteors – Meteors, or shooting stars, as they are more commonly called, are tiny specks of dust that burn up as they hit the Earth's atmosphere. They are seen as fast moving streaks of light that only last for a fraction of a second before being totally vaporised. If you look out on any dark and cloud-free night, the chances are that you will get to see at least one meteor whizzing across the night sky.

Fireball meteors are much larger. Weighing in at around 10 lb (4.5 kg) and upwards, fireball meteors survive for considerable lengths of time as they hurtle through the sky. As their name describes, they are literally blazing balls of light, complete with fiery tails, which, unlike regular meteors, are usually observed for periods in excess of eight seconds depending on the witness's vantage point. Unlike normal meteors, fireballs have much greater angular size, usually equal to the apparent size of the full moon. However, sightings of fireballs are far more rare than normal meteors. More often than not, people who witness fireball meteors report them as such, but there are occasions where they are reported as UFOs, mainly because many people are not aware that meteors can, and do, act in strange ways. To clear up some of the mysteries, here is a run-down of the basic characteristics of fireballs:

Colours/effects – The light emitted by a fireball meteor can be any of the following colours: white, red, yellow, green or blue. Sometimes the head is a different colour to the tail and, on occasions, can change colour several times throughout its flight. Different colours are produced by the different compositions of material which meteors are made of. For instance, iron-nickel meteors usually give off blue or green light whereas stony-iron meteors are more red/white in colour. An important point to note is that meteors do not diminish (fade out) in brightness but go out instantly.

Speed – Meteors travel incredibly fast, usually around 11-72 km per second (7-45 miles per second) and have average 'flight' path lengths of between 80-160 km (50-100

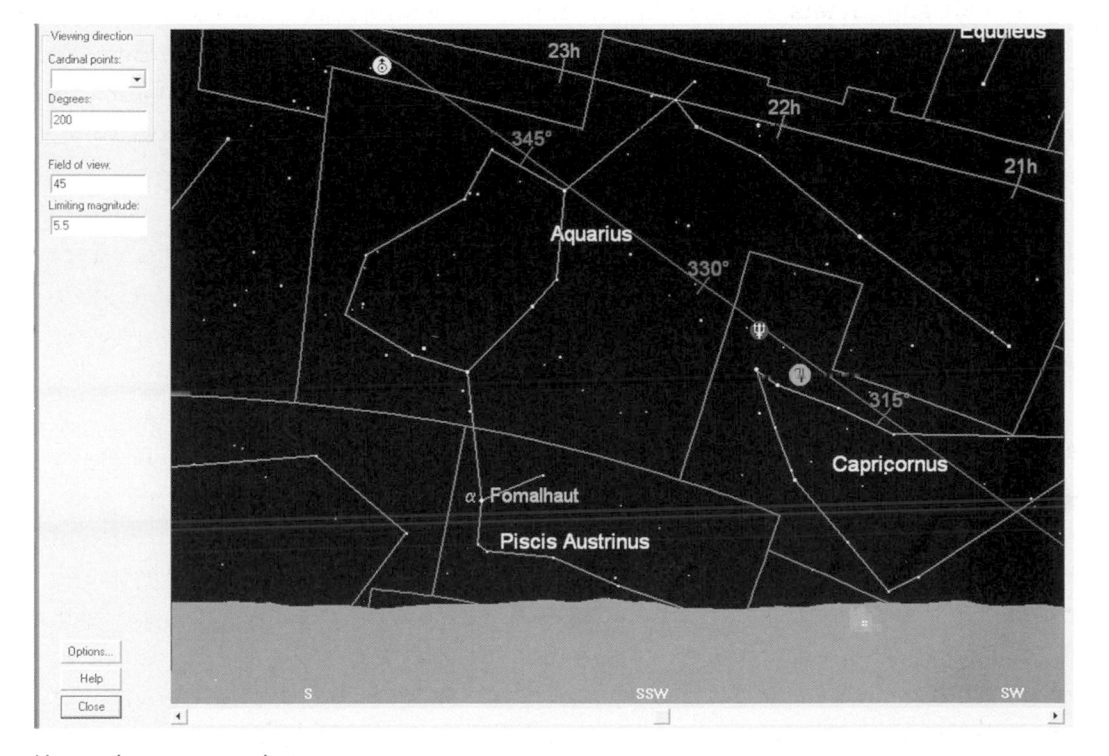

Home planet screen shot.

miles) before being completely vaporised. In some rare instances fragments survive to reach the ground, where they become known as meteorites.

Height and brightness - Another hallmark of fireball meteor sightings is that there are usually lots of witnesses. There are two reasons why fireball meteor events are spotted by many observers simultaneously. Firstly, fireballs begin to heat up and glow at around 160 km (100 miles) up, making them visible to a wider area on the ground, and secondly, they are exceptionally bright, sometimes as bright as the full moon, and have been known to turn night into day on rare occasions. In fact, some have even been seen in broad daylight.

Formations – More often than not, large fireball meteors break up into smaller fragments during their descent, giving rise to sightings of whole formations of fast moving lights. One such sighting over Cornwall in July 1998 had hundreds of people ringing the emergency services to report that they had seen the letters 'Z' and 'Q' shoot through the sky. Some people thought it was a message from alien beings.

Occurrences – Fireballs usually occur in connection with meteor showers. A meteor shower takes place when the Earth passes through a swarm of interplanetary dust or debris left behind from the passage of comets. As these debris clouds are in fixed positions along the Earth's orbit around the sun, the showers occur at the same time each year. Usually lasting several days, each shower has a peak time, where meteor activity is at its highest. The two most productive meteor showers in the northern hemisphere occur on 12 August (called the Perseids) and 17-18 November (called the Leonids). Here is a list of the dates of the more common meteor showers.

Quadrantids	1-5 January
Lyrids	16-25 April
δ Aquarids	19 April – 28 May
δ Aquarids	12 July – 19 August
α Capricornids	3 July – 15 August
Perseids	17 July – 24 August
κ Cygnids	3-25 August
α Aurigids	25 August – 8 September
September Perseids	5-17 September
α Aurigids	18 September – 10 October
Draconids	6-10 October
Orionids	2 October – 7 November

Taurids	25 September – 25 November
Leonids	10-23 November
Geminids	7-17 December
Ursids	17-26 December

In addition to knowing when meteor showers will occur, it is also possible to work out which part of the sky to look at in order to get the best chance of seeing meteors. Each shower has a fixed point in the sky from where all the meteors appear to radiate. This is called the shower radiant. The names given to the regular showers are derived from the constellations in which the radiants are located. Hence, Perseids appear to come out of a point somewhere in the constellation Perseus and Leonids from a point somewhere in the constellation of Leo. Familiarisation with the locations of the constellations, the times of the year when these showers occur, and the use of astronomy software is very useful when chasing up suspected meteor misidentifications.

Movement – Fireballs can appear to be stationary for short durations. This illusion is created when a meteor is observed coming straight over the horizon towards the observer (see diagram), giving the appearance of a bright object hovering in the sky, which then suddenly picks up momentum.

Sounds – Large meteors can create extremely loud noises. These are caused when the meteor, travelling at tremendous speeds, causes a powerful compression wave to build up ahead of itself producing a supersonic boom. Such booms are heard some time after the passage of the meteor, as sound travels considerably slower than light. In fact, the lag between sighting and sound can be quite long. For instance, the light from a meteor burning up at an altitude of 80 km (50 miles) would take only 0.0003 seconds to reach an observer on the ground, whereas the accompanying sonic boom would take in excess of four minutes!

However, there have been many reliable reports of instantaneous sound associated with meteors. These sounds have been described as 'rattles', 'low booms' and 'hisses'. In many cases it has been the sound that has caused the observer to look up! So, how is it possible to see a meteor and hear its sound at the same time? Some scientists believe that the plasma trail of the meteor generates extra low and very low frequency (ELF/VLF) radio emissions that travel at the speed of light which are then converted into sound at ground level by sharp objects acting as receivers, such as aerials, wires and even blades of grass. This idea is not as crazy as it might first appear, as it is possible to hear bursts of static on a carefully tuned radio when a meteor falls.

Meteor Resources – There are many online resources available. Here are a few websites that you can use to see if there have been any recent fireball meteor sightings:

Society for Popular Astronomy: http://www.popastro.com/sections/meteor.htm
International Meteor Organisation: http://www.imo.net/
British Astronomical Association: http://britastro.org/baa/

Alternatively, you could also contact your local astronomical society, who may be able to help you. You can find their contact details at your local library or in the monthly directory in the *Sky at Night* magazine.

Man-made Objects

There are quite a few man-made things that get misidentified for a variety of reasons. Aircraft in particular seem to be the source of a lot of sightings, closely followed by satellites, fire balloons (or Chinese lanterns) and special effects lighting. Let's look at each of these in turn.

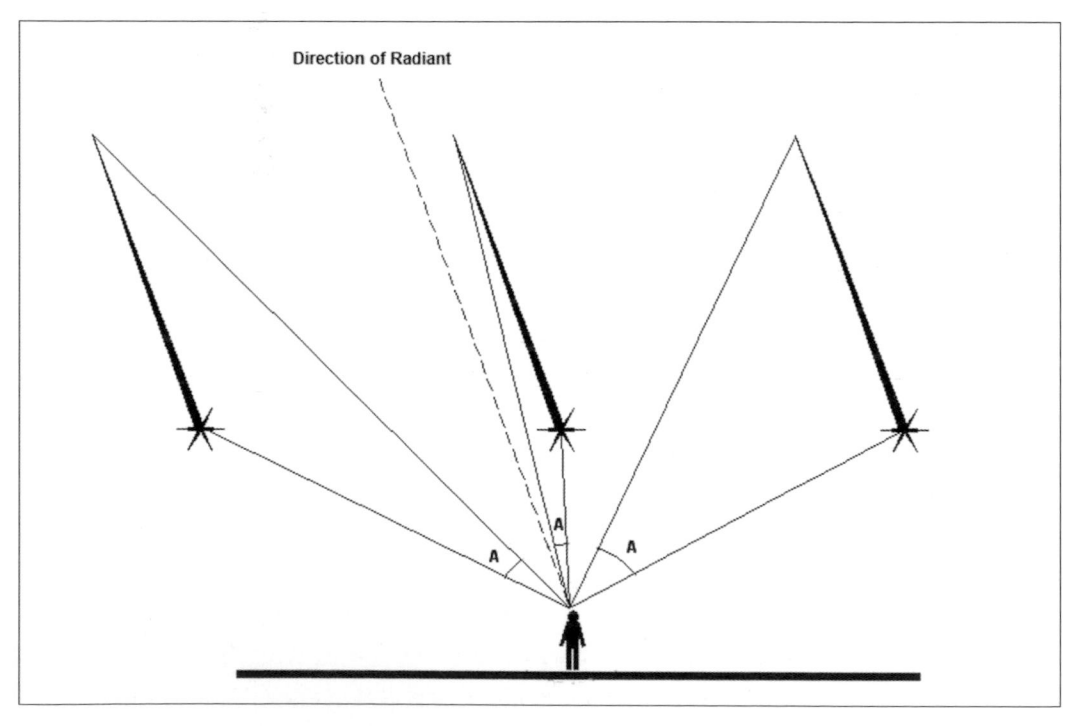

If a meteor is seen overhead, it can appear to hang stationary in the sky for a moment before you see any movement. Although the trail lengths of the meteor in this illustration are identical in length (and therefore duration) those seen lower in the sky will appear to be moving much more speedily than the ones seen overhead. Note the difference in angular size (A) of each trail despite them being identical.

Aircraft – High-flying aircraft can sometimes be misidentified as UFOs because witnesses see them but do not hear any noise from them. This can be caused by a number of factors such as background noises at street level masking the faint sound of the plane's engines, wind blowing in the wrong direction or the aircraft may be flying at such a high altitude that there is a slight delay in the sound reaching the ground.

Another common misidentification occurs when people see aircraft approaching them at night with their landing lights on. Approaching aircraft can appear to be stationary for several minutes, whereupon they appear to speed up as they near the witness. This is another example of motion parallax at work.

During the daytime, sunlight can reflect off an aircraft's fuselage and wings, making distant planes look like balls of light, or the true image of the plane can sometimes be distorted by atmospheric disturbances such as mirages, which can occur in both hot and cold conditions, or an odd distortion effect known as towering, where the shape of an object appears to be stretched in the vertical plane.

Retrospectively checking to see if there were any aircraft flying in the vicinity at the time of a sighting is a tricky business. More often than not, the best you will be able to manage is to check the likelihood of an aircraft being present.

All aircraft are required to stick to prearranged routes when flying from one destination to another. These are known as air traffic routes. There are maps available that mark out the major ones, which are handy to look at if you suspect that an aircraft may be the cause of the sighting. If the UFOs location coincides with an air traffic route, the chances are that the witness may have misidentified an aircraft. Maps showing these routes across the UK can be found on the internet. Here are two links to get you started:

Flightmapping.com. This is a very good site that has interactive maps of all air traffic routes from UK airports and the rest of the world. http://www.flightmapping.com/maps/UKIreland/

BAA Campaign for Dark Skies page. This astronomy page has a map of the UK air traffic routes and also includes the locations of aircraft holding areas (also known as stacks). http://www.britastro.org/dark-skies/bestukastrolocationmap2.html

If you are unable to obtain any maps showing the air traffic routes, you can do the next best thing and go to the sighting location and look out for aircraft. After a few hours, you will be able to see if the location is close to an air traffic route. In addition, if the location is situated near an airport, you will also become aware of the holding area or 'stack' where aircraft are made to circle the airport until a runway becomes available for landing. Another source of information on aircraft movements is local aircraft enthusiasts who you can contact to see if they have logged any aircraft at the time of the sighting. One thing we urge you not to do is to contact airport air traffic control staff to ask about UFO sightings unless you have a very extraordinary sighting on your hands. The chances are that they will be unwilling or unable to help you.

Satellites – If you look towards the heavens on a clear night in a location that has little or no light pollution, you will be able to see dozens of artificial satellites criss-cross the sky every hour. They appear as tiny specks of light that move at moderate speed across the sky. They look similar to the lights on high-flying aircraft, but unlike the former, their light is constant, not flashing or pulsing like an aircraft's anti-collision beacons. Since the light from a satellite is reflected sunlight, once the satellite passes into the Earth's shadow the light disappears instantly. Their brightness is usually comparable to that of an average star in the sky. However, there is a fleet of around ninety telecommunication satellites currently in low orbit around the Earth, called Iridium, that produce very bright flashes of light in the sky. This is because each satellite is equipped with three highly reflective antenna panels that reflect around 90 per cent of the sunlight that hits them. These flashes are known as Iridium flares.

When witnessing an Iridium flare, the observer will see a moving point of light that grows in intensity to around three quarters of the brightness of the full moon, momentarily peaks, then begins to dim again. Typically, Iridium flares last no more than eight seconds. It is important to note that some flares are so bright that they can also be seen in daylight. Iridium flares are spectacular, and since their occurrence can be predicted in advance, many people go out at night specifically to look for them. The Heavens Above website holds information on the previous forty-eight hours worth of flare observations, along with observation data for many other satellites. http://www.heavens-above.com/. Another useful online resource for all satellites is the NASA satellite tracking applets page, which can be found at http://science.nasa.gov/realtime/.

The most impressive application on this page is the J-Track 3D applet that plots around 500 satellite positions in real time around the globe. You can zoom into your location and find out what satellites are passing overhead. Another useful applet on this site is J-Pass that allows you to retrospectively check to see what was in the sky at any given date, time and location. However, this software is no longer maintained by NASA, so newer satellites will not appear on this.

Fire balloons or Chinese lanterns – In recent years fire balloons have become a very regular sight in the night sky. A fire balloon or Chinese lantern is basically a small hot-air balloon consisting of a plastic bag with an open flame underneath that heats up the air in the bag causing it to rise into the sky. Once airborne, fire balloons can be seen for many miles. It is currently a popular practice to launch them at weddings and other special events.

In recent years, hoaxers have launched whole fleets of fire balloons all over the country, which have fooled many people into believing an alien invasion was underway, which has led to many front page stories in national newspapers.

Fire balloons seen at distance normally give off an amber/orange glow and move at the same speed and in the same direction as the ambient air. If you suspect that fire balloons may be the cause, try to find the nearest local weather-monitoring station to the sighting location and gather information on wind speed and direction at the time of the sighting. A very useful online site that contains historical, regional weather data for most of the UK is Weather Underground, which can be found at http://www. wunderground.com/.

The site has a location search facility where you can type in a location name or a postcode, which then generates a list of nearby weather-monitoring stations.

As a non-internet alternative, you could always check the daily weather charts in newspaper archives at your local library. The information is not as detailed as you can find at the above site, but it will help in your investigation.

Effects lighting (also known as laser light shows) – Outdoor effects lights have been a major source of UFO misidentifications since the mid-1990s in the UK. These lights are usually set up on rooftops and fired skywards so that they project interesting patterns onto low cloud. These lights have been used for all manner of events, such as outdoor music concerts, advertising for night clubs, shops, taxi firms, pubs, etc.

The effects units are powerful spotlights that use mirrors and prisms to split up the light into intricate, moving patterns that can then be projected onto low cloud cover. The resultant light patterns often confuse people into thinking that they are UFOs because the beam leading up to the moving patterns is seldom visible, making people think that there is a formed object above the clouds projecting light downwards.

If you suspect that an effects light is the cause, you may be able to pick up clues from local newspapers. If you see any events/venues as possible candidates, there is no harm in contacting the organisers/owners to see if they have been operating effects lighting. It might then be possible for you to arrange a comparison demonstration for the witness.

Another useful source of information regarding effects lights is other local UFO investigators and groups. We (the authors) freely exchange any useful information with other investigators, as sharing information is mutually beneficial to all.

Fire balloon being launched.

Location Reconnaissance

If at all possible, it is always a good idea to visit the location where the witness had their sighting in order to see if there is anything in the area that could have been mistaken for a UFO. If the sighting occurred at night try to make two visits, one during the day and one at night around the same time as the witness's sighting. Here are a few things to look out for, on both a day and night visit.

Daytime

Sometimes, a visit during daylight hours is all that is needed to resolve a UFO sighting case. By standing at the same spot and looking in the same direction and elevation that the witness saw their UFO, you will be able to check to see if they have misidentified lights from lone buildings standing on hills or the headlights from cars moving along mountain roads, which can easily be mistaken for airborne objects in the dark. Also, keep a look out for aircraft to see if there are any obvious air traffic routes nearby. Try to gauge their speed, height and direction of travel and compare these against the witness's description of events.

It is a good idea to read through the witness's account of events whilst in situ to check that all site details match. In one case we investigated, we quickly realised that the spot where the witness claimed to have seen her UFO was suspect, as the view from the location she specified was too restricted for her to have seen anything in the sky for any length of time. We later discovered that the sighting was a hoax.

Depending upon the type of report you receive, you may need to visit as quickly as possible, especially if the witness claims that there is trace evidence present at the site, such as depressions in the ground, scorched grass or soil that has been desiccated (all the water removed) or anything else at the location that appears to have been physically affected by the presence of the UFO. If you do find anything unusual, it is vitally important not to disturb the evidence if you can avoid it, at least until you have thoroughly documented the find by taking photographs and/or video and making detailed measurements. When taking photographs of trace evidence, always include a familiar object in the picture, such as a coin or ruler, to give an idea of scale. Details like this are invaluable to anyone who may wish to review the evidence later.

Items to take:
Camera
Camcorder
Audio recorder
Notepad
Pens
Tape measure
Sample bags (resealable)
Copy of witness statement
Area map

Take soil and plant samples from the affected area, and place them in your sample bags, making sure that you label up each bag immediately. Also, take samples from a spot nearby that has not been affected. These are called control samples, and they can be used to compare the differences (if any) between the affected area and its immediate surroundings. Make a careful note of where each sample has been taken from. This can be done either photographically by placing the bags close to the spots you took the samples from and taking a general photograph of the affected area, or by sketching the scene and marking down the sampling points on the drawing.

If you are convinced that something anomalous has caused the traces, you will need to find someone qualified who will be willing to do some analysis for you. Larger UFO organisations may be able to help you to find a suitable testing facility, but be prepared for a hefty bill. Laboratory testing is very expensive, so only go down this route if you really think you have something out of the ordinary.

In 1996, we were lucky enough to receive a call from the local press who had got wind of a dramatic UFO sighting over Widnes, Cheshire, which had seemingly left ground trace markings. The incident occurred near Widnes railway station at around 2 a.m. on a fairly cold February morning. The witness, who had difficulty sleeping at night, had decided to go for a run in the hope that it would make him feel tired enough to sleep. As he ran along a footpath that followed the railway line, he became aware of a strange blue/white light in the sky. He stopped to look at it for a few seconds, and then realised that the light was moving towards him. In blind panic, he dropped his jacket and ran away as fast as he could. A few seconds later, the light overtook him and came to an abrupt stop about ten metres (approximately thirty-two feet) in front of him. Seconds later, the light faded a fraction and began to emit a noise that the witness described as sounding like a 'thousand wailing cats'. Now rooted to the spot in terror, the witness helplessly watched as the light began to 'fire' down beams of light towards a patch of ground about five metres away (approximately sixteen feet) from his position. He claimed that these beams hit a nearby pile of disused wooden railway sleepers, and burnt holes right through them.

Intrigued by the witness's report, we managed to get to the scene three days after the alleged event. We quickly found the sleepers in question and got to work documenting the evidence. We took samples of wood and excitedly sent them off for analysis. Several weeks later, we received the laboratory report, which stated that the wood's combustion had been aided by the presence of petrol, and that the wood had burned at a temperature consistent with that of a petrol-fuelled fire. In short, we had discovered someone's bonfire.

The fact that the witness saw something extraordinary that night is not in question, as there were two other independent witnesses who also saw the same bright light in the sky that night, along with several blinding flashes of light which they described to us as being like sheet lightning, only much brighter.

After a week of careful cross-checking, we came to the conclusion that the witness had wrongly assumed that the mysterious beams of light had burnt the sleepers – a conclusion he had come to only when he revisited the site several hours later with a police officer in order to retrieve his jacket. Both of them saw the burnt wood and made the same erroneous connection.

A simple check at the railway station confirmed that railway workers had made a bonfire out of several sleepers a week or so earlier during a station clear-up and the remnants of the bonfire had subsequently been scattered around the site by children. Although it turned out that there was no trace evidence in this case, it still remains a profound mystery as to what the witness encountered on that fateful night.

Night-time

Revisiting the site at the same time that the sighting occurred is a very good way of eliminating obvious IFOs, such as planets, stars and the moon. If you get to the scene of the incident within a week of the sighting, and the weather/atmospheric conditions are similar, you will be able to see these astronomical objects in more or less the same positions in the sky as they were when the witness had their sighting. If the witness

Holes burnt in wooden railway sleepers in Widnes, in 1996, thought to be caused by a UFO firing beams of light to the ground. (*Photo: Roger Ellison*)

has misidentified a star or planet, try to persuade them to return to the location as soon as possible to see it for themselves. That way you can physically demonstrate your findings, which is a powerful way of getting them to agree with your conclusions. By doing so, they are less likely to be fooled by the same thing in the future.

Also look out for tall buildings, radio masts or any other tall structures that may have anti-aircraft-collision lights attached to them. These have been reported to us as UFOs on more occasions than we care to remember. One such misidentification occurred because passing low clouds, invisible to the witnesses in the dark, scurried past the lights on a TV transmitter mast making them appear as if they were flashing on and off. The witnesses believed that the 'UFO' was trying to signal to them. The fact that these particular witnesses were trained observers goes to show that anyone can be fooled under the right circumstances.

Another fairly common night-time misidentification is caused when distant lights from towns and villages reflect off low cloud, giving rise to weird, illuminated shapes that, if there is sufficient breeze, can move swiftly across the sky, changing shape as they do so. If you aren't expecting it, they can look very out of place. Look out for obvious lighting hot spots that could cause this effect when cloud cover is present.

Finally, keep a look out for passing people, especially people walking their dogs, as they may regularly walk around the location at this time and may have witnessed something themselves, or have an idea of what could have been the cause of the sighting. It doesn't hurt to ask. Local knowledge is invaluable to an investigation.

Planning a Skywatch

Before we delve into the mechanics of organising a skywatch, it is important to understand why they are a vital part of UFO investigation.

Firstly, UFO sightings tend to occur in waves, where nothing is reported for months and then, out of the blue, investigators get inundated with dozens of reports, usually over the course of a few days or weeks. Therefore, if you receive two or more reports in the same week, it is a good idea to get out there as soon as possible to see if you can witness something for yourself. Waves of sightings occur for a number of reasons – mostly because something 'new' has appeared in the sky, such as unusual aircraft, effects lighting or advertising balloons. One very good example of this was a wave of sightings that occurred over Cheshire in the early '90s that were caused by an illuminated hot-air balloon flying over the region. The balloon was fitted with colourful lights that made the skin of the envelope shimmer in a dazzling array of colours, which from a distance, gave it a more bell-shaped, saucer-like appearance. During the wave, over seventy-five reports were received by local investigation teams in just over a week. Another reason why waves occur is because of popular media, such as UFO movies, documentaries, newspaper articles and TV dramas that fire up the public's imagination, prompting many people to believe that almost everything they see in the sky is a UFO. The film *Close Encounters of the Third Kind* produced a worldwide wave of sightings back in 1978-9 and, as we write, the return of Dr Who to our TV screens has been blamed for an increase of UFO sightings in South Wales.

The second reason why it is useful to conduct a skywatch is to get you and your team more familiar with the night sky. The more skywatching you do, the better equipped you will be at investigating other people's sightings. If you become better acquainted with the sights that the night sky can offer, you will be able to pick out vital clues in witness testimony that may lead you to finding a satisfactory explanation for what they saw. For example, the knowledge that an aircraft flying towards an observer can appear to be stationary for several minutes is very useful when assessing witness reports that contain words to the effect of 'The light hung in the air for ages then sped off rapidly'.

Choosing a Location

When selecting a location for your skywatch, you will need to find somewhere elevated, such as a hilltop or roof veranda that will give you all-round views of the surrounding horizon (or as much as possible), as well as unobstructed views of the sky. Ideally, the location should be as free as possible from light pollution. In addition, select a location that is not a regular haunt of unruly groups of people who could potentially cause trouble or damage your vehicles and/or equipment. The location should also be free of hazards such as uneven ground, pits, mine workings, or steep drops that become far more hazardous in the dark.

Another important thing is to make sure that you do not set up your skywatch on private property, unless you seek permission first. However, even land that is designated as having public right of way can, under certain circumstances, become off limits to the general public from time to time. For example, a number of years ago, Mark and a group of friends went skywatching in Warminster, where they set up camp on Cradle Hill, one of the most famous UFO hot spots in the UK in the 1960s. After observing the sky for a number of hours, Mark and friends called it a night and retired to their tents. Two hours later, they were rudely awoken by loud explosions and ground-shaking rumbling. Sticking his head out of the tent flaps, Mark stared in horror at streams of heavy machine-gun tracer bullets flying overhead, which were coming from the direction of the nearby army base. Mark and friends had unwittingly camped in the middle of a military live-fire exercise. The moral of this story is, be very careful where you set up camp!

Finally, on a much lighter note, make sure that you don't set up your cameras, scopes and binoculars in beauty spots that are popular with amorous couples, as you may end up having a bit of explaining to do to the police.

Team Size

The team size is only limited by the amount of equipment you wish to bring and the space available at the location. However, we recommend that team sizes should be no larger than ten to twelve people and no smaller than four. If the group is too large, it will be more difficult to manage. If the group is too small, vital observations may be missed.

Weather Conditions

Try to ensure as much as possible that you select dates where the weather is expected to be good. Although clear skies are preferable, a skywatch can still be undertaken in cloudy conditions, as long as it remains dry. Check local weather forecasts in the days leading up to the skywatch and be prepared to cancel if the weather is looking bad. A good practice is to make a list of all attendees' contact numbers, check the weather

Mark near Cradle Hill in Warminster in 1994. (*Photo: Julia Graham*)

conditions a few hours before, and then contact everyone to let them know if it is going ahead or not.

Remember that, especially on a clear night, temperatures will plummet on average to just above freezing, so it is important to dress for warmth. A top tip is to wear a few layers of clothing, so that if it is warm, you can remove a layer, if it is cold you can add a layer. Two thin layers of clothing are far more effective than one thick layer, as the air trapped between the layers is a good insulator against the cold. If you have the space, always pack an extra woolly jumper.

Sunset Time

Check the sunset time of the day you intend to do the skywatch. You should aim to arrive at the location with at least two hours worth of daylight available to allow you sufficient time to set up properly.

Sky Plots and Satellite Passes

If you are expecting a clear sky, it is a good idea to obtain sky plots, showing the positions of the planets and bright stars on the night you intend to do your skywatch. These can be obtained from websites such as Heavens Above, magazines such as *The Sky at Night* or from a laptop running a piece of astronomy software. Also, find out which satellites are due to pass over on the night, as these are fascinating to watch as they scurry across the heavens. Details of these can also be obtained from the Heavens Above website. If you don't have a computer and printer at home, you could always use the facilities at your local library.

Food and Drink

Taking a large thermos flask of hot water along will allow you to make hot drinks and instant soups, which will keep you alert and warm throughout the night. We also recommend that you pack high-energy foods like chocolate, mint cake or oatmeal bars. Stopping for regular breaks makes for more alert observation. Don't forget to pack enough cups for everyone and remember to take a bin bag to put the team's rubbish in. Make sure that someone takes all rubbish home.

Getting to the Location and Making it Safer

Make sure that everyone knows exactly where you are all going to meet and at what time. If driving to the location, where possible, try to share vehicles so that you won't have problems parking up a lot of cars when you arrive. Arrange to arrive in daylight so that you can check the area for obvious hazards, such as sheer drops or pits. If any are found, they must be pointed out to the whole team and, if possible, roped off to prevent people straying into them in the dark. To this end, remember to pack rope or string, stakes and a mallet in order to make warning markers. A top tip is to put up a rope or string and fold yellow Post-its onto it at regular intervals along the span to make it more noticeable in the dark.

Pre-brief

Once you have made your plan and selected your team, it is a good idea to assemble them in advance to go through the timetable for the night. This will include showing your team the sky plots, satellite pass plots, and making sure that everyone knows what equipment they need to bring along.

Running a Skywatch

When the whole team arrives, assemble all the equipment at the spot chosen for the skywatch. Get the team to look for potential hazards and rope off areas that are considered hazardous. Make sure the whole team is aware of the general layout of the location.

Equipment Set-up

Set up the tripods on the flattest ground possible and make sure that they are stable. Fold a yellow Post-it around the bottom of each leg of the tripods so that they will be easily visible in the dark. This will drastically reduce the risk of people tripping up and injuring themselves and damaging equipment in the process.

Once you have set up a still camera on a tripod, take a series of photographs of the horizon in a 360 degree sweep. Using a compass, note the direction the camera is pointing in for each picture. These can be used for comparison purposes if anything unusual is photographed in the dark, as they can later be compared with the night shots to help determine where the horizon is in relation to the anomaly.

Arrange the rest of the equipment you have available so that as much of the horizon as possible is covered by either a still camera or a camcorder. Obviously, the more cameras you have, the better your chances of successfully capturing something on the night.

Set all cameras and camcorders to manual focus, and while it is still light, adjust the image until the horizon is in focus. If your camera does not 'memorise' its settings once switched off, you may have to do this again just before beginning the skywatch.

Also, make sure that all camera flash units are turned off. The flash will be useless in the dark, as the average camera flash only illuminates objects effectively up to around 4.5 metres (15 feet), and if left to fire, you will be impairing the team's night vision every time you take a picture.

Things to take:

Stakes
Rope or string
Mallet
Yellow Post-its
Cameras
Camcorders
Tripods
Spotting scopes
Binoculars
Compasses (at least one for every two team members)
Watches (at least one for every two team members)
Spare batteries
Tapes
Torches (with red filter)
Area map
Sky plots
Laptop with astro software (optional)
Warm clothing
Food and drink
Folding chair or picnic rug
Bin bag for rubbish

Team Roles

When all the equipment has been set up and tested, split the team up into pairs and assign them to a particular piece of equipment, i.e., one pair on binoculars, one on camera, one on video, etc. One of the pair is the observer, and the second is their note-taker. If anything unusual is seen, the note-taker needs to note down details such as time, direction, elevation, and needs to time the duration of the sighting. This can either be done on paper or by speaking the details into an audio recorder. This leaves the observer free to concentrate on capturing evidence without having to worry about making notes at the same time. These roles can be swapped over throughout the night, as can the use of various pieces of equipment.

The team leader's role is to keep overall control of the investigation, and to remind people of timetabled events such as the passage of satellites or the International Space Station. The team leader should also make sure that people take regular breaks to make sure that they stay alert throughout the night. The general rule of thumb for skywatching is to do no more than fifty minutes of observation at a time, followed by a ten minute break.

Beginning the Skywatch

Make sure that all watches and internal clocks on equipment are all set to the correct time, so that all notes and evidence can correspond to each other when they are reviewed later. In addition, make sure that the correct time is logged if anything anomalous is seen.

As the sky grows dark, pay particular attention to any distant buildings, radio masts or any other structure that has lights on it. Make a note of what direction they are in and at what elevation (height) so as not to confuse them later for anomalous lights.

Make sure each pair has a compass, a watch, a notepad and pen or audio recorder, and torch fitted with a red filter. You can make your own red filter by wrapping red cellophane from sweet wrappers around the end of the torch and holding it in place with an elastic band. The red filters help people retain their night vision throughout the course of the night.

Once the sky is sufficiently dark, the skywatch can begin. Switch off all lights, torches, etc. and allow everyone's eyes to become acclimatised to the dark. If someone needs to switch on a torch, get them to announce it to the group so that everyone can shield their eyes. It takes several minutes for a person's night vision to return.

Eyes and Observation

In our eyes, there are two different types of light sensitive cells, called receptors, which allow us to see in both bright light and low light conditions. These are called rods and cones. The cones work best in bright light and are primarily responsible for providing us with colour vision. The rods, on the other hand, are 1,000 times more sensitive than the cones and provide us with our night vision. Rods are not colour sensitive, only allowing us to see in black, white and intermediate shades of grey. The cones form the centre of the retina (the back of the eye) and the rods are arranged all around them towards the outside edge of the retina. Therefore, in low light conditions, the corner of your eye is far more sensitive than the centre. In order to do effective skywatching, you will have to get used to looking slightly off to the side, using the corners of your eyes more when observing the sky. Practice looking at stars, and see how the fainter ones have a habit of disappearing once you attempt to look at them directly.

What to Do if You See Anything Anomalous

If anyone spots anything unusual in the sky, they should immediately call out 'event' to alert the rest of the team. Typical UFO sightings are measured in seconds not minutes, therefore, you will have to act fast. When confronted with a suspect UFO, it is vital to gather evidence first and ask questions later. To this aim, people operating any cameras or camcorders should try to secure stills and footage of the anomalous object as soon as possible. At the same time, the note-taker should immediately record the time, direction and elevation of the object before doing anything else. If doing this on paper, the note-taker should be careful not to let their torch light affect the observers night vision.

Teams should work as quietly as possible, so as not to mask any sound that could be coming from the object. In addition, observers and note-takers should look around to see if anything in the environment appears to be affected by the presence of the UFO, such as power drainage in vehicles, houses, investigation equipment, interference on walkie-talkies, etc.

Once the object has disappeared from view, note the time, its final direction and its final elevation. Once you have gathered all the information you can, try to assess what you have seen. Sometimes you will be able to determine what the 'UFO' is halfway through the observation, such as when an approaching aircraft eventually flies overhead and you get to hear its engines or see its red and green navigation lights. It is still important to log the sighting, as someone, somewhere else, may still report the same thing you have seen as a UFO, and your notes will be able to resolve the mystery. If, after careful thought, you cannot satisfactorily explain what you saw, continue to observe for as long as possible. It is not uncommon for anomalous objects to remain in a particular area for several hours.

Concluding the Skywatch

If any of the skywatch team feel overly fatigued or cold, or both, it is a good idea to draw the evening to a close as both of these things can drastically affect a person's ability to do effective skywatching. The team leader should note down the time that all observation has stopped and then get the team to start packing up.

If it is still dark, make sure that everyone packs away all their equipment and make careful sweeps around the area to make sure that nothing is left behind, such as lens caps, torches, tapes, memory cards or anything else small enough to be missed in the dark.

Also, make sure that all rubbish goes home with the team. The area should be left in the same condition as you found it. In fact, some of our skywatch locations have been left in a better condition than we found them, with diligent team members also removing rubbish left by previous visitors.

Once everything has been packed away, conduct a final sweep to make sure all equipment cases and holdalls have been removed and stowed away. When fatigued and cold, it is very easy to miss something.

Before the team leaves, the team leader should assemble everyone together to make sure everyone is present before driving off. It might sound silly, but in the rush to get home and warm as quickly as possible, people can easily be left behind. All it takes is for someone to answer the call of nature before leaving, and for everyone to assume that this person must be in another car. Treat team members like equipment. Don't leave without them.

Finally, especially if you are departing in the wee small hours, leave as quietly as possible so as not to disrupt other people living in close proximity to the location.

Post-skywatch Action

As soon as possible, all team members should write up their skywatch logs and pass them onto a designated team member for them to collate together into a master skywatch log. This is a log of everything seen during the skywatch, identified or unidentified. It may seem silly to log IFOs, but as previously stated, one person's IFO is another's UFO, and if you do receive reports that occurred in the same area while the skywatch was in progress, these notes may hold the key to what has been seen.

Recording Review

Unlike ghost investigations, pictures and video on skywatches are only taken when something is spotted, so there should not be too much footage to review. If at all possible, it is a good idea to retain any footage and/or stills of IFOs taken on the night, so that they can be catalogued and archived for comparison purposes in the future. These stills and clips may be useful to show to witnesses in future cases so that they can compare their sighting against the closest IFO match. Building up a visual IFO database is a powerful investigation tool and a good training resource for newer skywatchers.

The whole team should arrange to meet up as soon as possible to review the investigation and any evidence that may have been captured. If at all possible, try to make copies of the interesting segments from the original recordings, but do not get rid of the originals. If you have managed to capture anything interesting then you will need to retain the originals for others to review.

Similarly, if you have any interesting photographs, do not remove them from the camera's memory card or internal memory, as doing so may destroy vital file information (see Section 4: Photographic Anomalies).

Since the final stages in the Investigation Life Cycle: 'Writing up your findings' and 'Making your findings public' are identical for all types of paranormal investigation, we will cover them in more detail at the end of the book.

What to Do if You See a UFO

Since UFO sightings can occur anywhere and at any time, it is always a good idea to keep one eye on the sky every time you go out. If you are lucky and do see something anomalous when you are outside, but do not have any investigation kit at hand, there are still lots of useful things you can do.

Remember that most UFO sightings are measured in seconds and not minutes, so you have to act fast. Since it will be almost impossible to gather all the desired information about the sighting alone, we recommend that you concentrate on the four most useful elements of the sighting:

T – Time of sighting
I – I (Eye) witnesses – are there any other witnesses present?
D – Direction of sighting (north, south, east or west)
E – Elevation (how high up in the sky, in degrees)

In order to remember them, we have devised the acronym TIDE. These four basic pieces of information are massively useful when investigating any UFO sighting.

Think about what you have available. Do you have a mobile phone with you? Does it have the facility to take stills or video? If yes, try to capture images as quickly as possible. If you can, switch it to manual focus (some recent models have this facility built in). The problem with most footage shot on phones and camcorders is that they have been left on automatic focus, which works well in good light conditions on close up objects, but very poorly in the dark whilst attempting to zoom into something far away. By controlling the focus, you will improve the quality of the footage and also increase its usefulness as evidence.

Keep the camera as still as possible – rest it against a tree trunk, on top of a fence or a low wall, or against the edge of a building to eliminate camera shake. If the camera is moving it will be much harder for the investigator to determine if the object is moving or stationary.

While filming, try to include some point of reference along with the object you are trying to film, i.e., distant buildings, trees, etc. This will help when trying to gauge the object's size in relation to the surroundings.

Try not to zoom in to the object for the entire duration of your sighting. If you do zoom in, zoom back out again shortly after. Although zooming in does provides additional detail, it is also important to keep track of the object for as long as possible. Zooming in makes it much harder to keep the object in shot, especially if it is moving erratically.

If your phone doesn't come with a camera or video, try to call someone in the area to see if you can also get them to witness what you are seeing. If they can't see anything, ask them to note down details for you as you give them a running commentary of what you can see. In the past, we have rung home and left messages on our answering machines, which not only allowed us to describe what we were seeing in real time, but also, by timing the recording, gave us an accurate time for the sighting duration. In addition, on mobiles, the call duration indicator should also give you a decent estimate of how long you were observing.

If you haven't got a compass, or do not know which direction you were looking in, you can always mark the direction you were observing on the ground by using twigs or stones, or by looking out for a prominent landmark in the direction you were looking. This will allow you to come back to the spot later, armed with compass and maps. If you are in a built-up area, look out for satellite TV dishes, as they mostly point south (in the UK).

Determining elevation is not as hard as it first seems. If you hold your arm out horizontally, parallel to the ground, your arm is at 0 degrees. If you hold your arm vertically up, pointing towards the sky, your arm is at 90 degrees. The halfway point between the two is at 45 degrees. Using these three points it is possible to estimate how high up (elevation) the object is in degrees. Ask yourself, is the angle greater or less than 45 degrees? Then estimate how much greater or less it is. As with everything, practise makes perfect.

Once the sighting is over, write down what you saw as soon as possible. Try to include what you were feeling at the time. Go through all five senses to see if there was any sound, touch (heat/cold), taste or smell that you associated with the presence of the UFO.

Section 7

Concluding Your Investigation

The final two parts of the Investigation Life Cycle are all about something that is often missed in paranormal investigation – communication. In the final section of this book we briefly explain the importance and need to communicate – from forming collaborative alliances with fellow investigators and groups, to pooling information in the hope of solving some of the mysteries.

Writing Up Your Findings

Once you have completed your investigation, research and analysis, it is important to write up an account of what you did, and how you went about it, so that others can check your findings and also learn from them. Every investigation you undertake will teach you something new, such as a better investigation technique or a deeper insight into a particular phenomenon, which should be documented and shared.

Part of the job of paranormal investigation is managing the witness's expectations, which sometimes is not an easy thing to do if you find a rational explanation for what they experienced. If you were to just call up the witness and say 'Hello, we've just found out that the UFO you saw was actually Venus. Thank you, good night', there is a good chance that the witness will not agree with you. If, on the other hand, you can present them with a blow-by-blow account of how you came to your conclusions, with details of where Venus was in the sky, how bright it was and the atmospheric conditions which gave rise to the effects that made it look more unusual, then the witness is more likely to agree with your conclusions. More importantly, that particular witness will also be able to correctly identify the next 'strange-looking light' they see in the sky as a planet.

Wherever possible, you should get other (independent) investigators to read your account to double check your information and conclusions. This is called a peer review. Peer reviews are useful in spotting any errors or flaws in your assessment. Peer reviews also strengthen ties between different investigators and groups, which often lead to collaborative investigations.

What Should Your Write-up Include?

Ideally, it should contain information about the incident, the location and details of what steps you took in the investigation and what leads you followed. It should also include any evidence, such as weather data, star charts, site photographs and measurements you have made that were instrumental in helping you to determine the outcome of the investigation. For examples of investigation accounts, please see our website: www.para-projects.com.

What Should Be Excluded?

Since the account is being written for your witness as well as for fellow investigators to check your methods, it is essential to exclude the witness's identity if they do not wish it to be known. You can supply your peers with a write-up that excludes any sensitive information like name, contact details or anything else that may reveal the person's identity. Your peer reviewer only needs to know the details about the investigation to make a judgement on your methods and conclusions.

Making Your Findings Public

The main reason for making your findings public is to benefit the paranormal community as a whole. We all have so much to offer one another in the shape of practical expertise in specific areas, specialist knowledge, unique methods of working and different mindsets. We all possess different pieces of the same puzzle, and it will only get solved if we can pool our pieces. With this thought in mind, how do we go about getting our knowledge 'out there'?

Outlets

Online

If you own your own website, this is the obvious place to publish your information. If you don't have your own, maybe others will be able to include your reports on theirs. There are lots of sites that do round-ups of all the latest paranormal news, so if you have made an earth-shattering discovery or managed to obtain a compelling piece of evidence, they would be very happy to feature it for you. You could also email a summary of your account to other groups or individuals in the hope of fostering two-way traffic where information sharing is concerned.

Journals and 'Zines

Some investigation groups have their own journals and 'zines, which may be able to publish your investigation accounts. Many groups actively look for (and are often quite desperate for) new content, so you may be doing them a huge favour. There are also quite a few professional newsstand paranormal magazines around the world that may also consider publishing your findings. If you don't ask, you don't get!

Give Presentations

Libraries, institutes and other organisations are always on the look out for people to give talks. This is an excellent way of not only getting your information out there but also of attracting potential new cases to investigate. Women's Institutes, local historical societies, and other paranormal groups will especially welcome you with open arms.

Finally

We hope that we have given you sufficient insight into how effective paranormal investigations are conducted, and have also whetted your appetite sufficiently for you to start investigating the paranormal for yourself. We are confident that what starts out as a hobby will become a life-long pursuit that will take you on an amazing voyage of discovery. We wish you every success for a long and fruitful journey.

Appendices

UFO Incident Report Form
Paranormal Incident Report Form
Investigation Log Sheets

UFO Incident Report Form

Part A: About You

Title   Mr ☐   Mrs ☐   Miss ☐   Ms ☐   Other ☐ ▸ *please specify* _____

Full Name _____   Date of Birth _____

Address _____

Postcode _____   Telephone Number _____

e-mail address *(if any)* _____

Occupation _____

Interests/Hobbies _____

Part B: About the Incident: Please write an account of your experience

Continue on a separate piece of paper if necessary

Part C: Object Characteristics

Please use this space to sketch what you saw

Number of objects seen

Colour(s) of object(s) seen

Brightness of object(s) seen
(Compared to brightness of full moon)

Sound of object(s) seen

Smell of object(s) seen

Part D: Object Position

Object altitude

Overhead

Ground level   **X**

Imagine yourself at point '**X**'. Mark the curved line with an **A** where you first saw the object and a **B** where the object was last seen.

Object direction

N

W ——— E

S

Imagine yourself in the middle of the compass dial. Mark the compass with an **A** where you first saw the object and a **B** where the object was last seen.

Part E: Weather Conditions at the Time of your Observation

Please tick appropriate boxes

i) Clarity of atmosphere	Clear ☐	Hazy ☐	Foggy ☐		
ii) Cloud cover	None ☐	Quarter ☐	Half ☐	Three Quarter ☐	Total ☐
iii) Temperature	Freezing ☐	Cold ☐	Cool ☐	Mild ☐	Warm ☐
iv) Precipitation	Dry ☐	Rain ☐	Snow ☐	Lightning ☐	Other ☐

Please specify

v) Wind strength	Still ☐	Breeze ☐	Strong Wind ☐	Gale Force ☐
vi) Visible astronomical objects	Stars ☐	Moon ☐	Sun ☐	Aurora Borealis ☐	Shooting Stars ☐

Part F: Physical Characteristics of the Observation

Date, Time and Duration of observation

Day of week	Date	Month	Year	Time
				: AM/PM

Duration of observation		More than	But less than
Mins/Secs	*Or*	Mins/Secs	Mins/Secs

How did you gauge the **Time** and **Duration** of your observation? *(If estimated, please say how)*

Where were you at the time of the incident? *(Please include nearest street, town or village)*

What first brought your attention to the object(s)?

How did the object(s) disappear from view?

Comparing the size of the object(s) with the full moon, was it:-   *Give details

Same size ☐   Smaller* ☐   Larger* ☐ ⟶

Was/were the object(s) photographed, filmed or video recorded? *(If YES, give details)*

Were there any other witnesses to the object(s) you saw?
(If YES, give names, addresses and telephone numbers where possible)

Part G: Other Characteristics Relating to the Observation

Did you, or the surrounding environment, suffer any physical effects which you consider to be caused by the object(s)?

Were you aware of the passage of time around the time of the observation? *(If NO, please describe)*

Have you had any other 'unusual' experiences in your life? *(If YES, please describe them)*

You may feel unable to describe such events; if so, please indicate that there are matters you wish to discuss in a meeting with the investigator

Other than the events you have reported, did anything else 'odd' or 'out of place' occur around the time of the observation? *(If YES, please describe)*

Did any other witness experience anything in relation to any of the questions in Part G? *(If YES, please describe)*

Witness' signature(s)

Date

For Investigator use only

Reference Number

Evaluation

Further copies of this form can be downloaded from: www.para-projects.com

Paranormal Incident Report Form

Part A: About You

Title   Mr ☐   Mrs ☐   Miss ☐   Ms ☐   Other ☐ ▸ *please specify* _____

Full Name _____   Date of Birth _____

Address _____

Postcode _____   Telephone Number _____

e-mail address *(if any)* _____

Occupation _____

Interests/Hobbies _____

Part B: About the Incident: Please write an account of your experience

Please continue on the next page

Part B: About the Incident (Continued)

Continue on a seperate piece of paper if necessary

Have you had any other 'unusual' experiences in your life? *(If YES, please describe them)*

You may feel unable to describe such events; if so, please indicate that there are matters you wish to discuss in a meeting with the investigator

Witness' signature(s)

Date

For Investigator use only

Reference Number   Evaluation

Further copies of this form can be downloaded from: www.para-projects.com

Investigation Log Sheet

| Name | | Sheet Number | | of | |
| Investigation Location | | Date | | | |

Time	Location	Event	Notes